D0141781

THE WILL TO
WIN

Eberstadt appearing before the House Armed Services Committee in June 1949 to urge passage of bill amending the National Security Act. He was chairman of the Armed Services Task Force of the Hoover Commission reviewing the efficiency of the National Security Act that Congress had enacted into law two years earlier based on Eberstadt's original report on unification of the armed services. *Courtesy:* The Bettmann Archive.

THE WILL TO

WIN

A Biography of Ferdinand Eberstadt

Robert C. Perez

Edward F. Willett, Co-author

Contributions in Economics and Economic History, Number 96

Robert Sobel, Series Editor

GREENWOOD PRESS

New York • Westport, Connecticut • London

HG
2463
E34
P47
1989

ROBERT MANNING
STROZIER LIBRARY

DEC 4 1989

Tallahassee, Florida

Library of Congress Cataloging-in-Publication Data

Perez, Robert C.
   The will to win : a biography of Ferdinand Eberstadt / Robert C.
Perez, Edward F. Willett, co-author.
     p. cm. — (Contributions in economics and economic history,
ISSN 0084–9235 ; no. 96)
   Bibliography: p.
   Includes index.
   ISBN 0–313–26738–3 (lib. bdg. : alk. paper)
   1. Eberstadt, Ferdinand. 2. Bankers—United States—Biography.
I. Willett, Edward F. II. Title. III. Series.
HG2463.E34P47   1989
332.1'092'4—dc19
[B]   89–1898

British Library Cataloguing in Publication Data is available.

Copyright © 1989 by Robert C. Perez

All rights reserved. No portion of this book may be
reproduced, by any process or technique, without the
express written consent of the publisher.

Library of Congress Catalog Card Number: 89–1898
ISBN: 0–313–26738–3
ISSN: 0084–9235

First published in 1989

Greenwood Press, Inc.
88 Post Road West, Westport, Connecticut 06881

Printed in the United States of America

The paper used in this book complies with the
Permanent Paper Standard issued by the National
Information Standards Organization (Z39.48–1984).

10 9 8 7 6 5 4 3 2 1

Contents

Illustrations

Chronology of Eberstadt's Life

1890   Born in New York City on June 19, son of Edward Frederick and Elenita (Lembcke) Eberstadt.

1910   Graduates with honors from Newark Academy, N.J.

1913   Graduates from Princeton, Phi Beta Kappa, and spends next year in Europe in postgraduate study of economics and politics.

1914   Enters Columbia University Law School.

1916   Interrupts law study to join Squadron A Cavalry Troop on Mexican border in effort to capture the Mexican bandit leader, Pancho Villa.

1917–1919   Active military duty as captain in 304th Field Artillery, 77th Division, in France and Germany during World War I; receives Purple Heart for wounds received in action.

1919   Receives law degree from Columbia Law School and is admitted to the Bar. Joins Cotton and Franklin law firm as law clerk. Marries Mary Van Arsdale Tongue of Baltimore on New Year's Eve.

1921   Birth of daughter, Frances Stuart.

1922   Becomes partner in Cotton and Franklin.

1924   Birth of daughter, Mary Van Arsdale.

1926   Becomes partner in Dillon, Read and Co., New York in-
            vestment bankers, in charge of European financing activ-
            ities.

1926   Birth of son, Frederick.

1928   Birth of daughter, Ann Van Arsdale, in Paris.

1928   Withdraws from Dillon, Read.

1929   Member of the American delegation, headed by Owen D.
            Young, to the Reparations Conference in Paris on revision
            of the Dawes Plan; becomes partner in Otis & Co., Cleve-
            land investment bankers, in charge of New York office in
            October.

1931   Withdraws from Otis & Co.; forms F. Eberstadt & Co., Inc.
            in New York City on September 1.

1937   Completes construction of Target Rock mansion on Lloyd
            Neck, Long Island.

1941   Chairman of Army-Navy Munitions Board boosting ma-
            chine tool output by over 30 percent in four months.

1942   Vice chairman of War Production Board; develops Con-
            trolled Materials Plan to break up war production bottle-
            necks.

1943   Resigns from War Production Board.

1945   On October 22 completes and delivers report to Navy Sec-
            retary Forrestal on Unification of the Armed Services,
            which becomes basis for the National Security Act of 1947.

1948   Completes report evaluating National Security Organiza-
            tion as part of Hoover Commission.

1949   Recommendations to strengthen National Security Orga-
            nization enacted into law.

1950–1960   Works on private capital deals in partnership with Lazard
            Frères and other investment firms.

1962   Eight corporate finance partners separate from Eberstadt's
            firm to form New York Securities with Eberstadt concen-
            trating on investment management.

1962   Hospitalized three times for mental breakdowns.

1963–1967   Rebuilds investment banking operations of F. Eberstadt & Co., Inc.

1968   Donates Target Rock estate to the Department of Interior as wild life preserve retaining life residency.

1969   Suffers massive heart attack October 21 en route to meeting of Blue Ribbon Defense Panel to which he had been appointed by President Richard Nixon; dies on November 11 at Walter Reed Hospital in Washington, D.C.

Acknowledgments

I would like to acknowledge the valuable aid of Calvin Lee Christman, whose doctoral dissertation analyzed in detail the wartime career of Ferdinand Eberstadt. As part of his research, Christman interviewed Eberstadt over a two-day period in the summer of 1969, just months before Eberstadt suffered his fatal heart attack. Christman made available the transcripts of these far-reaching interviews which contain valuable insights on Eberstadt's views on the important issues that had a major impact on national security and finance during his career.

The efforts of several of Eberstadt's close associates who made important contributions to the biography are also acknowledged. These include Edward F. Willett, co-author, who contributed importantly to the planning, organization, content and writing of the biography, and Nelson Loud who supplied a considerable amount of information covering the period from the mid-1930s to the 1960s. Loud became the managing partner of the F. Eberstadt & Co., Inc. firm in the early 1950s and worked closely with Ferdinand Eberstadt on the highly successful private capital investments co-partnered with Lazard Frères.

Finally, I would like to express appreciation to members of my family who have taken a dedicated interest in this work. Barbara Ellen, my daughter, suggested the title of this biography and I thank her for her insight. I also would like to express my love and appreciation for the efforts of my wife, Mary Jean, who has suffered through five drafts of this work over more than five long years, helping me at every turn with editing, commentary, encouragement, typing the drafts on the word processor and helping with proofreading. I am indebted to her forever for her inspiration, which constantly drove me to excel.

Robert C. Perez, Ph.D.
Fall 1989

Introduction

Usually biographies attempt to reveal the inner drives and motives that lie behind a great man's actions in his lifetime. No one ever got close enough to Ferdinand Eberstadt, however, to know what really made him tick; one close associate commented, "He had a great sense of right and wrong, but how he would react to certain things was very difficult to fathom in advance."[1]

Lacking that kind of insight, this biography probes the inner forces that drove Eberstadt and tries to find answers to the many unanswered questions about this great American financier and public servant. It focuses on the periods of his greatest public and financial achievements, seeking his motives, and how his unbending character sometimes led to his undoing. A considerable portion of the biography is based on the recollections of close associates and family members who agreed to be interviewed to provide source material for this work. Although all the opinions of the persons interviewed represent their sincere beliefs, no representation is made that the opinions expressed are correct or incorrect.

Eberstadt played a major role in the mainstream of Wall Street's and Washington's power centers for almost fifty years during one of history's most turbulent periods of epic change. During the 1920s, young Eberstadt emerged as the foremost German financing expert in Wall Street. Using his superb negotiating skills, he soon propelled the firm of Dillon Read to the forefront of European finance, causing it to surpass even Morgan and Kuhn Loeb. Eberstadt had important assets working for him besides his innate brilliance. His fluency in German and French, his German heritage and the Grand Tour he had taken abroad after graduating from Princeton in 1913, when he studied European economic and financial theory at various universities prior to studying law at Columbia University, all contributed to his career as an investment specialist in European finance. Logically, Owen D. Young turned to Eberstadt to help negotiate with the German and French financial authorities at the Paris Reparations Conference in 1929.

In the 1930s, Eberstadt started his own firm and proceeded to revitalize many sound, temporarily depressed businesses (his so-called little blue chips) into healthy, growing businesses. *Time* later described Eberstadt as "a brave man with a shrewd sense of the times, rare in the . . . Wall Street of the 1930s."[2] Toward the end of the decade, Eberstadt followed up these initial successes with the launching of Chemical Fund, a mutual fund that enabled investors to share in the commercial successes resulting from research breakthroughs in medicine and a host of chemically derived products.

In the 1940s, Eberstadt came to Washington, D.C., at the request of his old Princeton friend and former Dillon Read partner, James Forrestal, to break up the serious bottlenecks impeding wartime production. Eliot Janeway, the columnist and economist, in his analysis of the war period declares that Eberstadt's war production strategy "saved a million lives and shortened the war by one full year."[3] Thereafter, Eberstadt helped revamp America's national security organization and worked with Bernard Baruch in the effort to harness the atom to peaceful uses.

Eberstadt's love affair with the chemical industry never diminished but, as evidenced by the history of his Chemical Fund, it expanded and changed direction several times. In the 1950s and 1960s, Eberstadt and André Meyer of Lazard Frères reinvented merchant banking with a series of spectacular private capital deals that remade a number of lackluster chemical and drug companies into corporate powerhouses. In the process, Eberstadt and Meyer helped to develop the leveraged buyout technique that is so popular today in the world of corporate finance.

There can be no greater testimonial to the outstanding genius and ability of Eberstadt as an investment banker than the phenomenal success of his firm when he was its undisputed autocratic ruler. Eberstadt had an uncanny knack for recognizing the future value of new developments and could make accurate appraisals of the investment merits of a venture, skimming the cream off the top for those who had confidence in his judgment.

But despite his spectacular successes in almost everything he touched, Eberstadt failed to achieve the single most important dream of his life—creating a family dynasty. Despite his best efforts, this dream eluded his grasp.

Notes

1. Interview with Walter Lubanko, former Eberstadt partner, April 16, 1984.
2. "Washington Tip-Offs," *Time*, January 12, 1942, pp. 62–65.
3. Interview with Eliot Janeway, April 3, 1984.

THE WILL TO
WIN

1

Saving the Nation

It had been raining heavily in Washington during much of the early fall of 1942 contributing to the depressing news flowing from the battle-fronts. On Guadalcanal, the Japanese, having assembled a large force for an all-out assault on the Marine positions, were threatening the main airfield. In Europe, the Axis powers controlled almost the entire conti-nent although American forces were now assembling in England in preparation for the main assault on Fortress Europe. In North Africa, British forces had suffered a major defeat during the summer, having been driven back to El Alamein near the edge of the Nile delta. Russia, having borne the full brunt of the German onslaught the previous year, showed signs of exhaustion and clamored for immediate action by her Western allies to ease the pressure.

This was the setting one Friday morning, October 16, 1942, at the War Production Board (WPB), the central control unit that directed the in-dustrial production effort that would later result in a flood tide of ar-maments to fight the Axis powers. Ferdinand Eberstadt, vice chairman of the WPB, received a call in his office from General Edwin Watkins, the president's personal adjutant, asking if he would come over to see the president that morning at 11:00 A.M.[1]

Eberstadt had moved up rapidly in the power structure directing the arms production effort. Shortly before the Japanese attack on Pearl Har-bor, he had become directly involved in the military buildup as an adviser to his old friend, James V. Forrestal who, along with another old friend, Robert Patterson, had been recruited by President Franklin D. Roosevelt to help prepare our national security organization in the event the United States should be drawn into the war.

Eberstadt had known Forrestal since his undergraduate days at Princeton, and in the 1920s he had worked with him as a partner in the Wall Street investment banking firm of Dillon Read. Eberstadt first met Patterson in France during World War I in which Patterson won the Distinguished Service Cross "for extraordinary heroism in action." Later, under Eberstadt's direction, Patterson, a topflight Wall Street attorney, helped to defend Dillon Read against the Goodyear Tire litigation during the 1920s. Patterson then became a federal judge and, later, secretary of the army during World War II.

After the fall of France in June 1940, Forrestal asked Eberstadt to help unsnarl the bottlenecks in machine tool output, an area that Eberstadt had helped to finance during the 1930s. Forrestal initially asked Eberstadt to conduct a survey of machine tool manufacturers, citing the number of conflicting reports he had received on the subject. Eberstadt's study covered the entire relationship of machine tools to defense mobilization. He concluded that there was still more juice to be squeezed out of the existing capacity by increasing shifts and using other means—as much as from 25 to 30 percent more without any superhuman effort.

The "other means" referred to Eberstadt's talent to ferret out hidden assets using his contacts and his powers of persuasion. Eberstadt had the notion that some automobile production people might have squirreled away vital machine tools in safe places for use after the war. He mentioned this to Walter Reuther, the fiery head of the United Auto Workers Union. Reuther, who admired Eberstadt's hard driving nature, replied, "I'll find out for you. I'll have a complete list of them in ten days—where they are and so forth," and he did indeed produce the inventory of the hidden machine tools.[2] Altogether, Eberstadt's efforts helped boost machine tool output by 30 percent in just four months.[3]

After that, Forrestal and Patterson asked Eberstadt to come to Washington and review the Army-Navy Munitions Board setup. He quickly proposed a reorganization of the board and the appointment of a full-time civilian chairman. Forrestal and Patterson accepted Eberstadt's recommendations, but Eberstadt declined their request that he assume the chairmanship, preferring to return to his investment banking business in New York. But after Pearl Harbor, Eberstadt impulsively picked up the phone, called Forrestal and asked: "When do you want me to start?" Forrestal replied, "I'd like you to start tonight, certainly tomorrow!"[4] Under Eberstadt, the Munitions Board suddenly emerged from obscurity and became a powerful advocate for the military services in directing the flow of materials to America's munitions factories.[5]

Shortly after the United States entered the war, the combined British and American commands held a series of conferences in Washington to plan the war effort. At the end of the meetings, Roosevelt committed the United States to launch an enormous war production effort to quadruple war materials output. The United States was to become the "Arsenal of Democracy," but many critics felt the goals were not attainable and might lead to morale problems when the inevitable failures became known.[6]

Roosevelt, however, doggedly stayed the course, and soon massive bottlenecks began to appear—tanks without treads, rifles without ammunition, and so forth. Part of the problem was the priority system that gave each manufacturer an equal claim on vital production. In Berlin, the Nazis were delighted by the creeping paralysis that had overtaken the United States' war production effort.

During this period, Eberstadt developed a close relationship with Bernard Baruch, whom he had first met when Eberstadt was at Dillon Read during the 1920s. They became dedicated and intimate friends. Baruch liked Eberstadt's determination—it reminded him of his own experiences as head of the War Industries Board which Baruch ran almost singlehandedly in World War I. The two thought alike about many things including what was wrong with the WPB and what needed to be done to remedy the situation. The spark that forged the close relationship between Eberstadt and Baruch was their common desire to expedite war production. Baruch, along with Patterson and Forrestal, maneuvered Eberstadt into favor with Roosevelt, although Eberstadt was a staunch enemy of the New Deal economic policies of the prewar Roosevelt administration. From that point on, Baruch and Eberstadt became almost inseparable, their common patriotism forging an intimate relationship that persisted for the remainder of their lives—some twenty-five years.

The WPB chairman, Donald M. Nelson, appeared to be inept at his job, and the situation was rapidly getting out of control. Nelson's personal habits and behavior did not help the effort to increase the output of munitions. He enjoyed the Washington social whirl, partying at favorite watering holes there as well as in New York City, which kept him out of the office a good part of the time.[7]

The situation deteriorated so much that many in government wanted to remove Nelson and bring in Baruch, but Baruch's physical condition and age prevented his taking on this awesome responsibility. Instead, Baruch played an influential role in the events that brought Ferdinand Eberstadt over to the WPB as vice chairman, with full authority to smooth out the clogged allocations of the crucial raw materials.

By the fall of 1942, production problems had become critical. Finally, in September 1942, under the threat of dismissal by the president, Nelson met with Eberstadt and agreed to his demands for full authority in materials allocation. Eberstadt then went to the WPB and, working on a crash schedule, twelve hours a day, seven days a week, he perfected an allocation plan to overcome the war production problems. After Nelson's failure in the previous two years, Eberstadt's plan, put into op-

eration by Roosevelt on November 2, 1942, created a miracle that broke
up the major bottlenecks in little more than a month and flooded the
fighting fronts with firepower. Although industrial expansion was actually curtailed, the output doubled in less than a year.[8]

Eberstadt calculated that by controlling the distribution of three vital
metals—steel, copper and aluminum—effective control of all other com-
ponents of war production would quickly follow. He explained how his
plan worked: "On one side of the table you put the people who make
steel and the other critical metals—and on the other side of the table,
those who need the materials [with the government in the middle as
the ultimate arbiter]."[9] To avoid inconsistent production flows, Eberstadt
hit on a scheme to allocate the scarce supplies among the myriad users.
He called it the Controlled Materials Plan (CMP).

As had occurred occasionally in his earlier career, Eberstadt's aggressiveness in seeking goals led to setbacks. Although his drive and dedication achieved startling results, it was sometimes so extreme as to be
obnoxious to some and ultimately self-defeating. Close associates could
anticipate Eberstadt's changes in disposition by watching his eyes. Although they sometimes twinkled with the enjoyment of a good joke or
anecdote, they more often penetrated his surroundings with a cold,
rational, determined gaze. Regrettably, his driving nature soon brought
him into direct conflict with Roosevelt over one of Eberstadt's early staff
appointments.

One of the critical areas under Eberstadt's control was foreign allocation of matériel. In early October 1942 he had appointed Thomas
Armstrong, a former Standard Oil vice president, to head up the foreign
allocations group. The press had greeted the Armstrong appointment
with considerable derision. They called attention to the fact that many
State Department officials feared that Armstrong would be too tough
with our Latin American friends because of his earlier effort to thwart
the Mexicans when they seized American-owned oil wells in Mexico.

When Eberstadt arrived at the White House pursuant to Roosevelt's
request, he was quickly ushered into the Oval Office; at first the president was very friendly and reassuring, but then he came to the point
of the visit:

"You have a man who works for you called Armstrong, Tom Armstrong?"
Eberstadt replied, "Yes, I have Mr. President." And FDR said, "I'm going to
have to ask you to do something very difficult. I'm going . . . to ask you to fire
Armstrong."[10]

Eberstadt was shocked and taken aback. He had known Armstrong
as an undergraduate at Princeton and had been impressed ever since
with his tough, no-nonsense approach to solving problems. Some time

before, Armstrong had stopped by Eberstadt's office to offer his help. To Eberstadt, Armstrong seemed to be the perfect man to solve the problems with foreign allocations for our allies and friendly neutrals, allocations which had fallen as much as eleven months behind schedule. Armstrong had excelled at handling the foreign business for Standard Oil of New Jersey and had risen rapidly to become a corporate vice president; he was well-versed in the intricate methods and policies of foreign countries. So Armstrong's offer was gladly accepted, and he was given charge of oil allocations for foreign nations. Within a week, Armstrong had reported for duty, having severed his connections with Standard Oil; in a month, Armstrong had cleared up the backlog of foreign allocations at WPB.

To Roosevelt's request for Armstrong's ouster, Eberstadt replied:

"Mr. President, I realize it is not becoming for me to try to cross-examine the President of the United States, but may I ask you a question or so?" FDR said, "Why, of course, ask any questions you want." Eberstadt said, "Are there any charges against his loyalty or patriotism or ability?" "None whatsoever." Eberstadt then said, "Mr. President, you understand that I am somewhat baffled."

Roosevelt remained charming, friendly and quite sympathetic during the interview, recalling that a similar request had been made of him when he had served as the assistant secretary of the navy in World War I. At the same time, however, he was quite firm, repeating that "for reasons of State Armstrong had to go!" However, in response to Eberstadt's inquiries as to Armstrong's character, the president firmly reiterated that his request to discharge Armstrong did not in any way reflect on Armstrong's loyalty, integrity or ability. FDR said, "All I can say is that for reasons of State, I'll have to ask you to discharge him."[11]

Eberstadt remembered that Armstrong and Sumner Welles, the under secretary of state, had clashed over what should be done when the Mexicans confiscated American oil properties in the early 1930s. It seemed probable that Welles had now gone to the president and had said, "You ought to fire that fellow Armstrong." Eberstadt then responded, "Mr. President, could affairs of state be a synonym for 'stale quarrels'?" "No, they couldn't be," FDR said.[12]

The president's order to dismiss Armstrong posed a serious dilemma for Eberstadt. Should he comply it would constitute a serious breach of his strict code of ethical behavior. On the other hand, Eberstadt had a greater allegiance to his country which clashed with his inherent sense of fairness. For if he were to back Armstrong to the limit with the risk of being dismissed himself, the war effort, so dependent on his embryonic allocations plan, would suffer interminable delays, resulting in untold additional and unnecessary American casualties.

Faced with this dilemma, Eberstadt believed Roosevelt also recognized the necessity of achieving war output goals with all else put aside for the duration of the war, including personal enmities. Defeating the Axis powers ranked as the top priority above all others. So, Eberstadt gambled and backed Armstrong to the hilt, counting on the President's recognition of the seriousness of the need to break up the production bottlenecks.

Summoning up his resolve, Eberstadt replied, "If you want Mr. Armstrong to go, he'll go, but I'm going to ask you at the same time to accept my resignation. I couldn't stay . . . under those circumstances after his sacrifices." FDR quickly replied, "No, no, no, we don't want you to do that. No, no, we want you to stay . . . I like the job you are doing. . . . I want you to finish the Controlled Materials Plan." Eberstadt then replied, "Mr. President, it would be a great help if Armstrong remained until I finish the Controlled Materials Plan and then we'll both go." "Why, of course, why, of course!" FDR exclaimed.[13]

Eberstadt heard nothing further from the White House after that, but persistent press reports claimed that Eberstadt had called FDR's bluff.[14] Although Roosevelt had reassured Eberstadt, his stand that rainy day in October 1942 sealed his fate at the WPB as subsequent events would prove.

Eberstadt hated the type of intrigue that existed at all levels of the Washington power structure. Eliot Janeway, the columnist, recalled: "Eberstadt was like a fish out of water in Washington."[15] He abhorred the carnival atmosphere that reigned after dark on the cocktail party circuit so much that Eberstadt himself had declared a personal moratorium on drinking to avoid any interference with his own effectiveness in achieving his goals in Washington. By Washington standards, therefore, Eberstadt was withdrawn and aloof.

Nonetheless, it is difficult to exaggerate the importance of Eberstadt's Controlled Materials Plan at the time because what the Western allies needed most from America in fighting Hitler was war matériel. As Churchill so aptly put it, "Give us the tools, and we'll finish the job."[16]

The CMP worked because it brought materials allocation into balance with production capabilities. Each order for one thousand tanks became an effective order for each item needed. Janeway adds, "In short, CMP ordered finished products on the business-like assumption that the home front high command meant to supply the fighting fronts with units of fighting power."[17] The CMP quickly became the linchpin of the nation's war production effort, balancing scarce raw materials with the needs of the country's fighting forces.

After his climactic meeting with Roosevelt, Eberstadt returned to his task, and the Controlled Materials Plan was unveiled formally at a press conference just two weeks later on November 1, 1942, right on schedule.

Within a few months of its first use, preliminary reports indicated that the CMP was a major success. By early 1943, the first allocations had been made, and output picked up markedly, so that for all of 1943 war production increased by nearly 100 percent over 1942, with about the same labor force and industrial plant. According to Janeway, by 1944 Eberstadt's plan enabled the United States to achieve war production levels so great that the problem shifted from scarcity to surpluses, and cutbacks became the order of the day.[18] The spectacular success of Eberstadt's CMP contrasts sharply with America's present military preparedness. For example, an Air Force study found that in 1984 it would take from twelve to twenty-four months to reach wartime production levels whereas it took Eberstadt's CMP just a few short months to achieve such levels in 1942.[19]

Following the Armstrong incident, however, Eberstadt's relationship with the White House cooled perceptibly. Eberstadt's strong sense of loyalty to his friend, combined with his innate aggressiveness, had probably alienated the president. Moreover, Eberstadt previously had been sharply critical of the administrative ability, character and personal habits of Donald Nelson, the WPB chairman. Nelson Loud, Eberstadt's close business associate, recollects that Eberstadt used to refer to the WPB under Donald Nelson as the "Arsenal of Hypocrisy." Eliot Janeway noted that, "One of the 'Janissaries' [at the White House] conspired with Nelson to oust Eberstadt. Nelson's White House accomplice figured he could crank Roosevelt up about it because they (Roosevelt and Eberstadt) never had a relationship, ever."[20]

The event that brought the long-simmering tension to the boiling point was the appointment by Nelson of Charles E. Wilson, the production genius from General Electric (nicknamed "Electric Charlie" to distinguish him from Charles E. "Engine Charlie" Wilson, head of General Motors) to head a newly created production committee at about the same time Eberstadt was appointed to the WPB in mid-September 1942. The Wilson appointment created an almost impossible situation at the War Production Board, for the boundary lines between Wilson's duties and Eberstadt's were extremely hazy. The official WPB release announced that Wilson would be responsible for production and schedules and that Eberstadt would be in charge of programs and schedules. Christman notes, "The potential for conflict under such an organization is all too clear."[21]

The strife and discord in the WPB greatly troubled Baruch. Baruch knew that Eberstadt was no one's man but his own. Combining tenacity with imagination, Eberstadt had no other purpose than to win the war as quickly as possible. In the hope of finding a harmonious solution, Baruch met one night with Nelson and canvassed frankly the subject of the internal conflict between Eberstadt and Wilson as well as Nelson's on-going, well-publicized feud with U.S. Army brass. Baruch thought when they parted that night that Nelson would seek to end the breach within the WPB and with the army, but that view proved to be wrong because Nelson considered Eberstadt an army Trojan horse.[22]

Notwithstanding Roosevelt's displeasure with Eberstadt, the White House had also become increasingly distressed over the quality of leadership that Nelson had given the WPB. According to Christman, the President wanted to replace Nelson with Wilson and ship Nelson off to some innocuous assignment in a nonstrategic region of the world.

At this point, Director of Economic Stabilization James Byrnes intervened, convincing the president that the appointment of Wilson to the chairmanship of the WPB would simply anger the faction supporting Nelson, thus further disrupting the WPB. "Instead," Byrnes continued, "the President should turn to Bernard Baruch since Baruch had the knowledge, the experience, the support of the Congress and the confidence of the President necessary for the position." Besides, Harry Hopkins, the president's closest adviser, supported the Baruch appointment. With the president's approval, Byrnes hastily prepared a letter, which the president signed, inviting Baruch to become the head of the WPB; Byrnes hand delivered the letter to Baruch at the Hotel Carlton.[23]

When Baruch recovered a little from his astonishment at Roosevelt's invitation, he questioned whether he should give up his work as an independent troubleshooter and he told Byrnes, "I can't answer you now. . . . I'm going to New York tonight. I'll give you my answer tomorrow." Byrnes was crushed that Baruch did not accept the appointment immediately. He had just spent a king's ransom in political capital, and Baruch wasn't sure he wanted the WPB job.[24]

Meanwhile Eberstadt, unaware of these developments, had decided to resign from the WPB. He was convinced that the new organization with Wilson controlling the operating divisions would not work. Moreover, his major contribution to the war effort, the Controlled Materials Plan, had been completed and was beginning to function efficiently. He composed a letter of resignation and took it over to show to Baruch at the Carlton, apparently arriving just after Byrnes had left. Eberstadt told Baruch, "Boss, I've had a belly full; I am going to get out."[25]

But Baruch asked Eberstadt not to send the letter. Pressed for a reason, Baruch would only say, "Something has just happened that I really can't tell you about, but please do not resign right now." And Eberstadt was left "holding the bag." Eberstadt later reflected in the Christman interviews, "[Baruch] was my dear friend . . . but maybe he shouldn't have asked me to [refrain from sending the letter] unless he was sure that he was going to take the post."

Early in the following week, Nelson received a phone call from an inside White House informer. The caller, apparently saying only that he had information vital to Nelson's interests, insisted on meeting the chairman at 7:00 A.M. the following day for breakfast. At that meeting the informer told Nelson that a White House conference was scheduled for 2:00 P.M. that afternoon at which the president would announce in the presence of the armed forces secretaries and Byrnes and Hopkins the appointment of Baruch as WPB chairman and Eberstadt as one of Baruch's chief deputies. Nelson took decisive action to save himself. He hurried back to his office and promptly issued a statement announcing that Eberstadt had been asked to resign and that most of the operating authority in the WPB had been transferred to Wilson.[26]

Nelson's coup d'état succeeded. Roosevelt was impressed by his decisive action and actually sent him a handwritten note that afternoon congratulating him on his courage in firing Eberstadt—this to a man whom Roosevelt earlier in the day had been poised to remove. John Fennelly, Eberstadt's deputy, describes this as a story of palace intrigue difficult to accept even after the passage of over twenty years.[27]

Although Eberstadt fell from power, he continued to play a major role in shaping the nation's defense organization through his close association with Forrestal and Baruch. As the war approached its end, congressional investigations focused much attention on the lack of coordination between the services which had contributed to the Pearl Harbor disaster. This had led to widespread pressure to unify the armed services under a single command. Convinced that unification would damage national security, Forrestal characteristically asked Eberstadt to undertake a thorough study of the nation's postwar national security needs, including the unification proposal. Eberstadt immediately came to Washington and assembled a task force to make an in-depth study of the problem, including all critical factors—political, diplomatic, economic and military—affecting the security of the country.[28] Edward F. Willett received the navy's highest civilian award, the Distinguished Civilian Service Award, for his efforts on this task force.

Eberstadt finished and delivered his massive report to Forrestal in September 1945. In it, he argued against army proposals for a centralized military structure and in favor of a decentralized alternative that preserved the individual services. Eberstadt and Forrestal lobbied aggressively for this proposal, but legislative infighting by opposing groups in Congress was intense and continued for almost two years.[29] The compromise that finally emerged was based essentially upon the original Eberstadt plan. This led ultimately to the enactment of the National Security Act in 1947 which maintained the separate services of the armed forces under a single secretary of defense. Forrestal was appointed the first secretary of defense by President Harry Truman on the day he signed the new National Security Act into law.[30] The Senate confirmed Forrestal as defense secretary one day later.

Somehow, during this period, Eberstadt also found time to run his own investment firm and to help Baruch and Forrestal with other plans directed toward national security. In January 1946, less than two weeks after Churchill's "Iron Curtain" speech, Secretary of State James Byrnes asked Baruch to head the American delegation to the United Nations Atomic Energy Commission (UNAEC) with the specific assignment of preparing and presenting the United States position on peacetime control of atomic energy.[31]

Baruch, after some earlier reservations, had accepted the call, asking Eberstadt to serve with him and other members of the "Baruch team" (John Hancock, Herbert Bayard Swope and Fred Searls, Jr.), with Eberstadt doing most of the strategy planning and actual writing of the Baruch plan. On June 14, Baruch formally presented the U.S. proposal to UNAEC. No nation actually voted against the plan, but Russia and Poland abstained from voting and it was never adopted by the United Nations General Assembly.[32]

In 1948, the Congress established a commission headed by former President Herbert C. Hoover to study the executive branch of government with the objective of making it more efficient. As part of this effort, Hoover asked Eberstadt to undertake a study of how well the national security organization was performing under the newly enacted National Security Act. Eberstadt immediately came to Washington and organized a task force of leaders from all sectors of the economy, government and the military which worked through the summer and early fall of 1948. As with the earlier task force on unification of the armed services, Eberstadt asked Dr. Willett to serve with this group. Eberstadt submitted the group's report in November; it recommended an increase in the overall authority of the secretary of defense, the creation of a permanent chairman of the Joint Chiefs of Staff and the strengthening of the secretary of defense's control over the armed forces secretaries as well as a number of other proposals designed to make the defense organization more efficient.[33] The following summer, after much heated debate, Congress enacted amendments to the National Security Act which embodied most of Eberstadt's recommendations; President Truman signed it into law on August 11.[34]

After the end of the war, Eberstadt's close associate, James Forrestal, became more and more obsessed with the growing threat of Russian expansionism in the immediate postwar period. After the British government decided to withdraw from the Middle East, Forrestal believed that the Soviet Union would try to influence Arabian oil sources to cut off the supply of oil to the West. To counter this threat, Forrestal urged that the United States refrain from giving too much support to Jewish causes, fearing that the Arabian oil sheiks might retaliate by depriving us of their oil. Over the next three years, Forrestal's position stirred considerable friction between himself and some of Truman's closest advisers.[35]

In the 1948 presidential campaign, the Palestine question became a crucial political issue, and Forrestal's attitude toward the Jews hurt him with the Truman administration. After the election, Truman decided to replace Forrestal and he named Louis Johnson as secretary of defense. This final blow combined with the tremendous pressure of nearly eight years in wartime Washington exacted a heavy toll on Forrestal. With the pressure mounting, Eberstadt advised his old friend: "Look, cut your losses and get out." Subsequently, Eberstadt tried without success on several occasions to convince Forrestal to join Eberstadt's Wall Street firm—a dream the two had harbored from their days with Dillon Read in the 1920s.[36]

Physical signs of Forrestal's decline included loss of appetite and weight, digestive disturbances, insomnia and chronic fatigue. Marx Leva, Forrestal's closest aide, became especially alarmed when he found Forrestal sitting in his Pentagon office wearing his hat and staring straight ahead at a blank wall. "Is there something the matter?" Leva asked. "You are a loyal fellow," Forrestal replied. Leva managed to get him home and then called Eberstadt who rushed over to talk to him. Forrestal finally agreed to see his old friend only after Eberstadt swore that he was alone. Once with him, Forrestal poured out his twisted emotions, telling Eberstadt that he was a complete failure, that Communists, Jews, and White House aides were out to "get" him, and that some of "them" were in his home right that moment. To prove his point, he began looking in closets. Eberstadt was able to get him on a military plane that night for Hobe Sound near Palm Beach in Florida, where his colleague and friend Robert Lovett cared for him at his winter home.[37]

Forrestal's condition continued to deteriorate, however, and he made at least one suicide attempt while at Hobe Sound, necessitating elaborate security measures in fear of a further attempt. After his arrival at Hobe Sound, Forrestal indicated that he would be willing to talk with Dr. William Menninger of the Menninger Clinic. Menninger had met Forrestal during the war and had served as a consultant to the navy's Research and Development Board. Menninger, then in New York to attend a conference, was reached by Dr. Howard A. Rusk at the instigation of Eberstadt. Menninger and Eberstadt flew to Florida in a private plane, and Menninger had several lengthy talks with Forrestal on the evening of his arrival. The following day, Menninger and Eberstadt met with Captain George N. Raines, chief psychiatrist at the U.S. Naval Hospital at Bethesda, Maryland. Menninger's opinion was that the patient was suffering from a severe depression of the type seen in operational fatigue during the war. After some discussion among the two psychiatrists and Eberstadt, Forrestal was hospitalized at Bethesda for the treatment of involutional melancholia.[38]

After a period of intensive treatment at Bethesda, Forrestal's condition seemed to improve, and he was permitted increased freedom, including the use of a small diet kitchen (e.g., pantry) across the hall. Because the window in this small room was not secured with a locked, heavy metal screen as in his bedroom, it was relatively easy for Forrestal to open the window and leap to his death sixteen floors below.

The major sacrifices made by both Eberstadt and Forrestal in the service of their country before, during and after World War II show clearly that, for each of them, love of country was a far more powerful motivating force than love of money. It is a sad commentary on our national politics that two patriots such as Eberstadt and Forrestal, each of whom made outstanding contributions to the American success in World War II, were betrayed by the president of their country—Eberstadt, with the active connivance of Roosevelt, was fired by Nelson in 1943; Forrestal was fired by Truman in 1949.

This portion of Eberstadt's life occurred roughly at the midpoint of his career, which had started in Wall Street at the beginning of the 1920s. Although somewhat matured, the basic tendencies and characteristics of the Eberstadt personality were quite evident in his brief tenure in wartime Washington. His autocratic methods made more enemies than friends. In the final analysis, he did not have enough important friends to help him in his battle with Donald Nelson in 1943.

Part of Eberstadt's lack of support resulted from his unwillingness to fraternize and develop harmonious working relationships within the WPB. He disliked the New Deal and all associated with it with the notable exceptions of Baruch and Forrestal. He avoided the after-hours Washington social scene with all of its intrigue. Thus, when the chips were down and the going got rough, Eberstadt had few to turn to except for Baruch, Forrestal and Patterson, who were regarded as too closely allied to the military establishment. He excluded others that could have helped, including Robert R. Nathan, Hopkins and Byrnes.

In the Christman interviews toward the end of his life, Eberstadt admitted that:

My greatest failure down there was [being] too shortsighted. . . . I was interested in doing a job, just as I would do it here, but Washington is very different from here; in Washington there is this complicated thing called "political atmosphere" [which] . . . depends on personal relations . . . recognition of the seats of power, . . . whereas I drove right smack for my objective. . . . I wouldn't survive five minutes down there now, because politics in time of war are a little bit in eclipse, but never completely. . . . I think that my survival, as long as it lasted, was simply due to the importance of the matters on which I was engaged and my ability to accomplish them.[39]

Eberstadt's aloofness during the war period is especially puzzling considering the vigorous efforts he made during the 1920s to cultivate personal relationships with a wide circle of financiers in pursuit of Dillon Read investment banking business in Europe. He knew the value of socializing after hours not only with these professionals but also with their spouses. However, the earlier failure in 1931 of Otis & Co., of which he was a partner, made Eberstadt more reclusive—thereafter he became a lone wolf. By 1942, he trusted only his closest aides. His self-imposed ban on drinking probably reflected his suspicion of others and his fear that drinking "loosens the tongue."

Ironically, as Eberstadt counselled his associates years later, "It takes ten friends to offset one enemy. I know," he added ruefully, "because I have made my share of enemies. So, the best course is to make as many friends as possible while avoiding making enemies."[40]

Notes

1. Calvin Lee Christman, "Ferdinand Eberstadt and Economic Mobilization for War, 1941–1943," Ph. D. diss., Ohio State University, 1971, n.p., p. 262 (hereinafter referred to as the Christman dissertation).

2. Interview with Lawrance K. Harper, Jr., Eberstadt's son-in-law, April 11, 1985.

3. Donald Robinson, *The 100 Most Important People in the World Today* (Boston, 1952), p. 155.

4. Christman dissertation, pp. 38–42.

5. "Munitions Board, Obscure in Peace, Now a Key Agency," *Wall Street Journal*, May 28, 1942, p. 1.

6. Robert E. Sherwood, *Roosevelt and Hopkins: An Intimate History* (New York, 1950), pp. 474–76.

7. Interview by Calvin Lee Christman with Ferdinand Eberstadt, July 17 and 18, 1969 (hereinafter referred to as the Christman-Eberstadt interviews), July 17, 1969, side 3, pp. 4–6.

8. Margaret L. Coit, *Mr. Baruch* (Boston, 1957), p. 508.

9. Ibid.

10. Christman-Eberstadt interviews, July 18, 1969, side 4, p. 2.; also Christman dissertation, pp. 262–67.

11. Christman dissertation, p. 266.

12. Christman-Eberstadt interviews, July 18, 1969, side 4, p. 4.; also I. F. Stone, "The Nation: N.J. Standard Oil Official Given Control of Exports," *PM*, October 6, 1942, p. 1; and I. F. Stone, "The Nation: FDR Orders Ouster of Standard Oil Man," *PM*, October 25, 1942, p. 9.

13. Christman-Eberstadt interviews, July 18, 1969, side 4, p. 5.

14. Ibid.

15. Interview with Eliot Janeway, April 3, 1984.

16. Winston Churchill, *Radio Broadcast*, February 9, 1941.

17. Eliot Janeway, "Mobilizing the Economy: Old Errors in a New Crisis," *The Yale Review*, vol. 40, no. 2, Winter 1951 (December 1950), p. 209.

18. Ibid.

19. "Arms in an Emergency," *New York Times*, October 19, 1987, p. A20.

20. Interview with Eliot Janeway, April 3, 1984.

21. Christman dissertation, p. 274. Also see Arthur Krock, "Tinder into WPB Set-up; Many Explosive Elements Remain to Threaten the War Program," *New York Times*, February 17, 1943, 11:2.

22. Bernard M. Baruch, *Baruch: The Public Years—My Own Story* (New York, 1960), pp. 313–14.

23. James Grant, *Bernard M. Baruch* (New York, 1983), pp. 297–99.

24. Ibid.

25. Christman dissertation, pp. 295–96; also Christman-Eberstadt interviews, July 18, 1969, side 3, p. 16.

26. Christman dissertation, pp. 302–4; also W. H. Lawrence, "Eberstadt Ousted; Wilson to Run WPB," *New York Times*, February 17, 1943, 1:5.

27. John Fennelly, *Memoirs of a Bureaucrat, a Personal Story of the War Production Board* (Chicago, 1965), pp. 69–70.

28. Arnold A. Rogow, *James Forrestal: A Study of Personality, Politics and Policy* (New York, 1963), pp. 216–19.

29. Letter to author from Marx Leva, February 12, 1985, and James Y. Newton, "The Man Behind the Big Brass," *American Magazine*, May 1949, p. 31.

30. "Bill Creating National Military Establishment Signed; Secretary Forrestal Appointed Defense Secretary," *New York Times*, July 27, 1947, p. 1:5.

31. Jordan A. Schwarz, *The Speculator: Bernard M. Baruch in Washington, 1917–1965* (Chapel Hill, N. C., 1981), p. 490.

32. Coit, *Mr. Baruch*, pp. 605–6.

33. Walter H. Waggoner, "Hoover Board Sees Waste in National Defense Setup; Blow to Economy Feared," *New York Times*, December 17, 1948, p. 1.

34. "National Military Establishment Becomes Defense Department; Joint Staff Chiefs Chairman Created; Offices of Deputy Secretary and Assistant Secretaries of Defense Created; Service Secretaries Subordinated to Give Defense Secretary More Power; Fiscal Methods Revised," *New York Times*, August 11, 1949, p. 1.

35. Rogow, *James Forrestal*, pp. 178–95.

36. Christman-Eberstadt interviews, July 17, 1969, side 1, p. 7; also telephone interview with John Davenport, former *Fortune* editor, March 12, 1985.

37. Walter Isaacson and Evan Thomas, *The Wise Men: Six Friends and the World They Made* (New York, 1986), pp. 469–71.

38. Rogow, *James Forrestal*, pp. 6–8.

39. Christman-Eberstadt interviews, July 17, 1969, side 2, pp. 6–7.

40. Based on author's recollection.

2

The Eberstadt Heritage

Edward Frederick Eberstadt had a major impact on his son Ferdinand during his formative years, from the time he first went away to camp as a boy up to the beginning of his career in Wall Street twenty years later. This influence continued even after Eberstadt's marriage to Mary Tongue. In the early 1920s, Eberstadt used to visit his father in East Orange, usually going alone for Sunday lunch and returning to New York in the early evening. Mary stayed home apparently because she felt uncomfortable with the excitable elder Eberstadt.[1]

The Eberstadt family roots are in both the northern sector of Germany in Hamburg and in the southern portion clustered around the Rhine valley. Many of Eberstadt's traits resemble those of his paternal grandfather, also named Ferdinand, who was described in one German biography as "a highly educated but ambitious man who was given to sudden anger and who had . . . many quarrels in his business and political life because of his independent views."[2]

The Eberstadts had deep roots in Worms, Germany, where they had settled in the seventeenth century. In the late 1840s, Worms was a town with a population of about 9,000, of whom 879 were Jews. A certified list of candidates in a municipal election in 1848 consisted of twenty-three names, of which thirteen were Jewish. Of these, five were named Eberstadt. This led the local newspaper to inquire ironically whether there weren't any more Eberstadts. Ferdinand Eberstadt, grandfather of the subject of this biography, served as mayor of Worms for several years.[3] Despite his Jewish heritage on his father's side, Eberstadt followed the Christian faith throughout his adult life; his Princeton yearbook listed Eberstadt as a Presbyterian[4] and in later years he was a

Eberstadt family in Worms, West Germany, circa 1860. Eberstadt's grand-father is in center, his father, Edward Frederick, is at top left. *Courtesy:* Stadtarchiv Worms.

member of the Brick Presbyterian Church on Park Avenue on Manhattan's upper East Side.

In 1860, Eberstadt's Aunt Emma married Benedikt Bernard Kahn who lived in nearby Mannheim. Emma's marriage produced a number of children including Otto Herman Kahn, who was groomed for his investment banking career at the Deutsche Bank in London before joining Speyer & Co. in New York City in 1893. Eberstadt's grandfather, as the mayor of Worms, had been instrumental in obtaining a permit for Solomon Loeb to emigrate to America. Then, in partnership with Abraham Kuhn, his brother-in-law, the two immigrants established a dry goods business in Cincinnati, Ohio, in 1867 which later evolved into the prominent investment banking firm of Kuhn Loeb. Subsequently, Otto Kahn became a partner in Kuhn Loeb in 1897 after his marriage to Adelaide Wolff, the daughter of one of Kuhn Loeb's senior partners. The Eberstadt family had other important banking connections; for example, Eberstadt's grandmother was related to the Paris Rothschilds.[5]

Both the Kahn and Eberstadt families in Germany were great supporters of the arts and other intellectual pursuits. For example, in the 1880s the two families organized the "Brahms' Circle," a salon devoted to the music of the German school as well as political and social discussion; two Eberstadt daughters formed similar salons in London. Otto Kahn, who continued the family's interest in the arts, became a major benefactor and guiding force in the development of the Metropolitan Opera Company of New York City into its present position as one of the great opera companies of the world.[6]

Eberstadt's father was a free spirit, a quixotic man with a romantic temperament. He had gotten himself into serious difficulty while attending Heidelberg University in Germany. The leader of one of the prestigious dueling clubs at the university, with a great scar on his face that he had received in dueling, he inexplicably killed a dueling partner, for which he was jailed. Subsequently the authorities banished him from Germany for this crime. He emigrated to the Western Hemisphere in the mid-1870s and became a U.S. citizen in 1879.[7]

Although his university career had ended rather abruptly following this episode, Eberstadt's father finally received his degree from the university,[8] and the Eberstadts remained friendly toward Heidelberg. In memory of his father, Ferdinand Eberstadt faithfully sent an annual donation to his dueling club to purchase beer for the student members.[9]

In the Western Hemisphere, Eberstadt's father initially travelled throughout the islands of the Caribbean and the countries of Central America as a roving correspondent for a German language newspaper. Articles under his byline appeared from time to time in the 1870s.[10] He then settled in New York City where he developed an export-import business as a principal of A. D. Straus & Co. He owned several sailing vessels as part of his business; the largest, the *Electric Light* was wrecked off Haiti.[11] Edward Eberstadt had many friends in the theatrical business, and romantic affairs flowed from that source. It was during this period that he met and had an affair with Josephine Emory, an entertainer, which resulted in the birth in 1883 of an illegitimate son, Edward Emory Eberstadt.[12]

Edward Eberstadt, eccentric and excitable, continued his bizarre behavior after he arrived in New York. In March 1883, the *New York Times* reported that he had assaulted a businessman and his son in a quarrel growing out of a name-calling incident on the street just outside his office in the financial district. Later in the 1880s, he was named in a suit for refusing to pay a tailor's bill because he claimed the tailor had failed to fit the suit properly. The tailor was so infuriated that he brought legal action to force Eberstadt to pay for the suit, all of which was dutifully reported in the *New York Times*. Finally, in 1898, the *New York Times* reported that the New York Produce Exchange had suspended Eberstadt from membership for improperly obtaining a quotation from a competing broker-member without revealing his identity, as required by the exchange's membership rules. He claimed it was just a "practical joke" on April Fool's Day. Thereafter, he became more discreet, and news items about him stopped—even his obituary notice did not appear in the *Times* when he died in August 1924.

Ferdinand Eberstadt's mother, Elenita, came from a Spanish-German family living in Venezuela. Nicolaus Adolph Lembcke, whose sister married a member of the noted Rachals piano manufacturing family of Hamburg, had been sent to Venezuela in the mid–1800s to represent the family's piano business. Later he became the Hamburg consul in Puerto Cabello, and in 1866 he married Mercedes Contreras de la Cruz, the daughter of a prominent Venezuelan family. The marriage produced four children including Juana Augusta Elena de la Cruz Lembcke (known as "Elenita"). Shortly after Elenita's birth in 1867, the family returned to Hamburg where she was reared in a strict German Catholic family setting. After Lembcke died in 1884, the mother returned to Puerto Cabello with her family.[13]

Elenita had musical talent and, when she was eighteen, she was sent to the conservatory in Hamburg where she studied the piano and stayed with her two maiden Rachals aunts. Elenita was a good student and by an early age had mastered seven languages. While she was in Hamburg, however, the unthinkable happened—she converted to the Lutheran faith. When word got back to Puerto Cabello, she was told to come home immediately. En route to South America, she befriended a Danish family. The head of the family (August S. H. Forlovere vare Kjoemandene p. g. Fangel) offered her a job as a music teacher and au pair to the Fangel's young daughter. Elenita, a strong-willed woman, debarked with the Fangels and lived in their house in St. Thomas where Fangel had his business. Shortly thereafter, Edward Eberstadt, then forty-seven years of age, met her while on a business trip from New York for his shipping business. She, anxious to end her career as a music teacher and enthralled by the tropical moonlight, married him in spite of a twenty-five-year age difference.[14]

The newlyweds moved to New York City after a bizarre honeymoon that included being shipwrecked for several months on a small island off French Martinique. The marriage resulted in four children: Zélie Mercedes and Ferdinand, named after their paternal grandparents, and Esther and Rudolph, all born before the turn of the century. When Ferdinand was two or three years of age, the family moved to East Orange, New Jersey, where Edward Eberstadt bought a ten-acre farm.[15]

Life in the Eberstadt home was very difficult. Edward Eberstadt was the archetypical German, a tyrannical father. On returning from his business, he frequently beat Ferdinand because he persisted in disobeying his parents. The beatings had a substantial impact on Ferdinand's mental attitude and probably contributed to his cold-blooded nature later in life.[16]

Ferdinand also suffered considerable mental anguish from the existence of his illegitimate half brother Edward Emory Eberstadt. Elenita Eberstadt offered to adopt him, but the elder Eberstadt steadfastly refused. According to his eldest daughter, Ferdinand Eberstadt was mistaken years later for the illegitimate son while with his son-in-law, Jack Payne. Eberstadt's reaction was violent and unforgiving.[17]

Eberstadt's brothers and sisters contrasted sharply in personality, the mixture of Latin and Germanic traditions making for a rare mosaic in the personalities of the four children. Zélie (German for Sarah), Ferdinand's older sister, tall, flamboyant, good-looking with gorgeous chestnut red hair, flighty and full of excitement, was liked by all. She was ultimately frustrated in her desire to become an actress.[18] She resembled in a way her Aunt Emma who was described as "one of those beautiful, romantic myths, the Eberstadt women."[19] Esther, Ferdinand's younger sister, smaller, more reserved and dour, resembled more closely her mother. Esther later organized an employment agency and was quite successful as a businesswoman. His brother, Rudy, the youngest, also redheaded, was fun-loving, not as brilliant as his brother nor as successful in business. Rudy was the first to die, tragically, in 1961 from bone cancer at the age of sixty-six.[20]

Short, standing about five feet eight inches, Ferdinand was nicknamed "Manny," meaning little man, by his older sister Zélie. Despite (or because of) his small size, he was very combative and as he grew older, his pranks took on a more serious tone. At Orange Public School he had an altercation with the principal and knocked him down the stairs. The

family decided to send Ferdinand to Newark Academy, one of the oldest
private schools in the country (founded in 1774) with a reputation for
classical education as well as a rugged athletic program. He entered
Newark Academy on February 1, 1904, in the middle of the upper in-
termediate level. There he learned to study, concentrating on Greek and
Latin.

The headmaster of Newark Academy, Samuel Farrand, quoted from
Juvenal, the second-century Roman poet and satirist, "Mens sana in
corpore sano" (a sound mind in a sound body) to stress the great objective of education. And that was the epitome of Newark Academy:
regular studies, high standards of scholarship and regular, healthy exercise.[21]

At Newark, Eberstadt was head linesman on the football team and
was a star on the field and track team. He valued highly the advice of
Charles Mayser, the head football coach (who coached Newark through
its memorable undefeated seasons of 1904, 1905 and 1906) on the subject
of competitiveness. Mayser counselled his players, on the football field
as in life, to "seek to exploit a competitive advantage—if you see a face,
kick it; if you see a hand, step on it."[22]

This competitive atmosphere at Newark became a trademark of Eberstadt's approach to deal making throughout his career. One of his partners noted: "Eber's philosophy was to extract the last drop of blood
from those with whom he negotiated. If his grandmother had gold teeth
and sat across the negotiating table from him, I'm sure the teeth would
end up in Eber's pocket."[23] Another old friend, Franz Schneider, noted,
"He was a very competitive fellow . . . he wanted to win intensely. . . .
Something was stirring and going on in him all the time."[24] Eberstadt
constantly urged his associates to "seize the opportunities that life pre-
sents."[25]

Eberstadt excelled at Newark, where he never received a grade lower
than a B in any course; in his junior and senior years, he received straight
A's. In his senior year, he was editor-in-chief of the monthly student
magazine, *The Polymian*. He graduated with honors in 1909 and entered
Princeton in the fall of that year.[26] Not many in the family thought that
young Eberstadt would last long at Princeton; within a week of entering,
he was in hot water for what was termed "roughhousing." Through the
efforts of his father, however, he was reinstated so that he did not lose
his position in the class.

Coupling his quickness with his brilliance, Eberstadt soon pushed
himself to the fore on the Princeton campus, and he was the outstanding
member of the class of 1913. With a particular penchant for wheeling
and dealing, he was nicknamed by his classmates "The King."[27] At
Princeton, he earned a varsity letter as a member of the wrestling team,
managed the 1912 varsity football team, was elected to Phi Beta Kappa

and was voted by his classmates as the one most likely to succeed.[28] As fellow classmate William Long, who later became head of and principal stockholder of the financial advertising agency of Doremus and Company, recalled, "Eberstadt ran everything that he ever had anything to do with."[29]

Eberstadt pursued studies in Latin and Greek at Princeton; he also tutored Greek and Latin on the side. The Heinrich Schliemann discoveries in Greece fascinated young Eberstadt, and he wanted to go to Greece to inspect at first hand the Schliemann excavations at Troy.[30]

David Lawrence, editor at the time of the student newspaper, the *Daily Princetonian*, and later a leading Washington columnist and founder of *U.S. News and World Report*, selected Eberstadt to serve as a cub reporter on the staff of the "Prince." Eberstadt applied himself to his reportorial duties with great energy and became editor of the paper in his senior year.[31]

This vigor and sense of mission attracted other friends at Princeton with similar qualities who played major roles in Eberstadt's later career at Dillon Read, especially James Forrestal, class of 1915. Forrestal was a brilliant scholar, as was Eberstadt, but he was a man given to liberal and somewhat socialistic causes, strange for a person who was later to become a leading investment banker.[32] Eberstadt asked Forrestal to serve on the *Princetonian* as a cub reporter, and Forrestal became one of the Eberstadt circle.

Another important friend whom Eberstadt met at Princeton and who remained a close business associate over the years was Dean Mathey who, a year or so older than Eberstadt, graduated in the class of 1912. Mathey followed the same path as Eberstadt at Princeton, becoming a member of the editorial staff of the *Princetonian*. Mathey achieved international acclaim during and after his Princeton career as a world-class tennis star who defeated Bill Tilden at Forest Hills in 1923.[33]

At Dillon Read, there evolved a theory that good investment bankers tended to either come from a law background or have writing ability as evidenced by becoming an editor of a college newspaper. The feeling was that a man who could achieve the editorship of a college newspaper demonstrated the key characteristic required in finance—the ability to take facts and information and to reassemble them into a persuasive format. The same theory applied to the law, which trained one to convert the bare essentials of a case into a persuasive framework. These three Princetonians then had the common bond of their college newspaper as they developed their careers at Dillon Read.[34]

Others have a more skeptical attitude toward Eberstadt's relations with others. James Benenson, a corporate finance associate of Eberstadt in the 1960s, comments, "Eber kept all of these contacts because they were extremely useful to him. . . . I don't think that he cared a 'fiddly dee' about [them or his family] . . . Eberstadt seemed to focus his attention and his affection only on his business."[35] Another partner, Robert L. Newton, adds, "In Eber's case, friends and enemies . . . were one and the same. I always had the feeling that he was constantly in combat . . . and he regarded everyone he knew . . . in a kind of love/hate relationship."[36]

A Princeton acquaintance was responsible for Eberstadt's first meeting with Mary Van Arsdale Tongue whom he later married. During his four years at Princeton, Eberstadt came to know and like a noted alumnus, Knox Taylor, who had starred as an All American tackle on the 1895 Princeton varsity football team. Taylor, the president of the Taylor-Wharton Iron and Steel Company in New Jersey, was a life trustee of Princeton. He returned to the campus at the time of Eberstadt's graduation and introduced Eberstadt to his cousin, Mary Van Arsdale Tongue of Baltimore, who earlier in the week had graduated from Bryn Mawr College and was visiting the Taylors. With the same acute judgment that he later showed in evaluating business investments, Eberstadt filed away his favorable initial impression of Miss Tongue until later when the "market" was right.[37]

Upon graduation from Princeton, Eberstadt, encouraged by his father, determined that the best course of action was to pursue subjects in which he was interested. Therefore he spent a year in Europe studying national politics and economics at the University of Berlin as well as at Munich and the Sorbonne in Paris. His Uncle Rudolph, a professor at the University of Berlin and a brilliant scholar with a number of learned publications to his credit, helped organize his study program. (Presumably, Eberstadt also managed to visit the Schliemann excavations.) This background in European affairs later played a major role in his law and investment career.

When Eberstadt came back from Europe, he decided to enroll in law school. His father had studied law at Heidelberg, and he had always wanted to become a lawyer, but he disliked the thought of attending law school for three years. When he finally entered Columbia Law School in the fall of 1914, his dread of three more years of schooling proved to be unfounded, for his law education was twice interrupted by military service.[38]

Despite these interruptions, Eberstadt's record at law school was brilliant, including an appointment to the law review in his first year. One of his professors recalled:

Eberstadt was an extraordinarily keen student but the factors most outstanding about him were imagination and an original mind. He knew the precedents and he knew the law most thoroughly, but in addition he had the capacity for expanding his point of view into a new realm if his case didn't find support in exact precedents. He had one of the most unusual minds of any of the students I had.[39]

The first interruption at law school occurred in the spring of 1916 when Eberstadt was called up to join his fashionable National Guard unit, Squadron A, New York Cavalry, which he, as had many socially prominent New Yorkers, had joined shortly after his graduation from Princeton. It was the place to be, and Eberstadt was very active in this unit.[40] Pancho Villa, the Mexican guerrilla *caudillo*, a cattle rustler and bandit for about fifteen years, had in early 1916 massacred sixteen American citizens in Texas, which enraged the American public. Following Villa's atrocity, President Woodrow Wilson sent an expeditionary force, which included Eberstadt's unit and was led by General John J. Pershing, to capture Villa, but Villa's cunning and popularity with the peasants in Chihuahua in northern Mexico stymied Pershing's efforts. Villa continued his bandit activities for several more years, but finally settled down in 1920 on a large ranch in Durango deeded to him by the Mexican government.[41] His retirement was short; he was assassinated in 1923.

Years later Eberstadt, a master raconteur, regaled his guests at client lunches in the firm's dining room with hilarious stories of his experiences on the Mexican border. The army food was terrible, and once Eberstadt and four other troopers, including his close buddy Auguste (Gus) Richard, went across the pickets to a Mexican house and paid them to cook a chicken dinner for them. The typhoid fever they caught as a result killed one of the troopers, and Eberstadt and Richard were hospitalized in San Antonio.[42] But Eberstadt and Richard recovered quickly and, with the aid of Eberstadt's father, returned home at the end of September on an extended medical leave.[43]

Soon thereafter and with the ill-fated Mexican campaign called off, Eberstadt was able to return to law school and pick up his studies in the fall of 1916. A more serious call to service awaited him in the spring of the following year. The United States formally entered World War I in April 1917 on the side of the Allies, and Eberstadt again left his law school studies to serve in the field artillery. Eberstadt's division, the 77th, was the first of the national army divisions to be sent to France and the first to see action at the front. Eberstadt told Christman that the 77th division captured more ground than any other American division in World War I. Eberstadt rose to the rank of captain and became a battery commander in the 304th Field Artillery; he was decorated with the Purple Heart for wounds received in action.

At the end of the war, the army needed an officer to act as liaison between the German civil government and the Army of Occupation headquartered at (C) Koblenz in the Rhine valley, not far from the Eberstadt ancestral home in Worms. With his command of German and

French providing the opening, Eberstadt was the logical choice for this post, and he spent the next several months at American Expeditionary Force (AEF) headquarters in Germany.[44]

Eberstadt was anxious to get back to his law studies. As he described the Army of Occupation, he thought it might more properly have been called an "Army of No Occupation." He told Christman that a typical day's work "consisted of about five minutes effort and if I had to do as much as 15 minutes work, someone else was shirking." But still it was an easy and happy time for him. Eberstadt later recollected, "The Rhine Valley in the spring was a lovely place and contrasted [sharply] to war in France, but time was passing!"[45]

With Eberstadt overseas for more than two years during and after World War I, the long-simmering romance with Mary Tongue went through some major upheavals, and according to family sources there was a breakup just before he sailed away with his artillery unit for the war zone in France. Mary, distracted and desiring a new challenge to help her forget what might have been, joined the field services of the American Red Cross and also embarked for France. Just after the armistice, a chance meeting of the two occurred on a train in France. Mary Eberstadt later told her oldest grandchild, John Payne, that the "chance meeting on the train in France was what got our romance going again seriously."[46]

After his discharge from the service in August 1919, Eberstadt wasted no further time—he courted Mary Tongue aggressively. He made a striking appearance in his twenties, strongly masculine and handsome. With a romantic flourish he married Mary four months later on New Year's Eve, just before the beginning of the fabulous 1920s. Probably the decision to go ahead with the marriage was aided by an increase of 50 percent in the salary that Eberstadt had been receiving from his law firm. With that good news in hand, Eberstadt calculated that the "market" was right, and Mary and he began the new decade as husband and wife, a decision that, Eberstadt later remarked to Christman, "never caused either one of us regret."

The children came fairly rapidly thereafter. Frances was born in 1921; Mary in 1924; Frederick, the only son, in 1926, the year in which he formally joined Dillon Read as a partner; and the last child, Ann, in Paris in 1928.

But Eberstadt was hardly the man to settle down to a comfortable career in law or finance. He had to be constantly in action—probably a trait acquired from his father and grandfather. Richly endowed with intellect, he could choose the direction he wanted to pursue in life and achieve greatness in whatever path he chose. Therefore, one naturally must question what motives drove Eberstadt. Was he driven by greed, or love of power or dedication to uplifting the human race? The impression remains that he was probably driven by a variety of sometimes conflicting motives.

Classical economists believe that the marginal utility of wealth declines as it grows, but entrepreneurial types like Eberstadt found that—rather than surfeiting their appetites—their first millions only stimulated their unquenchable thirst for further fortune.

Pike Sullivan, one of his closest partners in his later career, thinks that

Eberstadt was driven by the sheer love of doing deals. The money was important, obviously; that was the underlying factor [but] . . . he had plenty of money and he certainly didn't have to worry about doing the next deal. I think it was a game he liked to play; it was fascinating to him.[47]

Donald Young, the analyst who in the 1950s followed Xerox, one of Eberstadt's greatest investment finds, thought that

Eber had a higher purpose. . . . In my initial interview with him, he wanted to know if I felt that transactions in securities . . . were truly beneficial to the economy or the nation. . . . I think that Eber had a great respect for money and I think that money was his scorecard [but] that doesn't mean that . . . that is greed.[48]

Although brutally frank to his associates, Eberstadt's support was also legendary. Some claim this merely reflected his paternalism—or "Prussianism," but his reactions to crises often could be kind as well as fair. For example, in the early 1960s, one of Eberstadt's younger business associates had planned to buy a house on Long Island, but when his Spartan income was not sufficient to support the mortgage, he approached Eberstadt and said that he needed a salary increase. Immediately thereafter, he was informed that his pay would be increased by $5,000 a year, which put him comfortably ahead of the income needed to secure a mortgage loan on the house.

But all was not to go without a hitch. An Eberstadt tradition was the daily noon meeting at which all of the firm's business was reviewed for the benefit of the partners and key staff professionals. Knowing that the contract signing on his house purchase was scheduled for that day, the associate asked if he could be excused from the meeting to catch an early train for the contract signing. With that, Eberstadt chuckled with great glee, his eyes twinkling, and before ten or fifteen people present at the meeting he cried out, "Oh, that's the reason for the raise."

The story took still another bizarre and grim turn, two or three months later. The actual closing on the house purchase was to take place on November 22. As it turned out, the associate was involved again with

Eberstadt, this time at a luncheon meeting in the firm's private dining room with Irwin Lainoff, then financial editor of *Business Week*. He told Eberstadt before the luncheon that he would again have to leave early for the final closing.

The luncheon began, as usual, at 1:00 P.M. but then suddenly, at 1:22 P.M., the firm's trader burst into the dining room with the news that President John F. Kennedy had been shot and that turmoil and chaos had taken place on the "floor." To help Lainoff cover the story, Eberstadt installed him at his own desk in his private office and immediately converted the dining room into his command post with traders and other personnel rushing in and out with the latest news. The Stock Exchange closed down shortly thereafter with the Dow-Jones average down precipitously. The dining room, normally a serene and pleasant oasis, had become a battle station. In the midst of this bedlam—no one ate lunch—Eberstadt turned to his associate and said, "It's time for you to leave for the closing on your house." He had remembered despite all of the turmoil! Eberstadt's close associates remember incidents such as this about him.

Eberstadt, however, gets mixed reviews from his children. His son Frederick's comments are particularly poignant:

My father was the most complicated man that I ever expect to meet. He was warm and cold; he was up and down; he was a very difficult father and a very difficult man. He was somebody who didn't respond in any predictable way emotionally. I think he had some problems about his own feelings about himself and he was very, very prone to flattery and he was easily seduced . . . but the trouble with him, the difficult part of him, is whatever you say is true on the one hand, the opposite was true on the other hand. . . . He certainly could be extraordinarily cold and he was very manipulative.[49]

Eberstadt's oldest daughter, Mrs. Frances Payne, wrote, "I don't know what drove him—money, admiration, a fuss being made over him, honors, successes, achievements. . . . "[50]

Notes

1. Interview with Frederick Eberstadt, March 1985.
2. Fritz Reuter, *Wormaisa 1000 Jahr Juden in Worms* (Worms, West Germany, 1984). pp. 157–58.
3. Ibid.
4. *The Nassau Herald*, Class of 1913, Princeton University, Princeton University Press, June 9, 1913.
5. Reuter, *Wormaisa 1000 Jahr Juden in Worms*, p. 158; also Mary Jane Matz, *The Many Lives of Otto Kahn* (New York, 1963), pp. 6–14.
6. Matz, *The Many Lives of Otto Kahn*, pp. 9, 13, 55–144.

7. Interview with John Payne, Eberstadt's grandson, August 9, 1984.

8. Letter to author dated June 10, 1986 from Dr. W./Ha. Weisert, archivist of the University of Heidelberg.

9. Letter to author (mailed February 22, in 1986) from Mrs. Mary Harper, Eberstadt's daughter.

10. Interview with John Payne, Eberstadt's grandson, August 9, 1984.

11. Interview with Frederick Eberstadt, March 23, 1984.

12. New York City Department of Health, Records of Births.

13. Letter to author dated March 17, 1987 together with extracts from Das Staatsarchiv Sielemann, the archivist of the city of Hamburg (West Germany).

14. Interview with Frederick Eberstadt, March 23, 1984.

15. Ibid; also interview with Larry Harper, Jr., Eberstadt's grandson.

16. Letter to author dated June 23, 1984, from Mrs. Frances Payne, Eberstadt's daughter.

17. Letter to author dated July 10, 1984, from Mrs. Frances Payne.

18. Phone call to author on November 26, 1984 from Mrs. Frances Payne.

19. Matz, *The Many Lives of Otto Kahn*, p. 9.

20. Telephone call to author on November 26, 1984 from Mrs. Frances Payne; also letter dated June 23, 1984.

21. Interview by Calvin Lee Christman with Ferdinand Eberstadt, July 17 and 18, 1969 (hereinafter referred to as the Christman-Eberstadt interviews), July 17, 1969, side 1, p. 1.

22. Interview with Robert G. Zeller, May 1, 1984.

23. As related to the author by a former partner who requested anonymity.

24. Interview with Franz Schneider, May 7, 1984.

25. Based on author's recollection.

26. Letter to author dated October 24, 1984 from Leslie E. Byrnes, Jr., archivist of Newark Academy.

27. "Ferdinand Eberstadt," *Fortune*, April 1939, p. 72.

28. *Nassau Herald*, Class of 1913, Princeton University, pp. 67, 72, 77.

29. Interview with William H. Long, April 26, 1984.

30. "Business and Finance Leaders: Ferdinand Eberstadt," *New York Herald-Tribune*, April 25, 1951, p. 30.

31. James Y. Newton, "The Man behind the Big Brass," *American Magazine*, May 1949, p. 88.

32. Dean Mathey, *50 Years of Wall Street* (Princeton, N.J., 1966), p. 65.

33. "Dean Mathey, 81, Banking Official," *New York Times*, April 17, 1972, p. 36:3.

34. Mathey, *50 Years of Wall Street*, p. 61–62.

35. Interview with James Benenson, April 9, 1984.

36. Interview with Robert L. Newton, March 28, 1984.

37. Calvin Lee Christman, "Ferdinand Eberstadt and Economic Mobilization for War, 1941–1943," Ph. D. diss., Ohio State University, 1971, n.p., p. 5 (hereinafter referred to as the Christman dissertation).

38. Christman-Eberstadt interviews, July 17, 1969, side 1, pp. 2–3.

39. Christman dissertation, p. 7.

40. "Ferdinand Eberstadt," *Fortune*, p. 72.

41. "Pancho Villa," *Encyclopaedia Britannica*, 1988 ed., Micropaedia Ready Reference vol. 12, pp. 369–70.

42. Interview with John Payne, August 9, 1984.
43. Ibid.
44. Christman-Eberstadt interviews, July 17, 1969, side 1, p. 4.
45. Ibid.
46. Interview with John Payne, August 9, 1984.
47. Interview with Pike H. Sullivan, April 18, 1984.
48. Interview with Donald A. Young, April 5, 1984.
49. Interview with Frederick Eberstadt, March 23, 1984.
50. Letter to author from Mrs. Frances Payne, June 23, 1984.

3

Deal Making in Germany during the Roaring Twenties

Eberstadt was destined to become the leading American specialist on German finance in the 1920s. From his German parents, he learned to speak the language fluently and he also became conversant in French. Following his graduation from Princeton he had developed his knowledge of European affairs during a one-year tour on the Continent where he studied economics and national politics at several leading universities.

A brilliant opportunist, Eberstadt had the ability to size up the key factors likely to result in a given outcome and then aggressively concentrate his total energies on exploiting the opening provided by the window of opportunity. Like Winston Churchill, he had that "Cassandra" quality of being able to forecast accurately the likely outcomes of economic events. But, as in a Greek tragedy, he also possessed a fatal flaw, one that prevented his achieving even wider success and recognition. This flaw which bedeviled him persistently throughout his life was his tendency to overreach himself, which in turn led to monumental feuds with some of his closest associates and his own personal family.

Eberstadt had great family assets and he did not hesitate to exploit them. As noted earlier, his family was related to the great Jewish banking house of Kuhn Loeb. Otto Kahn, Eberstadt's first cousin, became head of Kuhn Loeb in the early part of the century. Throughout his business career, Eberstadt developed a wide circle of important Jewish friends and business contacts including Bernard Baruch, David Sarnoff, André Meyer, Arthur Krim, Robert Benjamin, Walter Heller, Ben Abrams, Billy Rose and many others, no doubt aided by his family's Jewish roots. Eberstadt's heritage must have helped open doors when he began to call on Jewish banking and business houses in Europe during the 1920s.

Other gifts of fortune helped Eberstadt. For example, after completing his wartime service in 1919, he found that two major hurdles facing him—obtaining his law degree and passing the bar exams—no longer existed. The dean of Columbia Law School had ruled that all senior-year law students with passing grades who had enlisted in the armed services would receive their diplomas without taking the final exams. Moreover, the New York State Court had ruled that all servicemen who had received their law diplomas but had been unable to take their bar exams because they were on active duty would be admitted by affidavit only, without taking the exam. The U.S. attorney general had made a similar ruling for the federal courts. Since he had completed two years of law school and had been on active military duty in France and Germany, he qualified under both rulings. As he later told Christman, "I was in the unique position of having received a [law degree] . . . without graduating and having been admitted to the bar . . . without taking the bar examination."[1]

Opportunity continued to beckon. Before being called up for duty on the Mexican border in 1916, he had clerked at the leading Wall Street law firm of McAdoo, Cotton and Franklin. Upon his return from overseas service in Germany in 1919, he was delighted to learn that his position with the firm was still open.[2] Joseph Cotton and George Franklin started their law firm prior to the war. Cotton, born and reared in rural New Hampshire, never lost his laconic country mannerisms and his matter-of-fact approach. A handsome man, looking not unlike his contemporary at Harvard, Franklin Delano Roosevelt, he had a country touch replete with corncob pipe, no matter how formal the occasion.[3] Eberstadt worked directly with George Franklin who was more reserved than Cotton, but Eberstadt got along famously with both men.

At Cotton and Franklin, Eberstadt did a considerable amount of work on the formation of RCA including the extensive negotiations leading to the acquisition of the Marconi Radio business. In addition, he played an important role in the formation of Allied Chemical and Dye Corporation, the largest chemical company in the world at the time, which involved the consolidation of five major chemical companies. He also assisted in the creation of United Artists, for which he drew up the original corporate charter.[4] Nearly forty years later, Eberstadt's own firm brought United Artists public for the first time, an ironic twist. He became a partner in Cotton and Franklin in 1922.

Fortune again beckoned. Earlier, Cotton and Franklin had sent Eberstadt to Germany to settle the war claims of several clients. He achieved such success in Berlin looking after American private interest that he was soon swamped with additional business.[5] Not long after he became a partner in the firm, one of Cotton and Franklin's major clients, Dillon Read, needed a foreign-trained expert to work on German financing deals. Clarence Dillon had decided that it would be futile to try to challenge J. P. Morgan and Kuhn Loeb head to head for control of the major domestic investment banking accounts, so he decided to exploit the emerging overseas markets. With an assist from James Forrestal, Eberstadt was soon actively working on Dillon Read's foreign business. In his new role, Eberstadt uncovered many investment banking deals for Dillon while working on legal details of other deals. He was the right man at the right place at the right time.

Earlier in the decade, Clarence Dillon had visited Germany and had canvassed the German financing needs with the Schroders and the Warburgs.[6] Europe's industries were devastated and its economies mired in debt; America, throbbing with revitalized factories, was in need of new markets. The situation was ripe for financiers with the foresight of Dillon and Eberstadt, who understood America's historic ties to Europe and felt comfortable with its growing involvement in global affairs.

The implementation of the Dawes Plan for German war reparations cleared the way for a major refinancing of German industry. Eberstadt's first assignment was to work on the financing program for August Thyssen, the giant German steel producer.[7] Soon, he developed other financing leads and, in a short time, he became the leading American specialist on German finance.

In one major deal, Eberstadt helped to negotiate the financing related to the formation of United Steel Works, a giant coal, iron and steel cartel, which ranked just behind U.S. Steel in the world steel industry. With the British merchant bankers, J. H. Schroder & Company of London, Dillon Read with Eberstadt in the lead negotiated $100 million in loans to finance this giant combination. Subsequently, Dillon and Schroder sold their interests at huge profits through large flotations in the New York and London markets. Dillon followed up this initial financing with a number of other offerings in New York for the new steel combine, with Schroder heading up parallel banking groups in London.[8]

As Eberstadt uncovered more and more financing prospects for Dillon, Eberstadt's law firm received an increasing volume of "finder" fees from Dillon. For example, Eberstadt was responsible for bringing to Dillon the German electrical colossus, Siemens & Halske. Dillon could see that this aggressive young lawyer had investment banking talents, and he decided to offer him a partnership in the firm to exploit his talents even further. Furthermore, Dillon's staff in Europe was lackluster and needed a tough operator like Eberstadt to turn the European operation into a profit center for the firm.[9]

In late 1925, Clarence Dillon asked Eberstadt if he "would consider leaving Cotton and Franklin and joining his firm as a partner." The offer included a salary that was more than three times what he was then earning in the practice of law. Eberstadt told Dillon, "I'll think it over and let you know." He then consulted with Joseph Cotton, his senior partner. After describing the offer, the somewhat iconoclastic Cotton replied, "I certainly advise you to take it." Taken aback by Cotton's ready acceptance of his possible departure, he asked, "How do you happen to be so sure, so quickly?" Cotton shot back with a chuckle, "The investment banking business is the only business I know of where you can make money without either brains or capital, and I think you are well-qualified on both scores."[10]

Although he regretted leaving, the opportunity to make a fortune in investment banking with Dillon Read was too much for Eberstadt to resist. Furthermore, since Cotton and Franklin continued as legal counsel to Dillon Read, he concluded that he could continue his long relationship with them, but from the other side of the desk.[11] Clarence Dillon had a great influence on Eberstadt, and the skills he developed under the tutelage of Dillon and his associates formed the basic mosaic of Eberstadt's financing technique.

After graduating from Harvard, Dillon married Anne McEldin Douglass and, after an extended honeymoon in Europe, Dillon decided to try his hand at the investment business. Through an old friend he was introduced to and joined the investment banking firm of William A. Read & Company, a successor to Vermilye & Company, an old-line firm whose roots went back to 1830. The firm, however, had developed major problems in distributing its securities underwritings, and Dillon devised a plan that overcame these problems. Two years later, at the age of thirty-four, Dillon became a partner in the firm. Shortly thereafter, Read suddenly died, and Dillon was named by the remaining partners to head the firm; its name was later changed to Dillon, Read & Co.[12]

By 1925, the firm under Dillon's leadership had raised $2 billion in new financing for American and European companies, placing it just behind Morgan and Kuhn Loeb as the leading investment bankers in the field.[13] Dillon did not play long shots as reflected in the care he used in preparing an issue for financing. This usually involved his professional staff's ironing out the myriad details as well as performing a rigorous "due diligence" analysis before Dillon was prepared to put his name on any deal.[14] Eberstadt would adopt this same careful approach in new business evaluation with his own firm years later; the training came from Dillon.

In comparing Eberstadt and Dillon, Dean Mathey once told his close associate, Peter Wastrom,

Eber was a very tough and uncompromising person and very difficult to work with [but] if you think Eber was tough, you should have known Clarence Dillon. He was probably . . . the meanest man that ever lived as far as we were concerned. To this day, I don't know whether he cheated us at the end of the year in divvying up the pie. He just called you in and told you what you were going to get with no rhyme, reason or calculations—very arbitrary.

Mathey then laughed, "Unfortunately I think Eber adopted or learned his toughness with other people as a carry-over from his days with Clarence Dillon."[15] Dillon's tightfisted methods and sage investment judgment paid off; he had amassed an estate estimated by *Fortune* at between $100 and $200 million in the early 1960s.[16]

The roaring twenties were an opportune time for aggressive men on the make such as Clarence Dillon and Ferdinand Eberstadt. The economy and the stock market were booming through most of the period, and the United States had emerged from World War I as a major creditor nation, in contrast to its debtor status prior to the war.

Not only had the financial position of the United States changed dramatically in the postwar period, but the American economy was so virile that the treasury piled up surpluses each year. Under the Republican administrations of Calvin Coolidge, three major tax reductions were made, which substantially reduced the tax burden for individuals and businesses. This spurred an increase in savings, permitting the expansion to continue. As John Kenneth Galbraith points out in his account of the stock market speculation in the 1920s, "The rich got richer much faster than the poor were getting less poor."[17] The spectacular growth of the American economy during the 1920s provided investment bankers with a highly stimulating and expansive environment for new securities issues. As chronicled by John Brooks, Eberstadt and Forrestal were two of the rising stars of this exciting period.[18]

From early 1922 until the stock market collapse in October 1929, except for slight setbacks, investment bankers enjoyed an unprecedented volume of business and prosperity as the security markets flourished. A significant part of this volume consisted of some $4.6 billion invested in foreign issues; America surpassed England as the world's leading exporter of capital. While most of America remained deeply committed to isolationism, a small group of Wall Street bankers and lawyers met in the clubs of London, Paris and Berlin as friendly competitors putting together deals for their firms. In a private and profit-seeking capacity, they were rebuilding a war-ravaged Europe in a manner much the same as would be employed by the United States under the Marshall Plan twenty-five years later.[19] To compete more effectively for the better foreign flotations, Dillon Read opened an office in Paris at 39 Rue Cambon in the late 1920s to find and prepare new issues of foreign securities for the American market.[20]

Not long after Eberstadt had become Dillon Read's European-based partner, however, a major incident occurred which forced him to return to New York in the fall of 1926. The firm was the investment banker for

Goodyear Tire and Rubber Company, having earlier in the decade restructured and saved that company when it was threatened with insolvency following the severe business slump of 1920–1921. As part of the
reorganization, Clarence Dillon and two others were appointed trustees
of Goodyear and granted 10,000 shares of management stock which gave
them control. Dillon Read then refinanced the company with a three-
part securities offering consisting of high-yield bonds, debentures and
preferred stock to raise $87 million of new capital. As part of the deal,
Dillon also received a very lucrative contract to manage Goodyear.[21]

By mid-1926, several dissatisfied Goodyear stockholders, particularly
the Seiberlings, the original founders who had been ousted in the earlier
crisis, brought lawsuits seeking to recover $15 million of alleged exces-
sive profits derived by Dillon from the reorganization of the company
in 1921.[22] Before the suits were settled, it was said that nearly every
major law firm in Cleveland, Akron and New York was involved in the
litigation in one way or another.

Dillon asked Eberstadt to coordinate the legal defense of the firm, the
staff for which occupied considerable space at 120 Broadway. Eberstadt
masterminded the handling of these lawsuits including a countersuit
brought by a Goodyear stockholder which sought to invalidate the position of the Seiberlings and to oust them as voting trustees for the
common stockholders of the company.[23]

The suits were finally settled after eight months of legal maneuvering.
Owen D. Young, one of the management trustees, acted as a mediator
at this point and helped bring an amicable settlement to the long legal
battle.[24] As part of the settlement, Dillon Read agreed to terminate its
management contract and to absorb all of the legal fees. It did this by
foregoing its underwriting fee on a subsequent offering of $60 million
of 5-percent bonds issued by the company in 1927 to refund the high-
yield securities still outstanding from Dillon's earlier financial rescue of
the company; in addition, Dillon agreed to sell a block of 50,000 shares
of Goodyear stock to certain employees designated by the company at
deep discounts from prevailing market prices. The legal fees came to
$2,225,000, a staggering sum at the time.[25]

After organizing Dillon's legal defense on Goodyear, Eberstadt returned to Europe in the summer of 1927 to continue nurturing German
financing deals. Economic conditions had become highly favorable to
German industry. The Dawes Plan had reduced the burden of reparations; German export industries such as iron, steel, coal and electrical
equipment thrived as European industry recovered from the postwar
business contraction. Preceding the favorable export trends, the German
government had finally brought under control the hyperinflation which
had brought the German economy to a near standstill.[26] Eberstadt's

newly revitalized European corporate finance staff aggressively pursued Dillon Read financings for those industries.

Eberstadt's record thereafter was impressive. In 1925 Dillon had total underwritings of $550 million, of which $139 million was foreign but only $39 million of this represented German deals. In 1926, Eberstadt's first year in Europe for Dillon, the firm's flotations totalled $485 million, but foreign financings rose to $192 million (about 40 percent of the total) including $117 million in seven German issues. In 1927 total deals for the firm came to $470 million with German issues accounting for $84 million; in 1928 almost 20 percent of Dillon's underwritings originated in Europe.[27]

While in Europe, Eberstadt met and maintained close ties with a number of leading financiers, government figures and captains of industry— the most powerful leaders of Europe. The list below indicates just a few of the prominent figures that he dealt with on a regular basis:

Hjalmar Schacht: President of the Reichsbank, the central bank of Germany, and later finance minister of the German Reich.

Gustav Stresemann: The leading politician of post–World War I Germany, initially chancellor of the German Reich and later the foreign minister responsible for negotiating the Lucarno Treaty and for bringing Germany into the League of Nations.

S. Parker Gilbert: Agent general for reparations, the official in charge of the all-important transfer of foreign exchange in Germany to pay private external obligations of German companies and governmental bodies. Later he became the managing director of J. P. Morgan.

Dr. Albert Voegler: Head of the United Steel Works, a company created by Dillon Read's merger of seven steel companies in 1926 to form the second largest steel concern in the world at that time.

Hermann Werner: Head of the Siemens & Halske electrical equipment concern, the largest of its kind in Europe.

Baron Henry Schroder: Head of the German banking firm of the same name with major branches in London and New York. Schroder and Dillon Read worked as partners on much German financing in the 1920s.

Max Warburg: Head of the Hamburg private bank of the same name. Eberstadt worked closely with Warburg on a number of German financing deals.[28]

Eberstadt's energy in this period is almost unbelievable. In the first year that he was in Europe he met literally hundreds of different people active in all levels of finance, industry and government in the course of his work.[29] Eberstadt needed to convert only a small portion of these contacts into viable deals to make a successful career.

Eberstadt's associate sheds light on how he organized his dealings in

Germany. A normal business day would consist of a half dozen or more important business meetings during the day, followed by a dinner and perhaps a performance at the opera with important clients. Finally, the evening would be topped off by visits to late-night cabarets with a few hours set aside for sleep. Dillon Read's surge in European financing seemed to thrive as a result of his grueling, whirlwind schedule.

Despite Eberstadt's eagerness to promote new deals, his penchant for autocratic control nearly lost the important Siemens account.[30] Eberstadt had completed the negotiations for a major financing for Siemens & Halske. The tombstone advertisements were to appear in the next day's papers in New York. At the closing on the evening before, however, Max Haller, the managing director of Siemens stated that Dillon would have to share with Schroder the top line in the offering prospectus. Dillon however would occupy the key left position.

Eberstadt made this a sticking point. He told Haller that Dillon Read would not underwrite the issue unless it had the top line all to itself as it always had before. Haller, who was red faced and stubborn, said that Siemens had had many years of profitable and pleasant dealings with Dillon Read and that he had hoped that they would continue, but that if this meant it must do this deal without Dillon, so be it; it would not consent to Dillon's being on the top line by itself.

Eberstadt's bluff was called; fortunately, he backed down at the last minute rather than risk losing the Siemens' business, and the deal went through with the two names on the top line. Although Eberstadt's over-aggressiveness had nearly lost the firm one of its prized accounts, he had the good sense to back off at the last moment.

Dillon's banking relationship with Schroder provided for working jointly on German financing with a fifty-fifty split of fees earned on such business originated by either house. Schroder later complained to Eberstadt that this formula should apply to any foreign business initiated by Dillon. Eberstadt stood his ground claiming that the formula applied only to the German deals originated by either house. This question became a source of continuing friction between the two houses.[31]

Among the many important political contacts developed by Eberstadt in Germany, and probably the most influential, was Gustav Stresemann, the leading politician in postwar Germany. Stresemann occupied a position roughly equivalent to that of Konrad Adenauer in the post–World War II period. In 1926, he was awarded the Nobel Peace prize for his continuing efforts to bring about a peaceful settlement to the World War I conflict. Although Stresemann's role in post-war Germany and Europe remains controversial to many historians, his untimely death in October 1929 removed the last obstacle to the rise of Hitler whom he had resisted.[32]

Eberstadt had extensive dealings with Stresemann regarding the concern that Dillon and other American investment bankers had with the maintenance of convertibility of marks to dollars. To float German debt and other issues in New York, the bankers had to be able to assure their clients that German corporations would have sufficient foreign exchange to meet their dollar obligations for dividends, interest payments and principal payments. For this and other reasons, Eberstadt and Dillon favored German corporations with a favorable trade balance in the form of exports over imports—primarily the export industries of coal, iron, steel and electrical equipment. These companies had sufficient foreign exchange income to meet the service charges on their foreign obligations.[33]

Eberstadt's frequent reports to Clarence Dillon, based on his close relations with Stresemann and many others, enabled the partners of Dillon Read to anticipate any changes in the thinking of the German authorities on this extremely critical factor affecting their financing business overseas. Stresemann valued Eberstadt's counsel as well, as noted in this excerpt from Stresemann's diaries on July 11, 1926:

> Mr. Ferdinand Eberstadt . . . came to see me today. . . . He had just come from an interview with Herren Thyssen and Voegler [with] whom . . . he had negotiated a part of the new shares of the Steel Trust, and he could assure me that there had never been so favourable a market for German securities in the U.S. A. as there was today. Two years ago he had been only able to negotiate German investments at an interest rate of 10 1/4 percent, but now shares bearing 6 3/4 percent stood above par. There was only one difficulty in the way of negotiating German shares, and that was the existing uncertainty as to the final sum which Germany would have to provide by way of reparations.

Stresemann added,

> Herr Eberstadt . . . thought he would be in a position to negotiate through his banking house in the next three or four years, one billion dollars' worth of these bonds, if Germany would undertake the payment of the interest and France stand security for it. Moreover, 300 million dollars' worth were immediately negotiable.[34]

Stresemann and Eberstadt continued their discussion, touching on such important topics as the German development of man-made oil from coal, the relations of Germany with France and England, the proposed revisions in the Dawes Plan and future relations with the Soviet Union.[35]

Even though Western nations had imposed a strict blockade on trade with the Soviets, Averell Harriman and others had begun talks with Moscow looking toward reestablishing joint trade between the West and the Soviet Union. Through his Berlin office, Harriman had begun discounting Russian trade paper growing out of exports to Russia. Harriman felt that these deals would benefit American business by allowing the Russian market to absorb German exports that might otherwise be dumped in the United States. Moreover, Harriman contended that trade and credit could be used as levers in gaining concessions from the Soviet leaders.[36] Armand Hammer would also exploit commercial opportunities with the Soviet leaders in return for humanitarian aid that Hammer used as barter. Although Eberstadt also explored opening up financing opportunities for Dillon Read in Russia, nothing came of it as Dillon did not put much faith in Soviet Russia's leaders.

Later, Eberstadt became disenchanted with the economic prospects for German industry.[37] Moreover, Stresemann suffered a series of debilitating strokes starting in the late 1920s, and this bastion of peace through rapprochement with France would soon be lost. Hitler was gaining political strength, and the shadows of anti-Semitism, extreme nationalism, violence and ultimate world war were lengthening. Eberstadt foresaw that investment prospects were becoming less attractive as the decade of the 1920s came to an end. His worst fears were ultimately realized.

Eberstadt's constant involvement with German politicians in Berlin in the late 1920s apparently led to a second straying from the marital hearth. According to family sources, Eberstadt had earlier in the decade had a long-lasting affair with Marie Norton Whitney, the socially prominent wife of Cornelius Vanderbilt (Sonny) Whitney in Old Westbury, Long Island. Later, in a bizarre turn of events, Averell Harriman, a close friend of Eberstadt, divorced his first wife, Kitty, and in the following year, 1930, married Marie, who had divorced Sonny Whitney in one of the most celebrated gossip stories of the time.[38]

The second Eberstadt infidelity occurred at about the same time but on a different continent. According to unconfirmed but reliable reports, Eberstadt had an affair with Stresemann's charming and elegant wife, Kathë, the daughter of Adolf Kleefield, a prominent Jewish Berlin industrialist.[39] Had the romance been discovered, it would probably have triggered an international incident between the two nations, but Eberstadt managed to conceal the relationship. He was also rumored to have had an affair with Greta Mosheim, one of the leading actresses of the Berlin stage, during this period. Many of his late-night companions were the wives of prominent financiers whom Eberstadt sought to cultivate as part of his growing network of investment banking contacts.[40]

During the 1920s Berlin emerged as the carefree sin capital of Europe. It seemed that the Germans wanted to forget their losses in World War I by drowning their sorrows in cabaret life. Berlin became a very seductive center. Since young Eberstadt was there, away from home much of the time, he could very well have had some alliances with attractive and prominent women.

After Stresemann's death, his wife stayed in Germany with her two baby sons for a time but fled to Switzerland when Hitler's plans for the Jewish people became clear.[41] Greta Mosheim also fled. It is not clear whether Eberstadt continued his relations with either Kathë Stresemann or Greta Mosheim.

Although Eberstadt's primary activity at Dillon Read was initiating and negotiating German deals, he played a major role along with Forrestal and Dillon in other financings. Forrestal's career at Dillon Read had been as meteoric as Eberstadt's. He became a partner in the firm at the end of 1922 and took charge of Dillon's syndicate operations. Forrestal drove himself without letup, frequently remaining in the office until late in the evening to prepare sales bulletins. When the firm floated a new issue, Forrestal and the other syndicate people often would not leave the office until after midnight.[42]

Forrestal and Eberstadt had that quality which another Princeton classmate, William Long, head of Doremus & Co., described as "the will to win." According to Charles Murphy, a former editor of *Fortune*, who knew both men intimately,

Eberstadt's relationship with Forrestal was, in many ways, a balance of opposite qualities. Eberstadt was brilliant, quick of thought and assertive . . . Forrestal was intuitive, hesitant, reserved and assailed privately by doubts and misgivings. However, separately and together, Eberstadt and Forrestal towered above the senior financial leaders of their day.[43]

Probably the most startling of the deals that Eberstadt and Forrestal put together at Dillon was the complicated merger of Dodge Brothers Motor Company into Chrysler Corporation in 1928. It all began in the spring of 1925 when Clarence Dillon shocked Wall Street by purchasing Dodge Brothers outright for $146 million in cash. The firm simultaneously arranged an underwriting and sold $160 million of newly issued Dodge securities, recovering its cost and netting Dillon and his group a quick $14 million profit.[44]

The two Dodge brothers had started up their motor car business at the beginning of the century initially as a supplier of parts to Henry Ford. They began manufacturing their own cars under the Dodge brand name in 1914 and, by the end of the decade, they had built up their business rapidly to a place just behind Ford. Then tragedy struck; the Dodge brothers had attended an automobile exposition in New York City in January 1920 and had become fatally ill from wood alcohol poisoning from a bottle of bootleg whiskey purchased from a bellhop at the Ritz Carlton Hotel. On their deaths, their widows became sole owners and ran the company for about five years, but the direction and profitability of the automotive business began to change rapidly. Intense and growing competition finally forced them to sell out.[45]

A professional business finder, Charles Schwartz, and his brother had heard that the Dodge widows might be interested in selling out, and they persuaded the widows to give them an option on the business. They took the option to Clarence Dillon, at the suggestion of their mutual friend, Bernard Baruch, and Dillon agreed to pay them a finder's fee based on a percentage of the eventual purchase price if Dillon got the business.[46]

When it became known that Dillon was negotiating with the Dodge brothers' widows for the purchase of the Dodge Company, J. P. Morgan demanded that Dillon discontinue his negotiations as Morgan was representing General Motors which wanted to acquire Dodge. Dillon countered by agreeing to a competitive bidding procedure whereby all interested parties, including the Morgans, would have a chance to acquire the Dodge business, but when the final bids were opened, the Dillon Read offer of $146 million was higher than any other. Dillon's successful bid exceeded the book value of the company by $50 million. Hugh Bullock notes, "The Dodge deal was the first time that the pricing of any new issue had been based on the premise that earning-power rather than assets was the important criterion in valuing a business."[47] As part of the deal, Dillon received all of the 500,000 shares of Class B voting common stock which constituted 100-percent control.[48]

However, the automobile business began to go downhill from that point, and Dillon's Dodge stock was worth far less in 1928 than in 1925. "Then one day," as Eberstadt later recollected, "God appeared in the guise of Walter P. Chrysler offering to buy the Dodge Company."[49] When Maxwell Motor Car went into receivership, Kuhn Loeb, their investment bankers, recruited Chrysler (then head of the Buick division of General Motors) to head up a new corporation to take over the Maxwell business with the name changed to Chrysler. Walter Chrysler, however, needed the popular Dodge brand name along with its production facilities and dealer organization to make his new company a success.[50]

As *Fortune* magazine noted, "by purchasing Dodge, Chrysler could put himself within a bowshot of his boyhood hero whom, all his life, he had hoped to emulate: Henry Ford."[51] Chrysler attached a condition on the acquisition, however, requiring that 90 percent of the stocks and bonds of each class of Dodge securities, issued and outstanding, be tendered before the merger could become effective.[52] Apparently Chrysler was concerned about the danger of having to pay excessive prices to acquire the interests of dissenting minority security holders after the merger became effective. In any event, Dillon and his partners devoted almost full time to the lengthy process of cajoling Dodge stock and bond holders to tender their holdings to meet Chrysler's 90-percent requirement.

The offering plan was made public on June 1, 1928. Originally scheduled to expire on June 30, it was extended three times; the final deadline
was set for Monday, July 30, 1928. As the deadline neared, Dillon still
did not have 90 percent of each class. The *New York Herald Tribune*
reported on July 23 that the Dillon group had 86 percent of the preferred,
76 percent of the Class A common stock (of which there were about two
million shares outstanding) and 99.6 percent of the Class B common
stock (all of which Dillon Read owned).

The stock was widely dispersed; many fathers and grandfathers had
bought shares for their children or grandchildren, very much as in the
original offering of Ford stock a quarter of century later. As the deadline
approached, the Dillon partners, despite Herculean efforts, were still
short of the necessary number of shares.

Time and again, as the difficulty of rounding up 90 percent of stock
issues held here and there and everywhere at home and abroad became
more evident, Dillon tried to change Chrysler's mind. But, according to
Fortune, "Chrysler, pacing the floor with his long Kansas stride, would
reply, 'No, Clarence. I can't do nothing for you.' "[53] A day or so before
the final deadline, Dillon was still short the necessary tender deposits
to make the deal effective.

At this critical juncture, just before time ran out, Eberstadt and Forrestal suggested to Dillon a brilliant though daring plan that saved the
deal. Their suggestion was adopted, and Wall Street was astounded to
learn that Dillon Read had gone into the open market and bought up
enough Dodge preferred shares and Class A common stock for its own
account to satisfy Chrysler's 90-percent requirement.[54] To hedge their
position (involving the commitment of about $5 million of firm capital),
the Eberstadt-Forrestal plan called for simultaneous short sales of Dodge
preferred and Class A stock to hedge the firm's long position.[55] With
this cunning and unprecedented move, the firm met Chrysler's demand
for a minimum of 90 percent of each class of security by the deadline of
July 30. The daring plan paid off, and Forrestal and Eberstadt became
the "golden boys" of the firm.[56]

The merger elevated Chrysler to the position of third-largest auto
company with over $450 million in assets. In addition, Chrysler Cor-
poration acquired 6,000 Dodge dealers, a key ingredient in Chrysler's
subsequent sales success.[57] Moreover, Dillon Read received 50,000
shares of Chrysler common with a market value of about $5 million in
exchange for its Class B stock and substantial fees for its assistance to
Chrysler in effecting the merger with Dodge.

Despite the accolades from his fellow partners and the Street, Eberstadt was far from satisfied with his position at Dillon Read, and he
pressed Forrestal to join him in forming a new firm which would cap-
italize on their combined genius and growing reputation in the Street.

Dillon had increased Eberstadt's partnership interest in 1927 and in the spring of 1928, but Eberstadt wanted more. It is difficult to say, more than half a century later, who was more at fault—Dillon or Eberstadt. Probably both were equally determined.

As to motives, Eberstadt had just bought an eighty-acre tract on a neck of land jutting out into Long Island Sound in the town of Huntington, within the so-called Gold Coast millionaires' preserve on the North Shore. Eberstadt wanted to build a mansion to rival the lavish estates of other multimillionaires—including the palatial eighty-room French chateau built for $4.5 million in 1917 by his first cousin, Otto Kahn, on 700 acres in neighboring Cold Spring Harbor.[58] Kahn's mansion was described at the time by the *New York Times* as the "finest country house in America"; it perfectly complemented Kahn's lavish Italian palazzo on Fifth Avenue.[59] Eberstadt felt that he needed to trumpet to the Wall Street establishment that he had indeed arrived. Therefore, it would be only natural for him to try to increase his partnership interest in order to pay for this vast undertaking. Furthermore, in the summer of 1928, Eberstadt felt the timing was propitious for him and Forrestal to go out on their own and form a new investment banking firm, given the wave of favorable publicity that had followed their success in the Chrysler-Dodge merger.

In the Christman interviews, years later, Eberstadt stated, "While I was very happy at Dillon Read, there were some things that I was not so happy about. My friend, Forrestal, a partner there, another friend by the name of Christie, and I had pretty well decided that we might go out on our own."[60] Eberstadt, with his characteristic aggressiveness, had leased office space for the new firm and had told Forrestal that the die was cast.

Forrestal, however, got cold feet and decided not to go ahead with the new venture. He asked Eberstadt, "Why don't we wait another year and see how things work out?"[61] Venturing out on his own was to Forrestal an unacceptable risk at that point in time. Although Eberstadt wanted to move ahead, the hesitation of Forrestal forced him to reconsider, and he decided to make one last effort to achieve a greater financial success at Dillon Read by demanding a steep increase in his partnership interest (perhaps with a greater management voice as well).

If Dillon met his conditions, he would stay; otherwise, he would strike out on his own. If Eberstadt did succeed in his demands, his partnership interest would be above that of William A. Phillips, second in command and Dillon's closest friend and ally from Harvard undergraduate days—an untenable position for Dillon. Dillon had always decided how the profits were to be divided among the partners. He made the division; no one knew what formula he used. André Meyer did the same later at Lazard; Eberstadt followed the same system when he set up his own firm in the 1930s.

Finally, Eberstadt decided to bring the matter to a head. Dean Mathey related the scene to Peter Wastrom years later:

One morning, while in the office during the Christmas holidays, Eberstadt stalked into Dillon's famed corner office and reviewed all of the profitable German bond deals that he had brought to the firm, resulting in millions of dollars of profits, as well as his role in completing the Chrysler-Dodge merger and his placements of millions of dollars of Dillon deals with the so-called Jewish banks in Europe. He had it right down to the penny. He knew exactly how much money Dillon Read had earned on every one of those deals and finally he told Dillon he thought his partnership interest should be increased to ten percent from three percent. Without blinking an eye, Clarence Dillon's answer was, "you're fired" and that was the end of it.[62]

Eberstadt's share of the partnership upon his withdrawal came to about $3 million, of which one-third was paid to him in cash and the balance in securities at market value. These included large amounts of shares of United States & Foreign Securities (a closed-end investment trust sponsored by the firm equal to about one half of the value), Louisiana Land and Exploration and twenty-odd other holdings, most representing important financings by Dillon Read in the 1920s.[63]

Although Eberstadt's holdings lost a major part of their value during the stock market crash, Louisiana Land, one of Dillon's legendary deals of the 1920s, more than made up for this drop in value in later years by virtue of the sensational oil and gas finds on its properties.

Dean Mathey developed the Louisiana Land financing for Dillon as a venture capital deal. As Mathey later related the story to Wastrom, "One day in the late 1920s this gentleman representing the ownership of Louisiana Land walked into Dillon Read and said they needed money." At that time, the company was a start-up speculation based on the prospects of developing oil and gas reserves on its 1,800,000 acres of swamps and bayous which lay across the southern portion of Louisiana. The company's only income consisted of modest fur-trapping fees from hunters who were using its vast land holdings which contained the nation's largest muskrat population.[64]

Dillon Read raised $1 million in capital for the company through an initial public offering of 500,000 shares of common stock at $2 per share. Much to the partners' dismay, the offering was unsuccessful and, as a result, the Dillon Read partners, including Eberstadt, were forced to take up the unsold shares.[65]

In late 1928, the company contracted with Texaco to explore and develop the company's oil and gas resources in return for a 25-percent royalty on all oil and gas produced from its lands.[66] A great quantity of oil and gas was found on the company's lands, and the discovery ranked among major oil finds of all time. The resulting royalties caused Louisiana Land's earnings to soar, and the Dillon Read partners and other stockholders made fortunes. One secretary, at the recommendation of her boss, a Dillon Read partner, bought 3,000 shares of Louisiana Land stock in the late twenties at 50 cents a share; that investment had soared in market value to over $6 million by the early 1950s.[67]

After leaving Dillon Read at the end of 1928, Eberstadt went fishing in the Bahamas with his family to ponder his next move and savor his outstanding financial success. About a week after he arrived, he received an urgent cable from Owen D. Young asking him to serve as one of Young's assistants on the U.S. delegation to the Reparations Conference to be held in Paris in the spring of 1929.[68] Eberstadt's reputation as an expert on German finance with intimate contacts at the highest levels of government, business and finance eminently qualified him for this important assignment. Accordingly, as reported in the *New York Times*, in early February Eberstadt sailed for Europe together with Young, J. P. Morgan, Thomas Lamont, Jeremiah Smith, and David Sarnoff, all members of the American delegation.[69]

The conference had been called to come to grips with the fact that the Germans were unable to pay the amount of reparations called for under the Dawes Plan. The Allies had to agree to reduce the level of these reparations in line with Germany's external trade balance. The French opposed these reductions because the reparations received by the French helped to balance France's trade position. Besides, the French thought the reparations burden would keep Germany, their long-standing enemy, in a weak economic condition.[70]

Upon arriving at the preliminary meeting in Paris, Eberstadt soon concluded that the conference had no hope of succeeding. On the second day, Eberstadt cornered Young and warned: "Hey, this thing's a fake—it will bust up because they are playing politics and have no concern for economics."[71] Ten years later, after Hitler came to power, Eberstadt reflected:

The conference might have saved the world from what has happened since—if they had had the vision and nerve to be realistic about reparations.... [P]olitical considerations remained uppermost in the minds of the representatives rather than economic realities and it had no chance for anything beyond ephemeral success. As it was, I was more of a financial "dirt farmer" to most of the people there and my views were outstandingly unpopular.... This is just another reason why wars make no sense; there is no victory in war ... nor in the peace following.[72]

The conference finally approved a new plan for German reparations with greatly reduced payments, but it was an empty achievement. Stresemann, the bastion of peace in postwar Germany, died in the fall of 1929, and Hitler's rise to power thereafter was irresistible. Moreover, the economies of the Western world were overexpanded and headed toward the worst economic disaster in history. Eberstadt would, unfortunately for him, change directions once again and reenter the investment business following his return to New York from Paris in October 1929. The ensuing crash destroyed much of Eberstadt's fortune as well as the fortunes and lives of many others and was followed by the longest, deepest depression in the nation's history. His fortune greatly reduced, Eberstadt had to rebuild from scratch, but his heritage and his aggressive character helped save him.

Notes

1. Interview by Calvin Lee Christman with Ferdinand Eberstadt, July 17 and 18, 1969 (hereinafter referred to as the Christman-Eberstadt interviews), July 17, 1969, side 1, p. 3.

2. Ibid, p. 4.

3. Dean Mathey, *50 Years of Wall Street* (Princeton, N.J., 1966), p. 56.

4. "Ferdinand Eberstadt," *Fortune*, April 1939, p. 72.

5. James Y. Newton, "The Man behind the Big Brass," *American Magazine*, May 1949, p. 88.

6. "Private Financing to Europeans," *New York Times*, July 19, 1922, p. 22.

7. "Ferdinand Eberstadt," *Fortune*, pp. 72–74.

8. James C. Young, "Clarence Dillon Became Banker through Chance," *New York Times*, January 10, 1926, VIII, p. 6; "Big Steel Merger Formed in Germany," *New York Times*, January 15, 1926, p. 1; Frank J. Williams, "A New Leader in Finance: Clarence Dillon," *American Review of Reviews*, February 1926, pp. 147–48; and "Offers $30,000,000 Reich Steel Bonds," *New York Times*, June 26, 1926, p. 21.

9. "Ferdinand Eberstadt," *Fortune*, pp. 72, 74.

10. Calvin Lee Christman, "Ferdinand Eberstadt and Economic Mobilization for War, 1941–1943," Ph.D. diss., Ohio State University, 1971, n.p., pp. 13–14.

11. "Eberstadt in Dillon, Read," *New York Times*, February 5, 1926, p. 29.

12. Williams, "A New Leader in Finance," p. 148.

13. Young, "Clarence Dillon Became Banker through Chance," VIII, p. 6; Williams, "A New Leader in Finance," p. 148.

14. Williams, "A New Leader in Finance," p. 148.

15. Interview with Peter Wastrom, March 29, 1984.

16. "Mrs. Anne Douglass Dillon Dies," *New York Times*, November 8, 1961, p. 35.

17. John Kenneth Galbraith, *The Great Crash* (Boston, 1955), p. 7.

18. John Brooks, *Once in Golconda: A True Drama of Wall Street, 1920–1938* (New York, 1969), pp. 59–60.

19. Walter Isaacson and Evan Thomas, *The Wise Men: Six Friends and the World They Made* (New York, 1986), p. 112.

20. "Dillon Read Opens Paris Office," *New York Times*, March 12, 1928, p. 35.

21. Williams, "A New Leader in Finance," pp. 146–7; Laura Jereski, "Clarence Dillon: Using Other People's Money," *Forbes*, July 13, 1987, p. 270; and *Poor's Industrials*, 1921 ed., pp. 1513–15; also "Goodyear Tire Plan Put into Operation; Bankers Announce Details by which a Readjustment Will Be Carried Out; Voting Trustees Selected; Disposition of Debt and Recapitalization Provided for in Plan of Committee," *New York Times*, May 17, 1921, p. 25.

22. "Sues to Oust Board of Goodyear Tire: Prosecutor in Ohio Attacks Reorganization of Company in 1921 as Illegal: Raps 'Management Stock': Action Begun to Take Control of Company 'Away from Wall Street,' Official Says," *New York Times*, August 24, 1926, p. 26:4.

23. "Goodyear Plaintiff Scores on Seiberling," *New York Times*, February 9, 1927, p. 33.

24. "Goodyear Suit Ends Outside of Court; Charges Dropped," *New York Times*, May 16, 1927, p. 1.

25. *Poor's Industrials*, 1927 ed., p. 2717; also "Goodyear Fight Is Ended," *Akron Times-Press*, May 12, 1927, p. 1.

26. "Years of Crises," *Encyclopaedia Britannica*, 1988 ed., Micropaedia Ready Reference vol. 20, p. 94.

27. Based on a survey by the author of deals done by Dillon Read from annual records of underwritings published privately by the firm.

28. As related to author by a former Dillon Read associate who requested anonymity.

29. Ibid.

30. Ibid.

31. Ibid.

32. Felix Hirsch, *Gustav Stresemann, 1878/1978* (Bonn, West Germany, 1978), pp. 10–84; also "Gustav Stresemann," *Encyclopaedia Britannica*, 1988 ed., Micropaedia Ready Reference vol. 11, pp. 316–18.

33. Edward F. Willett, "Coal, Iron and Steel in Europe," a brochure published in Paris by Dillon, Read & Co. (Paris, 1928).

34. Eric Sutton, ed. and trans., *Gustav Stresemann, His Diaries, Letters and Papers* (London, 1935–1940), vol. 3, pp. 415–17.

35. Sutton, *Gustav Stresemann*, p. 417.

36. Isaacson and Thomas, *The Wise Men*, pp. 98–101.

37. "Ferdinand Eberstadt," *Fortune*, p. 74.

38. Isaacson and Thomas, *The Wise Men*, p. 106.

39. As related to the author by a former Dillon Read associate who requested anonymity.

40. Ibid.

41. Hirsch, *Gustav Stresemann*, p. 16.

42. Mathey, *50 Years of Wall Street*, p. 263.

43. Letter to author from Charles J. V. Murphy, February 15, 1985.

44. Williams, "A New Leader in Finance," p. 147; "The Dodge Deal," *Literary Digest*, April 25, 1925, p. 80.

45. "John Dodge Dead," *New York Times*, January 15, 1920, p. 11; also Mathey, *50 Years of Wall Street*, pp. 12–14.

46. Mathey, *50 Years of Wall Street*, pp. 12–14.

47. Interview with Hugh Bullock, April 18, 1984.

48. "The Dodge Deal," *Literary Digest*, April 25, 1925, p. 80.

49. Interview with James Benenson, April 9, 1984.

50. "Chrysler," *Fortune*, August 1935, p. 37.

51. Ibid.

52. *Poor's Industrials*, 1929 ed., p. 2397; also "Chrysler," *Fortune*, August 1935, p. 37.

53. "Chrysler," *Fortune*, p. 37.

54. "Dodge Stock Buying Caps Chrysler Deal," *New York Times*, July 31, 1928, p. 1.

55. Interview with James Benenson, former Eberstadt associate, April 9, 1984.

56. Rogow, *James Forrestal*, p. 82; also interviews with John J. McCloy, April 17, 1984, Eliot Janeway, April 3, 1984, and Hugh Bullock, April 18, 1984; also, "Dodge Stock Buying Caps Chrysler Deal," p. 1.

57. "A Third Motor Car Colossus, The Chrysler-Dodge Merger," *Literary Digest*, June 16, 1928, p. 12.

58. " 'Citizen Kane' Site Changing Hands," *New York Times*, February 19, 1989, p. 61.

59. Mary Jane Matz, *The Many Lives of Otto Kahn* (New York, 1963), p. 20.

60. Christman-Eberstadt interviews, July 17, 1969, side 1, p. 7.

61. Interview with Eliot Janeway, April 3, 1984.

62. Interview with Peter L. Wastrom, March 29, 1984.

63. As related to author by a former Dillon Read associate who requested anonymity.

64. Interview with Peter L. Wastrom, March 29, 1984; also *Poor's Industrials*, 1929 ed., p. 2635.

65. Interview with Peter L. Wastrom, March 29, 1984.

66. *Poor's Industrials*, 1929 ed., p. 2635.

67. As related to the author by a former Dillon Read associate who requested anonymity.

68. "Ferdinand Eberstadt," *Fortune*, p. 74.

69. "Morgan and Young Sail with Advisors," *New York Times*, February 2, 1929, p. 1.

70. Christman-Eberstadt interviews, July 17, 1969, side 1, pp. 5–7.

71. Christman dissertation, pp. 18–19.

72. Ibid.

4

Making Money in the Depression Thirties

Following his sensational successes at Dillon Read, Eberstadt was riding high in the summer of 1929, as were many others in and out of Wall Street. After having met Cyrus Eaton through Owen D. Young, Eberstadt struck up a friendship based on mutual self-interest.[1] Eaton was interested in building up his New York operations to complement the rapidly expanding financial empire that he had constructed from his base in Cleveland, Ohio. The existing Otis office in New York needed a person like Eberstadt to revitalize it as he had stimulated the European operations of Dillon Read.

At this time, Cyrus Eaton was restructuring corporations thereby enhancing their value. Eaton even dreamed of transplanting the nation's financial center to the Midwest. By 1929 Eaton had emerged as a rising financial genius who in just two years had put together Republic Steel, the third largest steel corporation in the country, topped only by U.S. Steel and Bethlehem. His utility holdings in the Midwest represented $2 billion of invested capital; all of them were created through mergers and acquisitions as was his steel empire. These accomplishments were achieved through his use of other people's money in the closed-end investment trusts sponsored by his firm.[2] A short time later, Eaton launched his monumental battle to combine Republic with Inland Steel of Chicago and Youngstown Sheet & Tube (Ohio) to bypass Bethlehem and become the second largest steel producer.[3]

In August 1929, Eberstadt had changed his pessimistic view of the economy and fatefully decided to reenter the market. He became convinced that the business expansion and bull market in stocks had still a long way to go before reaching exhaustion, and he was fascinated with Eaton's success as were many others in the country. The incredible stock boom in the summer of 1929 excited Eberstadt, and he plunged back into the market, hoping to multiply his fortune quickly. He was not alone in this. Even the sage investment speculator, Bernard Baruch, was hurt badly in the ensuing stock market crash.

But Eberstadt made another more grievous error. He did not exercise proper due diligence in appraising a partnership interest in Otis. While considering Eaton's offer, Eberstadt had heard some disquieting rumors about Eaton, but Young assured him that the rumors were baseless and that the Eaton offer was a once in a lifetime opportunity.[4] Based on this reassurance, Eberstadt took the partnership offer without carefully inspecting the balance sheet and books of Otis. Thus, in October 1929, he purchased a 10-percent interest in Otis for $1.6 million, just before the stock market crashed later that month. After the market collapsed, he was shocked to find out that Otis & Company owed $260 million to the banks which had financed its customers' brokerage margin accounts. By then, the market crash had reduced the value of the collateral to below the required level, and the banks called the loans, making Otis insolvent.[5]

To compound Otis' problems, Eaton had thrown all of the resources of the firm and those of the firm's closed-end trusts into its titanic battle with Bethlehem Steel for control of Youngstown Sheet & Tube. The fight drained the firm's resources and helped force it into insolvency. Eberstadt, playing a key role in the reorganization of Otis, raised a temporary loan from the Chase National Bank which enabled Otis to meet the Stock Exchange's required minimum net capital; otherwise, Otis would have been closed down by the Exchange. Albert Wiggins, the head of the Chase Bank, arranged this loan based on nothing more than a handshake agreement with Eberstadt.[6]

The Stock Exchange stepped in and brought about the final reorganization of the firm with Otis' brokerage division spun off to become part of E. A. Pierce and Company. However, Eberstadt's 10-percent interest in the Otis firm was wiped out. Moreover, his remaining holdings in the stocks he received when he left Dillon Read had dropped precipitously in market value. After ensuring that the Otis brokerage dissolution was properly provided for, Eberstadt resigned and went fishing to contemplate his next move.[7]

Insiders claim that Eaton swindled Eberstadt because he never disclosed to Eberstadt the true nature of the firm's financial difficulties when he offered him a partnership. Eliot Janeway, the columnist, adds that Eaton knew all the time what he was doing and manipulated Eberstadt. Adds Janeway, "[D]espite the Otis failure, Eaton . . . got richer every year during the thirties; he was just too much of an 'Old Fox' for Eberstadt at that point in time."[8]

Eaton and the other Cleveland-based partners had systematically transferred most of their wealth outside of the firm and out of the reach of the bankruptcy courts. "The Cleveland partners of the firm were protecting their flanks by putting their capital and money in their wives' names so that when Otis went under, there was nothing to grab out in Cleveland," remarked Andrew W. Eberstadt, Eberstadt's nephew.[9] Later, when Eberstadt formed his own firm, he took a page out of Eaton's book and put all of his stock in the new firm in the name of his wife.[10]

Although financially the Otis disaster was a serious blow, it did not impoverish the Eberstadts. According to Baltimore probate records, Eberstadt's wife, Mary Tongue Eberstadt, inherited $156,105 upon the death of her father in 1929, a substantial sum at the time that helped cushion the disaster.[11] Moreover, Eberstadt no doubt had squirreled away in his wife's name a considerable portion of his now greatly diminished Dillon Read profits.[12] However, in view of his diminished assets, Eberstadt shelved the Delano and Aldrich architectural plans for the grandiose mansion at Target Rock and converted the four-car garage on the property into a temporary home. His New York apartment living was also reduced in scale; some of the children slept on sofa beds in the living room.[13]

After writing off his Otis losses, Eberstadt decided to be his own boss. He determined that from then on he would follow a lone wolf strategy.[14] During the 1920s he had excelled when he had worked as an independent, but he found that his freedom of action was limited when he had to conform to the requirements of the bureaucracy of a large firm. Thus, the idea of forming his own independent firm appealed to him.

With his characteristic energy and enthusiasm, he soon had the necessary capital lined up. The new firm opened its doors for business on September 1, 1931, with $100,000 in paid-in capital, which came equally from four outside investors: $25,000 from his old friends, brothers W. Averell and Roland Harriman; $25,000 from William Chester, a Milwaukee department store owner and a Princeton classmate; and $25,000 each from Joseph Cotton and George Franklin, Eberstadt's former law partners. Each of these four original investors received preferred stock plus a 5-percent common stock interest in the firm. They also agreed to put up an additional $100,000 in capital if Eberstadt deemed it necessary, but it never was. In a few years, all of the outside investors were completely repaid.[15]

The Harrimans, who had merged with Brown Brothers, offered their former office space to Eberstadt rent free. Since the Harrimans owned the building at 39 Broadway, they told Eberstadt that, since they were unable to sublet the space, he was welcome to use it for his new firm. The space was furnished with rugs on the floor, desks in place with telephones and pencils in the drawers.[16] For years thereafter, Eberstadt maintained a bank account with Brown Brothers Harriman in reciprocation for the free office rental.[17]

Among Eberstadt's major talents was his skill as a negotiator, a skill that had been finely honed in the numerous deals, underwritings, legal settlements and mergers of the 1920s. Though at times blunt to the point of being offensive, Eberstadt commanded an extraordinarily warm charm and subtlety of persuasion which he now turned to the task of staffing his new firm. Soon he recruited a responsive and loyal staff to launch his investment banking venture.

Several people came over from Otis, including Edward F. Willett (who had accompanied Eberstadt from Dillon Read to Otis) and Grinnell Martin, a slightly built man who served, as Eberstadt put it, "[i]n two wars with me, one in France and the other at Otis & Company."[18] He took with him his personal secretary, Isabel Laughlin, and Dan Breitbart, an accountant who had been with Otis since 1920. Ernest Brelsford, a close aide of Cyrus Eaton, joined Eberstadt a year later. Francis S. Williams became associated with the firm shortly afterward and remained with it throughout his career.

Williams, who previously had worked as a security analyst at the Old Colony Trust Company in Boston and with J. & W. Seligman & Company in New York, later made an extensive survey of the chemical industry which led to much investment banking activity for the firm and the launching in 1938 of Chemical Fund, a major success for the young firm.[19]

Nelson Loud, who later headed the corporate finance department, was hired after his graduation from Yale in 1935. He describes Eberstadt as "a startling man, 45 or so, bright eyes, very direct and if you didn't like it, that's all, he didn't spare any feelings." Loud notes that "a lot of people claim that Eberstadt had ice water in his veins. . . . He was straight forward, viciously hard; he could be as cold-blooded as anyone you ever saw . . . but he could also be a tremendously warm, charming man. . . . He was extraordinarily nice to me."[20] Even when Eberstadt had cornered an adversary, he offered generous surrender terms. Eberstadt used to counsel his close aides to always give their opponent a bridge over which to retreat.

Rounding out the early firm's operations was Eric (Rodie) Rodin, the big, affable over-the-counter trader. His job was to make markets in the stocks of the companies that Eberstadt began to underwrite in the mid-1930s, until the issues were thoroughly seasoned.

Rodie, one of the most colorful traders in the Street, was renowned for the practical jokes he played on fellow traders from other firms. He especially loved to play pranks on new recruits of the firm during their training programs. A large man, who stood six feet, five or six inches tall, Rodie was a heavy drinker, who took whiskey by the water glass.[21]

Eberstadt seemed to like Rodie's brand of humor which appealed to his own somewhat sardonic personality. Rodie represented to Eberstadt an independent spirit which, he felt, was good for the morale of the firm, although it was out of context with his own hard-nosed, no-nonsense business style. Eberstadt suffered few fools, but Rodie's brand of comic humor lifted the spirits of the firm during the difficult depression years.[22]

As the firm expanded its underwriting activity in the mid-1930s, Eberstadt hired Edward B. Conway, a Securities and Exchange Commission (SEC) lawyer with a flair for writing and an ability to work harmoniously with the SEC and the state securities commissioners on "blue skying" operations.[23] Conway, a classics scholar at Holy Cross, had graduated from Harvard Law School.

There was a considerable degree of loyalty in this tightly knit team. Eberstadt viewed the role of employees much as the Japanese do—the employee makes a life pact with the employer which lasts as long as the employee remains loyal and useful. Eberstadt also viewed investment banking as a family business very much along the lines of Lehman, Morgan, and Kuhn Loeb, where the house reflected the family.[24]

Since companies were going out of business right and left in 1931, the Eberstadt firm initially had little business to negotiate except for corporate reorganizations involving consolidations and mergers. Many of the corporate launchings of the 1920s had developed a considerable amount of excess overhead and, with reduced volume, many of them could not pay dividends or the interest on their debt. Eberstadt recapitalized such companies, modifying the positions of the various creditors and stockholders. Excess water was squeezed from balance sheets to give companies a chance to survive in the competitive world of the 1930s.[25]

An early reorganization involved the Steneck Trust Company, a small bank located in Hoboken, New Jersey, which had been closed down due to insolvency; its depositors were primarily Italian-American immigrants. They maintained their deposits in the bank through their benevolent society, *Society Fra'Malfatesi*. Eberstadt assigned Francis Williams to make the presentation of the firm's proposal to represent the depositors in the insolvency proceedings with hilarious results.

First, Williams went over to the bank to locate the principals of the Society to set up a meeting but the bank was closed down. Outside, he happened on one of the officers of the Society and Williams was invited to make a presentation to the executive committee of the Society that evening. Williams recalled the meeting in his broad Harvard accent:

I went to the meeting which was held in the back of a cobbler's shop behind drawn curtains at 10 P.M. The only light came from a single candle stuck in the top of a whiskey bottle. My presentation was followed by vigorous arguments with some shouting, all in Italian. Finally, the executive committee approved my appearance before the full membership of the Society the following evening.

The second meeting was also held late at night on the upper floor of a dilapidated warehouse. The house was packed solid and very noisy; apparently all of the members of the Society turned out to find out about their savings. However, as soon as I began my presentation, everyone fell silent. When I finished, the head of the Society came over to thank me and to explain that none of them knew any English but he would explain the proposal to them and recommend their approval.[26]

The Society approved the proposal and this bizarre story had a happy ending. Eberstadt represented the depositors who received a full recovery of their deposits—100 cents on the dollar.

Eberstadt worked on a number of such jobs for small companies during the early stages of his new firm. Although these jobs helped, the firm barely broke even in 1931; but in 1932 a plum landed on Eberstadt's doorstep, one that would make his firm profitable in the latter half of that year. This involved the monumental fraud surrounding Kreuger & Toll and its Machiavellian master, Ivar Kreuger, the "Match King." Kreuger had swindled American and European investors out of more than $1 billion in the 1920s.[27]

Eleven American banks had lent Ivar Kreuger $4,000,000 just before his suicide. Floyd Blair of the National City Bank, which headed the banking group, asked Eberstadt to try to collect. In the summer of 1932 Eberstadt, with Brelsford and his secretary, Isabel Laughlin, went to Europe to try to dig up the assets of the failed company to pay off the bank loan.[28]

Ivar Kreuger, who had for two decades dazzled Wall Street and the political leaders of the Western world, suddenly and without apparent cause committed suicide in his Paris apartment at the Ritz just before his worldwide holding company empire collapsed. At first the world was aghast at the death of this statesman-like leader who had, through the organization and sale of match monopolies, done so much to help finance the countries of Eastern Europe, as well as underdeveloped countries. His counsel was sought by governments around the world including the United States.[29] The Kreuger story continues to fascinate biographers and psychiatrists—more than fifty years after his death.

The American banks knew that, if they submitted their claims for repayment through normal bankruptcy court channels, it would probably be years before any payment would be realized. So they enlisted Eberstadt to represent them because of his reputation as a foreign expert based on his years of experience with Dillon Read and the German reparation conferences in the 1920s. If any American knew the favorite hiding places for money in Europe, Ferdinand Eberstadt was that person.

Eberstadt's response was that, if all the banks were united in the request and his expenses and a reasonable profit were assured, he would do it. After some haggling over whether his fee should be fixed or based on a percentage of any recovery, Eberstadt opted for a fixed fee.[30] Speed was of the essence because the Swedish government had declared a moratorium on payments which expired on August 31; a quick decision was needed.[31]

Eberstadt put liens on the pools of money that he was able to turn up all over Europe. By the time he was finished—a short time later—he had assembled enough assets to more than pay off the $4 million indebtedness to the New York banks.[32] As part of his campaign, Eberstadt propounded a novel theory which, while not having any legal basis, influenced the members of the creditor committee; this involved the application of the accounting principle of last in, first out (LIFO), in other words, the last claims should be settled first. The Swedes were persuaded that there was some merit to Eberstadt's theory, even though there was not any legal basis for it. Eberstadt's son Frederick notes, "My father made up [the LIFO theory] on sheer gall; but it gave the Swedes an easy way out."[33] In any event, it contributed to their decision to settle first the Eberstadt-represented claims.

As a final touch to Eberstadt's effort, the Swedes, being very proper, invited him to a farewell dinner after his job had been finished. As Eberstadt later recalled, "It was a charming affair—perfect Swedish hospitality—except that no one greeted me when I arrived, talked with me while I was there, or said good-by when I left."[34]

The firm's profits in 1932, its first full year, increased sharply in contrast to the dire results prevailing in Wall Street and industry generally. Business and economic prospects appeared to be in the process of firming. Reflecting its improved results, the firm distributed a Christmas bonus to its employees.[35] The firm was on its way.

Eberstadt turned to new challenges, financing the small, growing companies that were to lead the way out of the depression—what he would come to call his "little blue chips." Since the crash no Wall Streeter had bothered much about the financial air pockets enfolding small, sound companies temporarily out of funds in the trough of the Great Depression. Over the next several years, Eberstadt was to finance more than a score of such businesses, raising about $35 million in new capital for these companies or their owners.[36] These figures sound small today, but it would be difficult to name any other financial house, with the possible exception of Lehman, that was as active as Eberstadt during this period.

Eberstadt was able to take fundamentally strong smaller companies, many of them in the industrial Midwest, and arrange financing for them. He began this financing drive in advance of the new securities legislation of 1933 and 1934, which required full disclosure for new issues. His first offering consisted of 147,500 shares of Kingsbury Breweries at $11 a share on July 7, 1933.[37] Actually Eberstadt's offering prospectuses met most of the full disclosure requirements of the new legislation before it became effective, and Eberstadt had little difficulty conforming to the new securities regulations.[38]

No business in the country was more affected by New Deal reforms than the securities business. Together with the crash, the new rules had a devastating impact on the capital markets. New securities issues, which had hit a peak of $9.4 billion in 1929, plunged to $1.9 billion in 1939, just ten years later.[39] Many investment firms had vanished, and the survivors had contracted drastically or had merged with others to make a go of it. Against this grim background, Eberstadt doggedly plunged forward, turning his talents to making money where no one else thought it possible.

Performance of Eberstadt Stock Offerings during the 1930s

Name (year founded in parentheses)	-- Offering --		--% Change to --	
	Date	Price	1937 High	1946 High
Kingsbury Breweries(1918)	7/33	11	-71 %	-39 %
Mission Dry (1933)	12/33	11 3/4	--No Market Quotes--	
Square D Corp. (1903)	3/34	3	+3125	+4933
Allied Laboratories (1929)	4/35	17	+4	+50
Clevite Corp. (1919)(1)	4/35	17	+183	+353
Walter E. Heller (1919)	10/35	6 1/2	+58	+177
The Cliffs Corp. (1920)	11/35	17 1/2	+186	+97
Allen Industries (1927)	1/36	19	+47	+37
Detroit Gasket (1923)	3/36	18	+10	+196
Kalamazoo Stove (1901)	4/36	30	+53	+20
McGraw-Hill (1925)	4/36	20-24	+30	+120
Machine Steel Tube (1916)	6/36	19 1/2	-6	-8
Standard Products (1936)	6/36	10 1/2	+138	+124
Chamberlin Metal Weather Stripping (1907)	8/36	10	+100	+190
James Talcott (1914)	11/36	14	+13	+38
Hewitt Rubber (1904)	3/37	16 3/4	--	+136
Monarch Machine Tool(1909)	4/37	26	+35	+73
Victor Chemical Works(1902)	8/37	19	+33(2)	+179
Norwich Pharmacal (1890)	3/39	18 1/2	-------(3)-------	
W. L. Maxson (1935)	6/39	5	-------(3)-------	
Hydraulic Press (1887)	12/39	10 1/4	-------(3)-------	
Average Gain			+213%	+365%

(1) Formerly Cleveland Graphite Bronze Corp.   (2) 1938 high.
(3) Not applicable as offering made after 1937.

Source: Author's survey based on data in the 1938 and 1947 *Moody's Industrial Manuals*.

Many Wall Streeters tried to sabotage the new regulations. The SEC was established to try to make Wall Street safer for investors, but Wall Street reacted by trying to boycott the new regulations, refusing to float new issues under their requirements. Thus when Eberstadt and other firms broke the line and started to underwrite, many fellow Wall Streeters accused them of disloyalty.[40]

As reflected in this record of financings, Eberstadt moved into the small, closely held company field and, once there, he carved out a specialized niche for his firm. In early 1934, he worked out a sensational deal for Square D Corporation just after he had cut his teeth with his first underwritings the year before.

Francis W. Magin, the head of Square D Corporation, a privately owned manufacturer of electrical controls and switches in Detroit, had been caught up in the panic. He had put up 16,000 shares of Square D stock as bank collateral, and because there was no market for it, the bank threatened to clean him out. Eberstadt learned of this situation from a Princeton classmate. The block, consisting of 8,000 shares of preferred stock and 8,000 shares of common stock, was offered to Eberstadt for $40,000.[41]

Eberstadt asked Francis Williams to look at Square D; Williams' report encouraged Eberstadt to take the block from the bank. Eberstadt had hoped to place the block privately with institutions and investors, but when they were unsuccessful Eberstadt decided to buy it for the firm's account. Williams bought some shares for his own account as well.

Although Williams gave away more than three-quarters of his original investment to his children and to his alma mater, Harvard, he still owns about 7,000 Square D shares worth over $300,000, which cost him a little more than $200 in 1934.[42] Willett and Brelsford also participated in the Square D investment. According to *Fortune*, Eberstadt probably made close to $500,000 on Square D, and he kept quite a block of it in his own account thereafter as a private investment.[43]

Other deals logically followed in the wake of the success of the Square D financing, especially in Detroit and Cleveland. By distributing a part of the stock of a closely held company, Eberstadt created a public market for the stock so that when the owner passed on, his family would have cash and liquidity to pay the estate taxes. Moreover, these small companies would need financing in the recovery years ahead. By creating a public market, Eberstadt gave them broader access to the capital markets to finance their growth.[44]

Eberstadt's largest financing client during this early period was the factoring house of James Talcott, Inc., which operated principally in the textile field. Talcott, who learned about Eberstadt from a bank official, told *Fortune*, "I liked him at once. He attends to business."[45] In 1936, Eberstadt brought out two issues for Talcott, and in 1937 the stock was

listed on the New York Stock Exchange. Previously, Eberstadt had arranged financing for another factoring firm, Walter Heller, and Eberstadt
soon emerged as the major financier for factoring firms.

As for the Wall Street establishment, Eberstadt's attitude toward the
back-scratching ritual of the syndicates in the early 1930s, according to
Fortune, would be summed up in his own words, "Why should I take
them in as participants? As dealers, yes—if they can sell."[46] Although
Eberstadt worked with a few Wall Street houses as co-underwriters, he
preferred to operate independently.

Eberstadt's strategy was to cultivate regional houses which not only
sold the deals to the people out in the grass roots of the country, but
also brought him interesting issues that had never before been on the
public market and which met the criteria that he had set up to qualify
as one of his little blue chips.

The regional firms could trust Eberstadt because his firm, a wholesale
house, did not compete with them directly or indirectly. This informal
partnership between the regional firms and Eberstadt lasted well into
the sixties when regional firms began to be absorbed by national firms.
While it lasted, however, it accounted for a great deal of business for
the firm.

Among the major regional houses working with Eberstadt were Prescott of Cleveland; Shillinglaw, Bolger of Chicago; and Watling, Lerchen
of Detroit. Edward (Ned) P. Prescott was the principal partner of the
Cleveland house of the same name. He had known Eberstadt during
the time when both were partners of Otis. Watling Lerchen was brought
in through the efforts of Nelson Loud. Some of Loud's relatives were
principals in that firm; he introduced them to Eberstadt, and the relationship began on that basis.[47]

Moreover, Eberstadt tapped finder sources within the major law firms
that handled his securities filings, including White & Case, Cahill Gordon, Debevoise & Plimpton and Simpson Thatcher, all leading Wall
Street firms. He dangled the prospect of legal fees before the eyes of
these hungry firms during the depression-starved thirties, and they
brought deals to him. Eberstadt would say, "The way to keep them
bringing you business is not to give any firm all of your legal business—
just some of it, so that they would bring you more deals on the theory
that if 'you scratch my back, I'll scratch yours.' "[48]

To sell the deals, Eberstadt pioneered a marketing concept that he
called the "Distributing Group." Wall Street syndicates had developed
over the past century, and Eberstadt recognized that an investment
banker's word is his bond and that to finance companies he had to come
up with a fixed and firm underwriting commitment. Eberstadt's distributing group resembled the traditional underwriting syndicate except that
Eberstadt was the sole underwriter. The distributing group was in effect

a glorified selling group in which the smaller dealers received selling group concessions on their sales. Those dealers who agreed to take larger positions on a best-efforts basis received a larger commission.

Since Eberstadt was the sole underwriter, the entire underwriting spread went to the firm which, after paying the selling dealer's commission, benefitted from the leverage thus created.[49] By the same token, the firm took all of the risk. The risk was reduced to a minimum by waiting until the last moment before making a firm commitment to the issuing company. That gave the firm time to make sure that the dealers invited into the deal gave it reliable purchase orders ("indications of interest").[50]

The distributing group worked well on financings of relatively small size—under $3 million in total. Later on, when the deals involved from $5 million to $10 million or more, the sheer size of the underwriting risk forced Eberstadt to seek the safer harbor of the traditional underwriting syndicate which spread the risk among many houses.[51]

Eberstadt's genius was anchored upon two major traits: first, his uncanny knack of recognizing long-term investment opportunities long before others in Wall Street and second, his extraordinary negotiating skills which enabled him to put together a deal on advantageous terms and line up financial backing.

Buttressing these basic traits was Eberstadt's ability to focus his entire attention and energy on exploiting each new opportunity to the exclusion of all other extraneous distractions. This reflected the discipline of his training combined with his keen intellectual curiosity, which drove him relentlessly to uncover hidden values.

He favored management by conference. In the Christman interviews conducted toward the end of his life, Eberstadt explained: "You need to pick the brains of people whose opinions you value . . . to help you set your objectives." He loved to recall Greek philosophy, which stressed that "logic . . . flows from the exchange of views of informed people." He concluded by saying that, "While you can't govern by [conference] alone, group effort simplifies the exchange of opinions that helps a leader formulate policy and strategy."[52] He used the firm's daily noon meetings as his forum to review the progress of various financing programs with his aides and to sound out their views. Although open-minded throughout these meetings, Eberstadt remained in complete control of the direction and flow of the discussion and always made the final decision after having heard everyone's opinion.

Eberstadt's earlier legal training helped shape his negotiating style, and the many years of tutelage under Clarence Dillon had a major impact on his incisive judgment as an investment banker. Dillon's careful fact gathering and analyses were legendary on Wall Street; his staff would screen literally hundreds of proposals before choosing any for consideration by Dillon. Of these, Dillon took on only one out of the ten deals that were formally presented to him. One Dillon associate once re-marked,

[I]f Clarence Dillon were asked to finance a cattle ranch, he would first find out all about cows and cattle raising before making a decision. If he then agreed to take on the deal, he probably would know more about raising cows than the cattle rancher.[53]

Peter Wastrom, one of Eberstadt's later partners, recalled that "by his nature, Eber was . . . so devoted to working and to solving problems that he would literally work until he dropped.[54] In its final version, each financing concept would seem a stroke of genius, but it actually reflected a great deal of hard work by the old maestro along with his staff before it was perfected. Francis Williams recalled

Sometimes we would work until three o'clock in the morning for three or four nights in a row to get a job done and we had such a great feeling of accom-plishment when we finally finished it. Eberstadt had a certain thing about him. I can't put my finger on it but he loved to work on complex problems.[55]

This penchant for painstaking research and analysis paid off when underwritings fell off sharply in the fall of 1937 after the completion of the Victor financing. Eberstadt took the massive *Moody's Industrial Man-ual* and assigned sections of it to each of his corporate finance partners to screen each of the thousands of companies listed in the manual for new investment banking leads. Nelson Loud recalls receiving a special prospecting chore; he was assigned one of the Dun & Bradstreet direc-tories. Over the next year, Loud personally made new business solici-tations on every privately owned company listed in this directory having a net worth of $1 million or more.[56] In effect, Eberstadt was using the same barnstorming tactic he had used so successfully in Europe during the 1920s to develop new business for Dillon Read. As before, this marketing effort paid off by uncovering a number of valuable new clients for the firm.

Although Eberstadt typically delegated the day-to-day care of each banking client to one of his corporate finance partners, he himself took the lead in actual negotiations. As Ernest Brelsford put it, "Eberstadt took a leading part in the discussions with the principals of the com-panies involved—rightly so . . . in view of his wider experience . . . and the natural desire of a company president . . . to deal with his equivalent in our organization."[57] Loud adds that Eberstadt believed that only one person should lead the discussion with a client in a business conference without interruption by his associates. An aide should respond only if directly asked; it would confuse the client if each spoke separately.[58]

Eberstadt's day did not end when he left the office. Normally, he would take home a full briefcase of paperwork for further study late into the night. His son Frederick remembers his father reviewing important memoranda late into the evening, with his pencil carefully following the thought word by word to ensure that he did not miss any important details.[59]

Eberstadt exercised great caution to avoid backing unduly risky and speculative financings unless they fell into what he characterized as special situations. His analysis of these smaller situations involved the same effort as others would exert in researching much larger, well-known companies. He insisted that these smaller, unproven situations have unique state-of-the-art proprietary positions in their chosen fields and resourceful management. Eberstadt told his aides to avoid "machine shops that make products not protected by patents or special producing skills." He took the position that for a business to qualify as an investment, he had to have sufficient information on it so that he could project fairly accurately its future results. Thus, while many of Eberstadt's deals may have appeared to others to be risky, his methodical fact-finding and precision forecasting made them investments from his viewpoint.[60]

Before Eberstadt would take on a new underwriting commitment, he insisted that the client agree to send him monthly financial statements. This enabled Eberstadt and his staff to keep abreast of any problems that needed to be addressed or to recommend new financing programs to sustain a company's growth. For his part, Eberstadt committed his staff to make monthly visits to the principal operating facilities of each of his financing clients to supplement the ongoing analysis of the company's financial data. Eberstadt told the *Wall Street Journal* that this type of oversight "makes for a close relationship."[61]

Although Eberstadt believed that every deal should be beneficial to all parties, he sought out only the deals that would yield his firm handsome rewards. He constantly reminded his colleagues that "a deal that isn't a good deal for everybody, isn't a good deal for anybody";[62] nonetheless, he was ruthless in his quest for deals that were profitable to him and his firm.

Eberstadt's contacts both in and out of Wall Street were legendary and it was pretty difficult to resist his charisma if he needed someone's help. To maintain these contacts, he frequently invited the more important ones to lunch in the firm's private dining room. Often, when clients arrived early at Grand Central terminal for a conference later in the morning downtown, Eberstadt invited them to working breakfasts at his handsome apartment in the River House on Manhattan's fashionable East Side.[63] Wastrom notes, "Eber could be a very warm 'old school tie' person . . . to old business associates; people whom he had known or come in contact with over the years."[64]

Eberstadt kept what he called his personal "prestige" list of the business and government leaders that he carefully nurtured. From time to time, he would send them selected publications of the firm as they became available. He also used to purchase each year several hundred delicious Royal Victoria pears from the state of Washington at harvest time, and he had his staff send a basket to each of his important contacts as a special remembrance. These efforts paid off—whenever a problem cropped up on a financing, invariably Eberstadt's hand would reach for the phone to call one of his close contacts to help solve the problem quickly, thus permitting the financing program to move forward.[65]

Another important part of the Eberstadt technique was his commitment to his financings. Whenever a business financed by the firm faltered due to poor judgment or the failure of management, Eberstadt always stepped in to bring about improvements. This enhanced his reputation for standing behind his financings. In a merger negotiation, for example, Eberstadt insisted that an in-depth study of the situation be conducted to locate any problems and undisclosed liabilities as well as assets and earnings. Frequently, this involved independent surveys by outside experts. Sometimes this intensive study would lead Eberstadt to turn down a financing if it uncovered unsolvable problems. He had an uncanny ability to forecast future trends.[66]

On Wall Street during the depression thirties there was considerable uneasiness about this upstart firm whose financial alchemy was making what were incredibly large profits. It was not difficult to hear some hard things about Eberstadt from envious competitors who were part of the establishment.[67] Oblivious to these petty jealousies, Eberstadt savored the rewards of his new-found role as a lone wolf. Soon, he dusted off the architectural plans for the magnificent Georgian-style mansion at Target Rock, shelved after the crash, and in the spring of 1937 he commenced building this spectacular retreat.[68]

Notes

1. Interviews by Robert L. Newton of Franz Schneider on December 15, 1981, and February 10, 1982 (hereinafter referred to as the Newton-Schneider interviews).

2. Marcus Gleisser, *The World of Cyrus Eaton* (New York, 1965), pp. 40–41, and "Clash of Steel," *Fortune*, June 1930, pp. 68–69.

3. Ibid.

4. Newton-Schneider interviews.

5. Interview with Robert G. Zeller, May 1, 1984.

6. Newton-Schneider interviews.

7. "Ferdinand Eberstadt," *Fortune*, April 1939, p. 74.

8. Interview with Eliot Janeway, April 3, 1984.

9. Interview with Andrew W. Eberstadt, April 11, 1984.

10. Original incorporation papers of F. Eberstadt & Co. Inc., filed with Division of Corporations in the State of Delaware, August 18, 1931.

11. First and final administration account of Benjamin S. Tongue and Ferdinand Eberstadt, Executors of the Estate of Thomas T. Tongue, Deceased, in the Orphan's Court of Baltimore City, December 21, 1929.

12. As related to author by former Eberstadt partner who requested anonymity.

13. Interview with Mrs. Mary Harper, April 11, 1985.

14. Interview by Calvin Lee Christman with Ferdinand Eberstadt, July 17 and 18, 1969 (hereinafter referred to as the Christman-Eberstadt interviews), July 17, 1969, side 1, p. 7.

15. Interview with former Eberstadt partner who requested anonymity; also letter from E. Roland Harriman to Calvin Lee Christman, May 27, 1971.

16. Interview with Nelson Loud, April 2, 1984.

17. Interview by Robert L. Newton with Robert C. Porter in January 1982 and revised in March 1984 (hereinafter referred to as the Newton-Porter interview).

18. "Ferdinand Eberstadt," *Fortune*, April 1939, p. 136.

19. Interview with Francis S. Williams, by Henry Ansbacher Long, June 15, 1978.

20. Interview with Nelson Loud, April 2, 1984.

21. Telephone interview with William P. Sullivan, a former Eberstadt associate, May 26, 1984.

22. Ibid.

23. "Ferdinand Eberstadt," *Fortune*, p. 136.

24. Interview with Robert G. Zeller, May 1, 1984.

25. "Ferdinand Eberstadt," *Fortune*, p. 74.

26. Interview with Francis S. Williams, May 8, 1984.

27. Samuel T. Williamson, "The Mad Reign of the 'Match King,' " *New York Times* (book review of "The Incredible Ivar Kreuger" by Allen Churchill), January 22, 1957, VIII, p. 6.

28. "Ferdinand Eberstadt," *Fortune*, p. 74.

29. "Ivar Kreuger a Suicide; His Stocks Heavily Sold; Sweden to Protect Trust," *New York Times*, March 13, 1932, p. 1.

30. Interview with James Benenson, April 9, 1984.

31. "Moratorium Effective; Employees Prepare Statements for Government," *New York Times*, March 14, 1932, p. 2.

32. Interview with Nelson Loud, April 2, 1984.

33. Interview with Frederick Eberstadt, March 23, 1984.

34. "Ferdinand Eberstadt," *Fortune*, p. 74.

35. "F. Eberstadt & Co. Employees to Get Christmas Bonus," *New York Journal*, December 14, 1932, p. 25.

36. Based on a survey by the author of Eberstadt financings in the 1930s.

37. Tombstone Offering Advertisements in the *New York Herald Tribune, Wall Street Journal* and other newspapers.

38. Letter from Ernest C. Brelsford to Calvin Lee Christman, April 18, 1971.

39. Vincent Carosso, *Investment Banking in America* (Cambridge, Mass., 1970), pp. 243, 425.

40. Calvin Lee Christman, "Ferdinand Eberstadt and Economic Mobilization

for War, 1941–1943," Ph. D. diss., Ohio State University, 1971, n.p., p. 27; also John N. Brooks, *Once in Golconda—A True Drama of Wall Street, 1920–1938*, pp. 212–21.

41. "Ferdinand Eberstadt," *Fortune*, pp. 74–75.

42. Interview with Francis S. Williams, May 8, 1984.

43. "Ferdinand Eberstadt," *Fortune*, p. 75.

44. "Financial Services Industry and Investors," published by F. Elberstadt & Co., Inc. (New York, 1953), pp. 10–11.

45. "Ferdinand Eberstadt," *Fortune*, p. 136.

46. "Ferdinand Eberstadt," *Fortune*, p. 142.

47. Interview with Nelson Loud, April 2, 1984.

48. Newton-Porter interview.

49. Telephone interview with Craig Severance, former Eberstadt partner and syndicate manager, May 26, 1984.

50. Interview with Steven D. Fuller, former Eberstadt associate, May 4, 1984.

51. Letter from Craig Severance, June 19, 1984.

52. Christman-Eberstadt interviews. July 17, 1969, side 2, pp. 8–9.

53. Frank J. Williams, "A New Leader in Finance; Clarence Dillon," February 1926, p. 149; also interviews with former associates.

54. Interview with Peter L. Wastrom, March 29, 1984.

55. Interview with Francis S. Williams, May 8, 1984.

56. Interview with Nelson Loud, December 10, 1987.

57. Letter from Ernest C. Brelsford to Calvin Lee Christman, April 18, 1971.

58. Interview with Nelson Loud, December 10, 1987.

59. Interview with Frederick Eberstadt, September 7, 1987.

60. Interview with Nelson Loud, December 10, 1987.

61. "Wall Street Scene," *Wall Street Journal*, December 14, 1938, p. 6.

62. Interview with Frederick Eberstadt, March 23, 1984.

63. Interview with Nelson Loud, December 10, 1987.

64. Interview with Peter L. Wastrom, March 29, 1984.

65. Interview with Nelson Loud, December 10, 1987.

66. Letter to author from Robert C. Porter, September 28, 1987.

67. "Ferdinand Eberstadt," *Fortune*, p. 142.

68. Interview with Francis S. Williams, May 8, 1984 and Andrew W. Eberstadt, April 11, 1984.

5

Chemistry and Investing

Eberstadt's little blue chips fell into what might be broadly categorized as special situations. The key factors that he looked for were sound earnings record, compact management, explosive growth potential, a strong position in their fields, and an instinct for research.[1] Besides keeping his young firm going, Eberstadt's nurturing of smaller growth companies helped him exploit his next opportunity—financing companies operating in the fields of chemical and related activities.

The first of these opportunities was the Victor Chemical Works financing in 1937. The Victor business came to the firm through Joe Seaman, who formerly had been a partner in Dillon Read. He preferred to take the Victor deal to Eberstadt, and Clarence Dillon was furious when he learned that he had lost the Victor business.[2] Although he was fascinated with the prospects, Eberstadt knew little about the chemical business; he assigned the task of analyzing the company and business to Francis Williams, who had earned a bachelor of science degree in chemistry at Harvard.[3]

One of the hallmarks of the Eberstadt approach to financing was Eberstadt's insistence that, before the firm would do any public or private financing, he wanted in his own files a special report that analyzed the company in considerable detail. One of his key associates, Ernest Brelsford, had developed a checklist for this purpose, one which was especially helpful in performing the due diligence that Eberstadt insisted on as an investment banker. Most investment banking firms subsequently developed similar due diligence procedures.[4]

In addition to the study of Victor's business and prospects, Eberstadt asked Williams to look at other chemical companies and the chemical industry in general. The survey showed that chemical companies had weathered the depression quite well with very few losses and that the industry's future was bright indeed. Chemical companies had very consistent records of sales and earnings improvement, low labor cost and an emphasis on research. Williams and Eberstadt were particularly impressed with the chemical industry's research in developing more economical processes and new products. It seemed to them that chemical and related companies were an excellent field for investment, with outstanding opportunities for profit.[5]

After the Victor offering was completed, underwritings began to dwindle, and Eberstadt began to look for something to fill the void. Victor had given Eberstadt a good look at the chemical industry, and he liked what he saw.[6] His eyes gleamed when he pondered the long-term prospects of chemical science. He liked to compare the excitement of discovering the chemical field to that of the first Schmeling-Louis prizefight (Eberstadt loved boxing matches). Before the fight, the newspapers had reported that Schmeling thought he saw a weakness in Joe Louis' boxing style. The papers quoted Schmeling in his broken English, "I sink I see somesing!" Well, Eberstadt said, "I sink I see somesing, too," and that "somesing" was Chemical Fund—born from his hunch that chemistry and other scientific developments would represent one of the great investment opportunities of the twentieth century. Eberstadt loved to retell this anecdote to dealer groups when relating how he came to form Chemical Fund.[7]

The year 1938 was a difficult time to bring out a new mutual fund. The fund business had a bad reputation because its "second cousins," the closed-end trusts, had developed all sorts of unsavory practices during the 1920s and had performed poorly during the depression years. As a result, Wall Street was littered with investment trusts of almost every kind, and a lot of Eberstadt's friends told him to stay out of that business.[8]

But Eberstadt thought the basic idea of the mutual investment fund was sound, and he was enthusiastic about the prospects for the chemical industry. He therefore made a thorough study of the bad practices that had taken place with the older closed-end trusts in the past, and he set up internal controls to avoid these unsound practices. He subsequently included these rules in the original Chemical Fund offering prospectus. Furthermore, he discussed them with the Securities and Exchange Commission (SEC) so that, when the Investment Company Act was passed in 1940, he didn't have to make any major changes in the fund's prospectus.[9] Eberstadt formed Chemical Fund in July 1938 with $100,000 of capital which he and his associates put up for 10,000 shares.

Although initially Chemical Fund was not an outstanding sales success, it had a good beginning for a new fund, considering the unfavorable popular view of investment trusts in the 1930s. The fund gave dealers a constant supply of quality merchandise to sell when new capital offerings dried up. In the investment banking business there can be prolonged dry spells between underwritings. Having something to sell in these periods kept fresh Eberstadt's contacts with the dealers.[10]

It also gave the firm a new source of income. The firm received an annual management fee based on the fund's total assets, plus a bonus (under a later change) if the fund's performance was better than that of the market as a whole. The firm also retained a portion of the selling commission on sales of new shares.[11]

Another benefit the firm gained from Chemical Fund was the enhanced image it received as an investment banker in the rapidly growing fields of chemistry and related sciences. One of the problems of a small investment banking firm is that its name is not widely known; Chemical Fund helped to improve the visibility of the firm. Eberstadt financed quite a number of chemical and drug companies that came to the attention of the firm because of its growing reputation as a specialist in these fields. Nelson Loud, who for many years was Eberstadt's closest partner on investment banking deals, relates that, because of the firm's chemical expertise, "[P]otential clients would come to us and say, 'you guys know what is going on in this field . . . help us out with our financing needs.' "[12] Loud adds,

The fund also benefitted from this relationship. Investment bankers can see so much more about a business by talking with the people who are running it and then looking ahead for five years and appraising the opportunities and prospects. Ferd and his investment banking associates had a great deal to do with some of the more forward-looking advances in managing money.[13]

Eberstadt leaned over backward, however, to keep an arm's length relationship between the fund and the investment banking business, waiting six months to a year after an initial financing before considering a banking client as a possible investment for the fund. On balance, the fund helped the investment banking business, probably as much as the investment banking relationship helped the fund.[14]

Reflecting its emerging role in chemical and drug company financing, the firm soon became investment bankers for Chas. Pfizer & Co. With Pfizer the firm enjoyed a particularly close relationship after Maynard Simond, one of Eberstadt's senior partners, became a Pfizer director in 1942 and chairman of the board of its international division in 1953.[15]

Although the first public financing for Pfizer came in May 1942, the firm's relationship with the company began in 1940. At first Eberstadt was asked to help solve some of the problems the company had encountered as a privately held business. Pfizer used to buy back stock held by the heirs of the founders as they died or needed funds. These purchases ultimately caused financial problems for the small firm, forcing it to build up a considerable amount of debt.[16]

Actually, one of Eberstadt's few retail salesmen, Steven Fuller, introduced the firm to Pfizer. He had made some cold calls on some of the top officers at Pfizer, which at that time was located in an old warehouse building owned by the company at 81 Maiden Lane in downtown New York City. Pfizer fitted nicely into the kind of little blue chip the firm thrived on. A small, fine chemical producer founded in the 1840s, Pfizer had developed a process for making citric acid by fermentation, thus relieving the U.S. market of the need to import it from Italy at very high prices.[17]

The initial public offering of Pfizer consisted of 240,000 shares of common stock priced at 24 3/4, which raised over $5 million for the company. Pfizer used the proceeds to retire all of its bank debt and preferred stock and added $1 million to working capital. In addition, it purchased and retired all of the remaining common stock held by the estate of Emile Pfizer, son of the founder. After the financing, the company had 500,000 shares of common stock outstanding, with no debt, a very conservative balance sheet.[18]

During the late 1930s and early 1940s, Eberstadt also made several secondary offerings of chemical company stocks, including Westvaco Chlorine Products, Texas Gulf Sulphur, Union Carbide and Norwich Pharmaceutical. Later, in 1944, Chemical Fund purchased shares of Pfizer common stock for its investment portfolio, which turned out to be one of the fund's stellar performers. In the early 1950s, after Pfizer's stock price shot up sharply, based on rapidly increasing earnings, Clayton DuBosque, an Eberstadt partner, thought the fund should lighten up on its investment and take some profits since the dividend yield was quite low. Williams' response was a classic—in his broad Harvard accent, he replied—"In a pig's ass, we will!"[19]

In addition to Pfizer, Chemical Fund's investment record over the years includes a number of other major investment finds. For example, one of its most successful investments was in the antibiotic business, particularly penicillin. In 1944, research scientists at Pfizer discovered a commercial method of manufacturing penicillin in large quantities through an improved fermentation process. Thus chemical producers such as Pfizer, Commercial Solvents and American Cyanamid became profitable holdings for Chemical Fund.[20]

John F. Van Deventer, who became the firm's drug company specialist in the 1950s, uncovered a number of additional investment opportunities in this field including Lilly, Merck, G. D. Searle and Schering. Van Deventer's studies in the field opened Eberstadt's eyes to the broad range of wonder drugs that was flowing from chemists' test tubes. *New*

York Times columnist Robert Metz described Eberstadt as "a socially concerned man who seems almost messianic when he speaks of the eradication of some of the great killer diseases through chemical research."[21]

Another major challenge and investment opportunity in the late 1930s and 1940s arose from the specter of inflation, based on escalating wages and war-induced shortages. Eberstadt foresaw that the labor movement (however meritorious it might be) would add to these unfavorable trends and create a need for more efficient use of labor to offset cost increases. He concluded that the chemical molecule was the only sensible means available at the time to offset such increases.[22]

Eberstadt recognized that there were only two ways to shape and transform matter: one the physical, involving casting, molding, cutting and so forth; the other the chemical, whereby scientists change the form and nature of materials through the industry of the molecule and the atom. He used to tell dealer sales groups that "the chemical molecule was an ideal employee working 24 hours a day, seven days a week and never time off for holidays, sick leave or vacations."[23]

Eberstadt was, however, a great supporter of the labor movement. In fact he wanted to solve the problem of crippling national strikes that caused havoc in the economy by creating a special section of the judiciary system dedicated to handling grievances between labor and management in the courtroom and not on the picket line.[24]

Chemical Fund was highly rewarding for investors as well as for the firm. An investment of $10,000 in Chemical Fund when it began in 1938 would have multiplied over a hundredfold to more than $1.5 million by the end of 1986 on a total return basis.[25]

In the early 1950s Chemical Fund made its single most successful investment in the shares of Haloid Company, a small Rochester-based photo supply company and the predecessor of Xerox. Actually this investment coup had its genesis many years earlier in the little-noticed merger of a small investment trust into Chemical Fund. Barely a year after the fund had started, Chemical Fund acquired Rochester Capital Corporation, adding about $10 million to its assets. Far more important than the assets acquired (although they included such profitable Rochester firms as Eastman Kodak), the acquisition of Rochester Capital had a much more lasting benefit.[26]

The University of Rochester had a relatively large holding in Rochester Capital. Accordingly, the merger agreement stipulated that the person who was in charge of the university's investment portfolio would sit on the board of Chemical Fund to act as an overseer for the interests of the university as long as the university continued to hold the shares of Chemical Fund it had received in exchange for its holdings of Rochester Capital. In the 1950s, that investment officer was Hulbert W. (Bert) Tripp.

Later, when Tripp became a director of Haloid, he suggested to Eberstadt that, if he could find time, it might be of interest for him to go and talk to the people at Haloid and see what he thought of their work.[27]

Eberstadt dispatched Williams to visit the company. Bert Tripp introduced Williams to both of the Wilsons (the father and son who controlled Haloid), and Williams made the original study and report on the business. At that time xerography was little more than a Wilson dream. Haloid, founded in 1906, was a marginally profitable producer of photographic print paper and equipment; it had a good yield and low price earnings ratio but its record was not very impressive. The real kicker in the business was the potential from the development of the xerography process which had been patented in 1938 by the inventor, Chester F. Carlson.[28]

Haloid was developing xerography under rights obtained from the Batelle Memorial Institute of Columbus, Ohio, which held the patent rights. Under Batelle's sponsorship, twenty-one major industrial companies including RCA, Remington Rand, General Electric, Eastman Kodak, Minnesota Mining and IBM looked into Carlson's invention, but they all turned it down because each thought its own technology offered better commercial prospects than the electrostatic method of xerography. Their indifference to the new process partially reflected an Arthur D. Little study that cautioned its clients on the commercial potential of photocopying.[29]

In 1948 Haloid looked at Carlson's invention. John Dessauer, a German scientist just hired by Haloid to head its research department, had read of the new electrostatic copying process in a technical bulletin. Dessauer was so entranced by the xerographic process that he convinced Haloid's management to develop it under the Batelle license.[30]

After studying Haloid's xerography process, Williams became very excited about the prospects and recommended to Eberstadt that Chemical Fund make a modest investment in Haloid.[31] Chemical Fund's initial investment in 1953 consisted of the purchase of about $300,000 of Haloid's convertible preferred stock—the common stock was not readily available in the market, and the preferred provided a better yield than the common stock—with a call on the common at a fixed price which provided all the leverage that the fund desired. Later, Chemical Fund doubled its investment, but the original and second-round purchases never exceeded more than 1 percent at cost of the fund's investment assets.[32]

After ten years of development, Haloid introduced the first Xerox machines to the market in 1959; thereafter, sales volume soared, and Haloid (renamed Xerox Corporation in 1961) soon became a billion-dollar company.[33] Chemical Fund was the first institutional investor to recognize the investment merits of xerography. The investment was extremely rewarding to the fund, which held Xerox until the mid–1960s when it began to sell some of its holdings to reduce overexposure (Xerox had so appreciated that on one occasion it represented 20 percent of the fund's total assets, four times the normal limit). Later in the decade, the fund sold the balance of its position as growth slowed down and Xerox began to develop problems related to its inability to manage and diversify its huge business, a problem often faced by rapidly growing one-product companies. According to company records, Chemical Fund realized a profit of $112 million on its investment over the fifteen-year span that it held Xerox; its total cost had been about $600,000.[34]

The later development of xerography into a multibillion-dollar business far exceeded Eberstadt's wildest expectations and ranked with his earlier legendary investments in Louisiana Land in the 1920s and Square D in the 1930s—both "once in a lifetime" success stories. But, whereas Louisiana Land and Square D had enriched Eberstadt personally, Xerox enriched the many thousands of public investors who held Chemical Fund during the "golden era" of the 1950s and 1960s.

On the horizons of chemical research were more potent antibiotics and a new field in health care—diagnostic medical equipment. Other chemical companies pursued more versatile plastics that could be engineered to achieve specific levels of heat resistance, strength and durability in place of metal, wood and other materials. Dupont and others continued to introduce and perfect new synthetic fibers that could be woven into long-wearing, washable and wrinkle-resistant clothing. Finally the merger of the chemical sciences with the physical sciences made possible the miniaturization of electronic circuits into microchips combining all the properties of a computer in a tiny chip.

Some claim that Eberstadt's launching of Chemical Fund ranks with his earlier great achievements—his role as a production expediter and planner in World War II and his success in financing the little blue chips in the 1930s and the German economy in the 1920s. While Kuhn Loeb had grown great as a specialist in railroads and Bonbright in utilities, Eberstadt had staked his future on chemistry. By the early 1970s, Eberstadt's Chemical Fund had reached over one billion dollars in assets and had enriched hundreds of thousands of small and large individual and institutional investors.[35]

Notes

1. "Ferdinand Eberstadt," *Fortune*, April 1939, p. 75.

2. Interview by Robert L. Newton with Francis S. Williams, November 18, 1981 (hereinafter referred to as the Newton-Williams interview).

3. Interview with Francis S. Williams by Henry Ansbacher Long, June 15, 1978.

4. Letter from Ernest C. Brelsford to Calvin Lee Christman, April 18, 1971.

5. Interview with Francis S. Williams, by Henry Ansbacher Long, June 15, 1978.

6. "Ferdinand Eberstadt," *Fortune*, April 1939, p. 140.

7. Based on author's recollection.

8. Newton-Williams interview.

9. Ibid.

10. Ibid.

11. "Ferdinand Eberstadt," *Fortune*, p. 142.

12. Interview with Nelson Loud, April 2, 1984.

13. Ibid.

14. Ibid.

15. Newton-Williams interview.

16. Interview of Robert L. Newton with Robert C. Porter, January 1982, revised March 1984.

17. Newton-Williams interview.

18. Original offering prospectus, Charles Pfizer Co., Inc., 240,000 shares common stock, ($1 par value), June 22, 1942, pp. 1, 3, 8, and 9.

19. Based on recollections of various members of the firm.

20. Interview by Robert L. Newton with John F. Van Deventer, January 19, 1982, revised in April 1984.

21. Robert Metz, "Market Place: Chemical Fund 30 Years Later," *New York Times*, August 9, 1968, p. 48.

22. Interview by Calvin Lee Christman with Ferdinand Eberstadt, July 17 and 18, 1969., July 17, 1969, side 1, p. 8; and Metz, "Market Place: Chemical Fund 30 Years Later," *New York Times*, August 9, 1968, p. 48.

23. Based on author's recollection.

24. Ibid.

25. Semiannual report, June 30, 1988, of Alliance Fund (successor to Chemical Fund, Inc.), pp. 10–11.

26. Ferdinand Eberstadt, from an address before Rochester Security Analysts, Rochester, N.Y., June 12, 1962.

27. Interviews with Francis S. Williams, May 8, 1984, and Donald A. Young, April 5, 1984; also written statement from Hulbert W. Tripp, May 25, 1984.

28. Interview with Francis S. Williams, May 8, 1984.

29. Walter Guzzardi, Jr., "Life after Xerox," *Fortune*, January 6, 1986, pp. 121–22.

30. Ibid.

31. Interview with Francis S. Williams, May 8, 1984.

32. Perez, *Inside Venture Capital*, pp. 98–99.

33. Perez, *Inside Venture Capital*, p. 98.

34. Perez, *Inside Venture Capital*, p. 99.

35. Letter to author from Robert C. Porter, May 23, 1985.

Eberstadt family at home in Orange, N.J., circa 1898. Clockwise from right front: Ferdinand, Esther, Rudy, Zélie, Edward (father), and Elenita (mother).
Courtesy: John Payne.

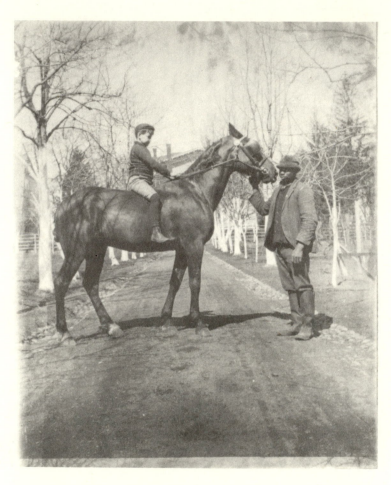

Eberstadt as a boy astride carriage horse, circa 1900, with stable boy Boone. *Courtesy:* John Payne.

Eberstadt at Princeton, circa 1913. *Courtesy:* John Payne.

Eberstadt's troop, Squadron A, New York State National Guard, on parade in New York City, circa 1910. *Courtesy:* Squadron A Association.

Eberstadt as captain in the 304th Field Artillery after World War I.
Courtesy: John Payne.

Eberstadt's mother, Elenita, in 1924 or 1925. *Courtesy:* John Payne.

Clarence Dillon appearing in October 1933 before Senate committee investigating the causes of the 1929 Crash. *Courtesy:* The Bettmann Archive.

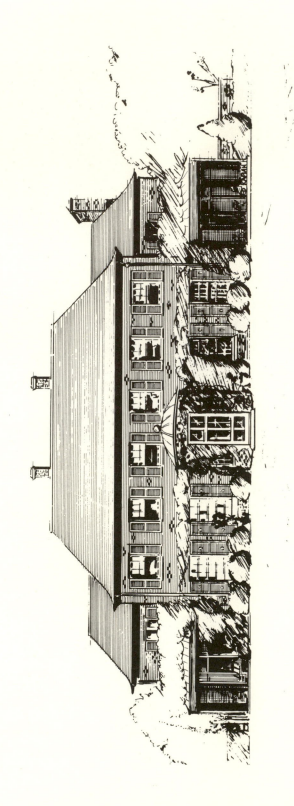

Eberstadt's mansion at Target Rock as it appeared in the late 1960s. *Sketch Courtesy:* Edward Kaplan.

Eberstadt's wife, Mary, gardening at Target Rock, spring 1958. *Courtesy:* John Payne.

Eberstadt aboard his yacht, "Target," fishing for Swordfish off Cuttyhunk, Mass., with Auguste Richard (right), August 1961. *Courtesy:* John Payne.

James Forrestal, the nation's first Secretary of Defense, meeting with Dwight D. Eisenhower who served as advisor to the Defense Department in February 1949. *Courtesy:* The Bettmann Archive.

Bernard Baruch, with Eberstadt as his Deputy, led the U.S. delegation to the United Nations in proposing peacetime uses for atomic energy. Photograph shows Baruch presenting the U.S. proposal on June 25, 1946. *Courtesy:* The Bettmann Archive.

Eberstadt (center) conducts a Chemical Fund board meeting in the early 1950s. Photograph from author's personal collection.

André Meyer of Lazard Frères, shown in September 1957, reinvented merchant banking (with Eberstadt) with a series of spectacular takeovers in the 1950s. *Courtesy:* The Bettmann Archive.

Eberstadt in a contemplative mood in the late 1950s. *Courtesy:* William P. Sullivan.

6

Creative Financing and the Fabulous Fifties

Having survived World War II, the Eberstadt firm entered the first postwar decade with renewed vigor and aggressiveness. In fact, this decade probably represented the most creative and clearly the most profitable period in Eberstadt's long and brilliant career.

In the 1950s, the firm conducted three distinct activities: first, for a handsome fee, it managed the investments of Chemical Fund; second, it raised capital as a small specialty investment banking firm for Eberstadt's little blue chips through public offerings or private placements; and third, it developed private capital deals in partnership with Lazard Frères and other prominent firms in Wall Street.[1]

Chemical Fund's assets had multiplied tenfold from their prewar levels to over $100 million by the mid–1950s. The management and distribution fees on these assets exceeded $1 million a year, which more than covered the expense of the firm's staff of about fifty employees and partners. By the late 1950s, the fund's assets doubled again to over $200 million and then more than doubled again to just under $600 million by the end of the next decade.[2]

The development of xerography in the mid–1950s (see Chapter 5) stands as Eberstadt's greatest single investment coup for Chemical Fund. During the 1950s, he made changes in the fund's investment policies which had a significant impact on its performance for many years thereafter. Before then, the portfolio had been very heavily weighted with basic commodity-type chemical companies. Eberstadt shifted the portfolio's emphasis in the late 1950s from these increasingly cyclical sectors of the economy to companies with more proprietary products such as the pharmaceutical companies, the graphic arts companies and companies in specialty chemical fields.

The second activity of the firm was the continuation of its original investment banking business started in 1931, which had pioneered the little blue chips, along with its emerging role as a financier of chemical and drug companies. This activity later branched out into and nurtured other technology areas including electronics and medical diagnostic equipment. The breadth of Eberstadt's financing was striking, ranging from airlines and textile factoring firms to pharmaceutical companies and motion picture producers. Franz Schneider remarked, "Ferd could tackle anything."[3] (The firm's third activity, private capital deals, is discussed at length in Chapter 7.)

The public and private placements of securities for its on-going investment banking operation came under the direction of Robert C. Porter who came to Eberstadt from Pfizer to help handle the increasing volume of financings which reached the imposing total of $610.5 million during the 1950s, more than four times the business financed in the 1940s which in turn had been four times the level of the 1930s.[4] Porter had been a practicing attorney with the prominent Wall Street firm of Cravath, Swaine & Moore for about eight years before joining Pfizer as its legal counsel in 1951.[5]

In the spring of 1951, Eberstadt had put together the firm's largest financing up to that time—a $30 million issue of common and preferred stock for Pfizer. With the success of Pfizer's new broad-spectrum antibiotic, Terramycin, and its program to expand its foreign business, Pfizer turned to its investment banker, Eberstadt, to help raise needed additional capital. Eberstadt arranged a $15 million rights offering of common stock to existing stockholders combined with a simultaneous public offering of $15 million of 4-percent convertible preferred stock.[6] The underwriting in mid–1951 was an instant sellout.

Eberstadt's first airline financing involved Braniff Airways, then a small regional airline. After the colorful founder, Tom Braniff, died tragically in an airplane crash in 1954, the airline had to raise a considerable amount of new capital to finance the purchase of new equipment to meet competition from the larger airlines. Eberstadt raised $15 million privately from a small group of life insurance companies to cover Braniff's aircraft purchases and then raised $5 million of additional equity capital by offering subscription rights to its common stockholders.[7]

The rights offering was risk free to Eberstadt because Braniff's successor as president, an American Indian named William A. Blakely, agreed to purchase personally all stock not subscribed to by existing stockholders. Blakely told Eberstadt, "Ok, you put oversubscription rights in there and I, as the largest stockholder in the company, will agree to subscribe whatever part isn't subscribed by the other stockholders." At the closing, Blakely brought three certified checks—one for $1 million, another for $2 million and a third for $3 million—and he asked Eberstadt, "Which one do you need?" Porter observed, "Eberstadt had a way of getting people like that to use his name but their cash to support a deal." He later arranged several additional financings for Braniff, each involving rights offerings to existing stockholders with Blakely committed to take up any unsubscribed stock.[8]

Another unusual financing was the United Artists (UA) offering. In the spring of 1957, Eberstadt took the company public for the first time with a $17 million combination debt and equity offering. United Artists had been formed in 1919 by four legendary movie artists—Mary Pickford, Douglas Fairbanks, Sr., Charlie Chaplin and D. W. Griffith (the producer).[9] Eberstadt had actually drawn up the original charter of the United Artists Corporation as one of his first assignments at Cotton and Franklin.[10]

In 1951, however, UA was in serious financial straits. It had lost money for several years, and the surviving owners, Mary Pickford and Charlie Chaplin, could not agree on what should be done. At this point a new management team consisting of two young lawyers, Robert Benjamin and Arthur Krim, who had substantial experience in the entertainment business, took control of the company. They received an option from UA to acquire 50 percent of its stock for $8,000 provided they were able to show a profit in any year during the three-year period ending 1953. The two lawyers were granted voting control during this three-year period, and if they produced a profit in any of these years, their option would vest and they would gain full voting control for a period of ten years.[11]

The Benjamin-Krim team had a unique program in mind to promote UA's special niche with independent film producers. It offered them complete freedom to shoot their films anywhere in the world since UA was not saddled with expensive, antiquated Hollywood studios. In selecting new film proposals, the Benjamin-Krim approach focused on four key ingredients: script, financing, cast and director. Using the UA approach, the independent producer-actor gained a better share of a film's overall distribution profits, thus creating major incentives to control costs to enhance the profits. Later, other major film companies followed UA's lead in focusing on distribution profits rather than on the up-front studio production fees, which had been the customary source of income in the industry.[12]

This program paid off with profits generated in the first year of the Krim-Benjamin regime. During this period the company repurchased the Chaplin stock for $1.5 million and later the Pickford stock for $3 million, partly out of accumulated earnings and partly with money borrowed from the banks. The net result was that Krim and Benjamin owned 100 percent of the outstanding stock for an out-of-pocket cost to them of just $8,000.[13]

The next phase of the plan was the initial public offering of securities of United Artists. Although Eberstadt was familiar with the company from his earlier work, he became much more aware of its need for permanent financing after Al Feinman, a blind printing salesman for one of UA's suppliers, came to F. Kenneth Melis, one of Eberstadt's partners. Feinman explained the need of the company to raise fresh capital to finance its motion picture production program and pay off the bank loans used to finance the repurchases of Chaplin's and Pickford's stock. With the opening provided by Feinman, Eberstadt aggressively pursued a public financing for UA thereafter. For his efforts in finding the deal, Feinman received 10 percent of the firm's profits from launching UA's initial public offering.[14]

Krim and Benjamin, however, preferred a private merger which would preserve their independence, give them some profit for their success to date and provide them the capital they needed to develop UA's business. They approached CBS, Twentieth Century Fox and MGM on the basis of a buyout in which Krim and Benjamin would remain as the management in a subsidiary. Krim and Benjamin preferred that to going public.[15]

But Eberstadt persisted. He was literally the first investment banker that had showed any interest in the company. He talked about the benefits of going public, and since the other options with CBS, Fox and MGM fell through, Eberstadt's plan finally won out. His persistence earned the respect of United Artists' management; Krim and Benjamin never considered any other investment banker. Krim recollected, "We had come to know Ferdie, trust him—he was by then receiving quarterly financial reports to aid him in his counselling of us."[16]

Eberstadt led United Artists' initial public offering. Since motion picture stocks were out of favor at that time, it was necessary to organize extensive road shows to help sell this film producer as having unique qualities that set it apart from the rest of the industry. During that period the noted public relations expert, David Karr, was retained by UA to help put together the initial publicity and, as a result of his efforts, the deal went public with all of the fanfare of a major movie premiere.

Another major client that came to Eberstadt in the 1950s was Becton-Dickinson (B-D), a pharmaceutical firm founded in 1897. It had developed and introduced commercially plastic disposable syringes and hypodermic needles that have now become standard in hospitals and doctors' offices throughout the world.

William Engstrom, then chairman of Irving Trust Company and an old friend of Eberstadt, came to the office one day and told him that Irving had this nice privately owned company that had been a long-term banking client. Its working capital loan had increased almost five-fold to $14 million and in effect had become permanent capital. Engstrom

told Eberstadt that they had introduced the company to Prudential In-
surance but that the Pru wanted to put restrictive covenants in the loan
agreements. These covenants, which would greatly limit future borrow-
ings and put a lid on salary increases and new hirings, were unacceptable
to B-D's management. What could Eberstadt do to refinance the company's loan with external investors?[17]

As a result of this meeting and a subsequent meeting with Fairleigh
Dickinson, Eberstadt, assisted by his close aides, Nelson Loud and Joseph Dineen, worked out with New York Life a refinancing of the Irving
loan. New York Life knew that Becton-Dickinson had been turned down
by Prudential so it took some courage and arm twisting on Eberstadt's
part, to get them to agree to the financing.[18] Although the restrictive
covenants were eliminated from the loan agreement, they remained in
force in a gentleman's agreement with Eberstadt as the overseer or en-
forcer to ensure that the company lived up to the agreements.[19]

As part of the gentleman's agreement, Eberstadt insisted that the
company adopt a more professional approach to management. His analysis of the business set forth what needed to be done to put the company
on a sound basis. He found that the trouble with the company was that
the owners were not paying enough attention to the business. Fairleigh
Dickinson, son of the cofounder, had to reduce his outside interests on
St. Croix in the Virgin Islands, tend to the store and stop hiring old
cronies. Moreover, they needed a tough financial vice president and a
controller. B-D's management agreed to these conditions.[20]

However, just one year after Eberstadt raised the money, Becton-
Dickinson reported the first loss in its sixty-year history. Eberstadt invited Dickinson over for lunch for one of his so-called frank talks. According to Porter, Eberstadt brought out the agreement and checked off
each point and asked, "What have you done about this, what have you
done about that?"[21]

Eberstadt then reached the part of the agreement dealing with the
financial vice president. "Who's the financial vice president?" Eberstadt
answered his own question, "This fellow, Thibault de St. Phalle, a lawyer
and a crony—very nice, sociable chap but surely not a financial vice
president." Eberstadt asked, "Well, have you hired a controller?" Dickinson replied, "No, we have not hired a controller." "Why not?" Eberstadt shot back. Dickinson hesitated and then said, "Well, we thought
we didn't need one if we had a financial vice president." Eberstadt said,
"Well, you have neither a financial vice president nor a controller."[22]

Dickinson left the luncheon meeting feeling very chagrined. The next
year, with their financial statements much improved, B-D's management
came back again for a much more pleasant luncheon. Dickinson told
Eberstadt, "We have now hired Ben Harter, who is not a crony, as our

financial vice president and I am liquidating my real estate in the Virgin
Islands. Moreover, we brought in Dick Simmons to be controller and
executive vice president."[23]

The second luncheon was cheerful and pleasant in contrast to the
bleak affair the previous year. During the luncheon, Eberstadt noticed
that Dickinson had brought in a large hat box tied with a fancy ribbon
and had set it on one of the side chairs. Curious, Eberstadt asked Dickinson what was in the box. With that, Dickinson handed the box to
Eberstadt who, upon opening it, found it contained a stuffed crow.
Dickinson explained to Eberstadt, "We had felt so badly after your Dutch
Uncle's talk last year that we told ourselves we were going to make you
eat crow next year, so here is the crow; would you like it fricasseed,
fried or broiled?"[24] Eberstadt laughed as he relished the joke. Adds
Porter, "Eberstadt cherished that crow and it became a fixture in the
firm's dining room, providing a good talking point for what an investment banker does for his fees."[25] B-D thereafter became one of the most
active clients of the firm; its sales and earnings soared in the 1960s,
requiring new capital to expand facilities to meet the increased demand
for its products.

Chock Full O'Nuts, another very successful deal, had an important
human interest aspect. William Black, the founder, wanted to make a
grant to Columbia Medical School for research on Parkinson's disease,
and he was going to sell his company to Consolidated Foods in Chicago
which had offered him $10 million in stock. Glover Johnson of White &
Case was his lawyer and was on the board of the company at the time.
He told Black, "Before you decide to do that deal, I want you to meet
Eberstadt and maybe he'll have some better ideas." Eberstadt met with
him and said, "Well, if you agree to go public, we can make a lot more
than $10 million by creating a public market for your stock." Eberstadt
proposed selling part of Black's stock to the public and added,

When your company gets better known, the stock will go up in price and you'll
be able to give $6 or $7 million to Columbia and have a building named after
you and still have in your retained holdings as much as you gave away.[26]

Using this strategy, Eberstadt brought the company public in 1958
with an initial offering of 400,000 shares at $15 a share, netting Black $6
million. In the aftermarket, Chock Full O'Nuts was a star performer and
tripled in price in a little over a year. Eberstadt brought another offering
of 126,000 shares at $45 a share in early 1960, which raised $5.7 million
for Columbia Medical School.[27] After the Eberstadt firm split up in 1962,
the Chock Full O'Nuts account was assigned to New York Securities.

Eberstadt originated other interesting deals including the initial public
financing for American-Saint Gobain Corporation (ASG), the American

subsidiary of Saint Gobain, a centuries-old major French glass producer with a long history of innovation in glassmaking technology. Saint Gobain, the parent company, had developed a revolutionary although untested new process for producing glass in a continuous strip with a twin grinding and polishing technique which promised major efficiencies. The technology was intended to enable the production of glass of uniform thickness and smoothness without requiring a separate polishing process for each side.[28]

With $40.7 million in new capital raised by Eberstadt, ASG acquired several small domestic glass companies into which it installed the new process. The new technique proved to be technically inferior, however, and the French parent sold it to an American investor group headed by Nelson Loud. It was subsequently merged with another glass producer, Fourco, and now operates under the name AFG Industries, Inc.[29]

Although Eberstadt was a specialist in developing creative financing, Porter notes that he avoided like the plague getting involved with start-up venture capital deals. As an investment banker, he was not interested in wet nursing new businesses.[30] As *Fortune* noted, "Ferdinand Eberstadt won't touch capital for *new* enterprises. . . . Ferd likes nothing better than to discover a new piece of research to pass on to his financial clientele . . . but further he will not go."[31] Nelson Loud adds, "When the firm came upon things like seed or venture capital deals Eberstadt took them to Jock Whitney or the Rockefellers."[32]

But there were occasional exceptions to this general rule. One such exception was Colchem, a venture the firm promoted unsuccessfully in the early 1950s to produce gasoline and chemicals from coal, based on the hydrogenation process. Eberstadt wanted a sure thing, however, and refused to go ahead with this venture unless he received a government guarantee to cover the investors' original capital. However, Colchem never got off the ground; it was killed by politicians who could not see the long-term need for such a project and by the chemical and oil industry lobbyists, who regarded the venture as a threat to their businesses.[33]

If Colchem had materialized, it might have provided a long-term solution to America's energy problems by converting its vast coal resources into a source of gasoline as well as a host of other chemical derivatives. Even in the early 1950s, oil geologists were warning that America's bountiful supplies of petroleum were likely to run out by the end of the century.

The problem in 1951, as today, is that coal hydrogenation requires large quantities of heat and pressure to make the chemical recovery process function. This in turn requires highly specialized equipment to contain and handle the tremendous pressures and heat required. Eberstadt calculated that it would require about $400 million in capital to build such a plant. Colchem's hydrogenation plant, sitting on top of a huge coal pile in southern Illinois, could have become the prototype of a vast synthetic fuels business based on America's almost inexhaustible supply of coal.[34]

The new plant would depend heavily on the coal hydrogenation technology developed by two German scientists, Franz Fischer and Hans Trosch. Eberstadt first encountered this new technology when he was active in Germany during the 1920s. The German process greatly reduced the required heat and pressure, making the process commercially feasible. Subsequently, Germany used coal hydrogenation to build a synthetic fuels industry that helped power its war machine in World War II.[35]

Eberstadt's team, working with the Bureau of Mines and the Koppers Company, had adapted the German technology to a process for the direct conversion of coal into gas and thence into synthetic fuels. Interior Secretary Oscar Chapman, seeking a partnership program with private industry to produce liquid fuel from coal, decided to announce publicly Eberstadt's plan to build the plant with minimum government price guarantees for the gasoline produced.[36]

However, the Bureau of Mines, the U.S. Government agency that controlled authorization of guarantees for projects of this sort, turned against the Eberstadt plan, damning it as a "Socialist Scheme." Nelson Loud lamented,

[T]hat aborted deal . . . could have made the energy crisis of the 1970s and 1980s a nonevent. . . . Everything was working along fine but the Secretary of the Interior made a premature announcement about the damn thing before we had it all done and of course everybody ran away. . . . They are really trying to do the same thing today but the costs have skyrocketed—the price is twenty times higher.[37]

Twenty years later, when the energy crisis got out of hand in the early 1970s, David Lilienthal, the former head of the Tennessee Valley Authority (TVA) power program and the first chairman of the Atomic Energy Commission, was quoted in the press denouncing the government's shortsighted policy in the early 1950s which aborted Eberstadt's synthetic fuel effort.

When he failed to get the government guarantee, Eberstadt wrote off his development costs on the aborted deal, and unfortunately Colchem never got off the drawing boards. One can only speculate about what might have been. Perhaps Eberstadt's instinct to avoid high-risk ventures was the culprit in this situation; perhaps Colchem's time had not yet come. But Francis Williams recalled, "The concept was sound and we would have been way ahead of where we are today if they had gone ahead with it."[38]

Notes

1. "Financial Services to Industry and Investors," a brochure published privately by F. Eberstadt & Co., Inc. (New York, 1953), and internal firm memorandum, March 21, 1968.

2. Annual Reports to Stockholders of Chemical Fund, Inc., for the years indicated.

3. Interviews by Robert L. Newton with Franz Schneider, December 15, 1981, and February 10, 1982.

4. Based on author's survey of the firm's financing activities as contained in the "Corporate Financing Directory" published annually by the *Investment Dealer's Digest* for the periods covered and the Eberstadt brochure, "Financial Services to Industry and Investors."

5. "Who's Who in America," *Marquis Who's Who, Inc.*, 40th ed., vol. 2, p. 2602.

6. Robert C. Porter, "Importance of Financial Planning to a Growing Corporation," an address before the Pharmaceutical Advertising Club, New York City, May 9, 1957, reprinted in the *Commercial and Financial Chronicle*, June 6, 1957, pp. 2–3.

7. Ibid, pp. 5–6.

8. Interview with Robert C. Porter, August 27, 1984.

9. Porter, "Importance of Financial Planning," pp. 3–5.

10. Interview with Robert G. Zeller, May 1, 1984.

11. Porter, "Importance of Financial Planning," pp. 3–4.

12. Interview with Arthur Krim, former head of United Artists, April 12, 1984.

13. Porter, "Importance of Financial Planning," p. 4.

14. Telephone interview with Nelson Loud, February 28, 1986, and letter from F. Kenneth Melis, March 3, 1986.

15. Interview with Arthur Krim, April 12, 1984.

16. Ibid.

17. Interview by Robert L. Newton with Robert C. Porter, January 1982, revised March 1984 (hereinafter referred to as the Newton-Porter interview).

18. Ibid.

19. Interview with Nelson Loud, April 2, 1984.

20. Newton-Porter interview.

21. Ibid.

22. Ibid.

23. Ibid.

24. Interview with Fairleigh Dickinson, September 19, 1984.

25. Newton-Porter interview.

26. Newton-Porter interview.

27. Moody's Industrial Manual, 1961 ed., p. 2925.

28. Interview with Nelson Loud, December 10, 1987.

29. Preliminary prospectus, June 9, 1983, for NL Capital Associates, pp. 19–20; also interview with Nelson Loud, December 10, 1987.

30. Telephone interview with Robert C. Porter, January 31, 1984.

31. "Ferdinand Eberstadt," *Fortune*, April 1939, p. 140.

32. Interview with Nelson Loud, April 2, 1984.

33. Interview with Francis S. Williams, May 8, 1984.

34. "The $400 Million Colchem Question," *Fortune*, November 1951, p. 76.

35. "Hydrogenation," *Encyclopaedia Britannica*, 1988 ed., Macropaedia vol. 21, p. 408.

36. David E. Lilienthal, *The Journals of David E. Lilienthal* (New York, 1964–1981), vol. III, p. 247.

37. Interview with Nelson Loud, April 2, 1984.

38. Interview with Francis S. Williams, May 8, 1984.

7

The Lazard Connection

Many people feel that Eberstadt reached the pinnacle of his creative financing skills in the 1950s when, in partnership with André Meyer of Lazard Frères and Robert Lehman of Lehman Brothers, he engineered a number of financial coups. These private capital deals were largely unknown to the public although they were frequently intertwined with the firm's public deals. Five major and a score of smaller ones took place during the 1950s and to some extent the 1960s. Most of them were done in partnership or coventured with Lazard Frères. By style and training, André Meyer, the dynamic head of that firm, was just the sort of plunger to push forward the giant deals that Eberstadt was dreaming up.

Their method typically involved buying control (largely with bank loans) of an established company and then restructuring its operations by selling off unprofitable divisions, buying up more profitable businesses, upgrading management, changing the nature of the business and thereby creating more valuable properties.[1]

Eberstadt and Meyer pioneered many of the investment banking techniques that are so popular today in the world of corporate finance. The leveraged buyout, which had its genesis with their deals in the 1950s and 1960s, revived the merchant banking techniques of the 1920s. Eberstadt and Meyer never went into a deal unless they could finance most of it with loans from banks or other institutional lenders.[2] According to Robert C. Porter, "Eber, despite his great wealth, never put much of his own money at risk; he was basically a very cautious man. . . . In addition, he liked to get André or Lehman in there . . . to have them . . . check out his thinking."[3]

James Benenson, a close Eberstadt associate, recalled:

Eberstadt and Meyer each knew the other was super smart and could be relied on in a deal. Eber would bring André in on the other side of a deal because he knew that André would not "put it to him" and vice versa. And André used to bring Eberstadt into deals. They each wanted a friend on the other side of the trade. It was not an adversarial relationship. Eber's interest was in seeing the deal happen and so was André's—not in busting it up and saying the hell with you, we can get more money down the street—Eber was not a "shoot 'em up" guy at all.[4]

Nelson Loud said that the deals were not really venture capital deals in the sense of backing some young inventor. Most of the investments however contained a special situation quality to them. The primary concern of Eberstadt was that the downside risk should be low enough to minimize the loss should everything go wrong.[5] Loud continued, "In all, I worked on six or seven private deals with Ferd and André but with the exception of Borax (which came from the English Lazards), we originated all of the deals, not André." Some of the restructurings were complicated, some simple, but all were constructively handled in an imaginative way.[6]

The two deal makers combined a rare blend of talents. David Lilienthal, a former director of Tennessee Valley Authority (TVA) and the Atomic Energy Commission, who became a confidant of Eberstadt and Meyer, described in his *Journals* the two deal makers in the midst of a negotiation:

Eberstadt enjoys the "hunt"; his eyes take on the intense look of a man in the midst of an absorbing game. André takes it in still another way; he meditates, sitting way back in the corner of his big room, . . . appraising risks, trying to see ahead, letting his sense of "feel" tell him when is a good time . . . to go to market![7]

Lilienthal adds,

"[I]t was always fun to watch Eber's way of going at the financial aspects. It is a form of wizardry; I am always half-persuaded that it is done with mirrors, by which the whole is made to add up to more than the sum of the parts."[8]

In addition to Lazard, Eberstadt sometimes invited as coinvestors Ladenburg Thalmann, Lehman Brothers, Paine Webber, Reynolds, Wertheim, and White Weld, as well as the senior managements of the corporations involved. Institutional investors playing major roles as senior lenders included Bankers Trust, Chase Bank, Chemical Bank, Equitable Life, Guaranty Trust, Prudential and others who put up over $12 million to help finance these ventures. Each transaction was initiated under a written joint partnership agreement with Lazard and any other participant. None of them was done under so-called hand shake, gentleman's agreements.[9]

When Eberstadt and Meyer sold part of their positions, they normally used other investment bankers to handle the initial public offering to gain reciprocal benefits. For example, Eastman Dillon underwrote Carter Products; Blyth sold their Filtrol holdings; Lehman handled the Minerals & Chemicals offering; Morgan Stanley handled Warner-Lambert and First Boston engineered the U.S. Borax distribution. Each of these firms subsequently reciprocated by offering Eberstadt and Lazard better underwriting positions in their deals.[10]

Although the exact history is hazy, Eberstadt probably first met Meyer when Eberstadt headed Dillon Read's European operations in the 1920s. Meyer was then putting together deals at Lazard's Paris office. In addition, Eberstadt and Meyer were both deputies at the 1929 Reparations Conference in Paris—Eberstadt with the American delegation, Meyer with the French.[11] Moreover, Eberstadt had cultivated a number of Jewish banking houses in Europe probably benefitting discretely from his family heritage, and it is more than likely that his path crossed that of Meyer on several occasions in Paris where Dillon had opened an office and where Eberstadt lived for a considerable period during the 1920s. Meyer fled France at the time of its surrender to the Germans in 1940 and came to New York where he soon took active control of the New York–based Lazard operation along with Pierre David-Weill, a descendant of the founding Lazard brothers and a majority controlling partner of the firm.[12]

The Eberstadt-Meyer relationship was based on two distinctive traits of the two men. Eberstadt originated the deals and the ideas; Meyer was the promoter, the person who pushed them through. Meyer stiffened the resolve of Eberstadt and provided him with the needed financial backing to go ahead. John Vogelstein, a former Lazard partner, recalls, "Eber had the ideas, but André had the guts."[13]

Although Eberstadt and Meyer saw eye to eye on deal making, their investment styles differed considerably. Meyer typically stayed in a situation just long enough to build it up to a holding substantially more valuable than it was when he went into it. At that point, Meyer unloaded his shares and moved on to something else.[14] Eberstadt's approach was quite different. When he died in 1969, he still held in his own, in his wife's accounts and in the numerous trust accounts for his children and grandchildren portions of his holdings in many of his earlier financial successes.[15]

Meyer's attitude may have reflected his European roots, namely the fragility of fortunes and wealth as reflected in the collapse of France and his own fortune in France after the German invasion. Even though this was New York, not Paris, Meyer never got over the fear of losing it all.

"André's attitude," said one of his closest Lazard partners, "was if you made some money, put it in your pocket. Don't be a wise guy." Adds another Lazard partner, "André wanted to make sure he could sell it, and how did he make sure? He sold it."[16]

By contrast, Eberstadt felt that "if you had a good thing, why sell it?"[17] Eberstadt took profits too but just enough to recover his original investment plus pay the capital gains taxes on what he had sold. Thereafter, Eberstadt carried the balance of the investment at zero cost.[18] However, Eberstadt did not ignore the downside risks. He once remarked to David Lilienthal, "[W]hen I start out on a new venture, I want to be sure I know how much a return ticket will cost"—in other words, if all goes wrong, how much will it cost to get out?[19]

Eberstadt and his partners invested about $14 million in the five major private investments discussed in this chapter. These five investments resulted in total realized values approximating $136 million, or capital gains of $122 million equal to more than 800 percent over their original capital investment. At no time did Eberstadt or Lazard have more than $7.5 million of their own capital at risk, the greater part of it Lazard's. Moreover, the retained holdings of the original investments in the Engelhard Minerals & Chemicals, Warner-Lambert, Carter-Wallace and U.S. Borax transactions continued to multiply in value in later years from further company growth.[20]

Probably the most spectacular of these five deals was the Engelhard Minerals & Chemicals deal; it was also the first. In the spring of 1951 Eberstadt received a call from Frederick H. Bedford, Jr., a former director and top executive of Standard Oil Company (New Jersey), asking him to help find a buyer for its 50-percent interest in Attapulgus Clay Company. The other 50 percent was owned by Atlantic Refining. Attapulgus had a substantial business in the mining and beneficiation of Fuller's Earth, a type of clay used for petroleum refining and oil-well drilling, as well as in products used as adsorbents for the purification and clarification of lubricating oil.[21]

Eberstadt was attracted by the Georgia company. Besides being the country's leading producer of Fuller's Earth, Attapulgus owned 50 percent of Filtrol Corporation, the only processor of bentonite and halloysite clays used in petroleum-cracking catalysts—the chemicals that break down heavy crude oil into gasoline and other petroleum products. The other 50 percent of Filtrol was owned by Filtrol Company of California, a company whose stock traded inactively in the over-the-counter market.[22] As Eberstadt toyed with the idea of buying up this small clay company, he suggested to Loud that they discuss the matter with Meyer who was making some fairly daring moves at Lazard.

Meyer was definitely interested; on April 21, 1952, Eberstadt and Lazard agreed to buy 50 percent of Attapulgus for $4.5 million. Half of the purchase price was backed by a loan from the Chase Bank. However, Myron Bantrell, a former Rochester, New York, chemist and chairman of Filtrol of California, which owned the other 50 percent of Filtrol, wanted full control of Filtrol.[23]

The transactions involved were exceedingly complex, a hallmark of the Eberstadt-Lazard deals, involving spin-offs, reorganizations and restructuring of Attapulgus and Filtrol together with the merger of the clay business into Minerals Separation North America. This company, which held the patents for numerous mineral-extraction processes, was then renamed Attapulgus Minerals & Chemicals.

Lazard and Eberstadt sold their Filtrol stock, which permitted Bantrell to assume complete control of Filtrol. The public offering was made through Blyth & Company at a price which more than recovered their entire investment while retaining majority ownership of Attapulgus at no cost. Eberstadt and Meyer divided $5.4 million in profits on the sale of their Filtrol shares.[24]

Despite these moves, the remaining holding in Attapulgus Minerals & Chemicals was disappointing. Earnings sagged although they took a turn for the better in early 1954. But then Eberstadt and Meyer pulled off the coup that assured the company's success: a merger with Edgar Brothers, a company which produced kaolin, also known as China Clay, a form of clay used in the coating of paper. More importantly, the new company—now renamed Minerals & Chemicals—was developing new uses for kaolin as a petroleum-cracking catalyst.[25]

Getting the new process for the catalyst off the ground, however, involved many severe operating problems. Finally, Julian Avery, a Chemical Fund director, recommended a retired chemist in Florida who had been a specialist in the field. Francis S. Williams recalled that the chemist told Eberstadt that he would look at the process provided Eberstadt would be "willing to pay the cost of my private plane to fly up to Georgia and fly back home again."[26]

This agreed, the chemist flew to Georgia, put on his overalls and traced the process all the way through, from the mining and mixing through the acid treatments; finally, he discovered the cause of the trouble—a broken titrator, which measured the needed concentration of sulphuric acid in the process. When a new titrator was installed, the process worked. Subsequently, the directors of the company presented Eberstadt with the defective titrator to be joined later by Becton-Dickinson's stuffed crow in Eberstadt's growing collection of memorabilia.[27]

The new petroleum-cracking catalysts and other chemicals developed from kaolin caused a marked improvement in the company's earnings. Just four months after the merger had been consummated, Minerals & Chemicals stock had soared to $22 a share compared to $5 a share when Eberstadt and Meyer made their original investment. At that point, the two bankers were eager to take some profits. They arranged a February 1955 offering of 436,000 Minerals & Chemicals shares at $24.50 a share through Lehman Brothers, and the stock was listed on the New York Stock Exchange. Within two years after the offering, the retained stock had more than doubled in price.[28]

In the late 1950s, Meyer struck up a friendship with the principals of an international metals trading firm, Philipp Brothers, which had leveraged their superb trading instincts and international contacts into a $200 million business. Although their operation was regularly churning out profits of $5 million or $6 million a year, they knew full well that they had to take the company public to cash in. They went to André Meyer for advice. Meyer asked Eberstadt, "Why not bring Philipp Brothers public by merging it with . . . Minerals & Chemicals?" That way Philipp's two owners would get a public market for their holdings, and Minerals & Chemicals would get an important source of financing for its rapidly growing petroleum catalyst line.[29]

For Eberstadt and Meyer, the Philipp merger into Minerals & Chemicals was a sensational success. The stock in the new company, now renamed Minerals & Chemicals Philipp, jumped 40 percent in price within a year, and Eberstadt's remaining 150,000 shares of stock had a value of $4.2 million.[30]

According to James Benenson, Eberstadt had earlier considered selling off the chemicals division to National Starch, an investment banking client of his firm. Although this incident is amusing, it also illustrates Eberstadt's eclectic negotiating style. Eberstadt asked Benenson one day, "Jimmy, do we have anybody on the board of Minerals & Chemicals?" Benenson answered, "Yes, we do." "Well," he said, "go do a spread sheet on the chemicals division and let's go uptown and sell it to National Starch." Benenson got all the statistical studies together and packed them in his briefcase, and they went to meet with Frank Greenwall and Donald Pascal who ran National Starch.[31]

They sat down at Greenwall's octagonal desk covered in green leather, and Eberstadt began to tell them what a grand company this chemicals division was and what a wonderful fit it would make for National Starch. Benenson recalls, "When Eber started to extol a company, he would get this faraway look in his eyes, just like he was talking about girls."[32]

Everybody was sitting there just mesmerized, and Eberstadt said, "Jimmy, give me those figures." (This was the first time he had taken a close look at them.) After he stared at them in disbelief for a minute, he looked at Benenson and said to him in a confidential tone, as if no one else could hear, "Jimmy, for God's sake, this is a terrific company. We're not going to sell this. Put these away and let's get out of here." Greenwall and Pascal stared at each other in disbelief and chased after Eberstadt and Benenson all the way down the hall to the elevator saying, "Can't we talk a little more about this?"[33]

But Eberstadt shooed them away, just as if he were shooing away flies. The last thing Benenson remembers seeing was two faces leaning in as the elevator doors closed, staring and wishing that something would happen to change Eberstadt's mind. Eberstadt had decided there were better ways to deal with the financing needs of the company.[34] Eberstadt's inexplicable failure to study the figures before meeting with Greenwall and Pascal was completely atypical.

At this point, Meyer came up with the solution to the company's financing needs—namely, a merger with Engelhard Industries, the world's largest refiner and fabricator of precious metals. In the mid–1960s, Meyer sat down and discussed with Eberstadt his ideas for an alliance of Minerals & Chemicals Philipp and Engelhard Industries. Meyer also suggested that the group might later include Harry Oppenheimer's Anglo-American mining empire which controlled most of South Africa's gold and diamond mining. Engelhard agreed to the merger in mid–1967, and the stock of the new company, now renamed Engelhard Minerals & Chemicals, soared in the market further enriching Eberstadt and Lazard who still held large blocks in the combined company. For his assistance on the deal, Meyer remitted to Eberstadt 25 percent of the $1.1 million fee that Lazard received for arranging the Engelhard merger.[35]

All told, Eberstadt and Meyer made more than ten times their original net investment of $2.25 million in what started out as a small, unknown clay company located in a rural, remote part of Georgia, and Eberstadt retained a large block as an investment which continued to multiply in value.

Although the Engelhard Minerals & Chemicals deal was spectacular, Warner-Lambert was probably the best example of how Eberstadt and Meyer employed the rebuilding process in their coventures. Benenson notes, "Eber and André built Warner-Lambert through a brilliant series of mergers [which] . . . restructured a go nowhere business into a dynamic powerhouse."[36]

The financing began when Eberstadt brought public in early 1951 the old Warner-Hudnut common stock raising $6.3 million for the company. The company's main products were a stagnant line of home remedies and the Richard Hudnut line of cosmetics which continually lost money. On the other hand, the Warner business, founded in the 1880s, had some interesting proprietary drug products, and it had recently acquired Chilcott Laboratories, an ethical drug producer. The company was still privately controlled; the controlling block, consisting of 56 percent of the outstanding stock, was in the hands of the Pfeiffer family foundation.[37]

The William R. Warner Company, as it was originally known, had been controlled by the Pfeiffer family since the 1880s. By the early 1950s, Gustavus Pfeiffer, fearful of losing control of the business, put his hold-

ings into a foundation dedicated to medical research with the stipulation
that after he died the stock be sold.[38]

Pfeiffer's death in 1953 thus presented serious complications for the
company, complications which became apparent soon after Nelson Loud
received a call at Eberstadt from Alfred Driscoll, an ex-governor of New
Jersey, who was then president of Warner-Hudnut. All Driscoll could
say on the phone was, "We've got to come and see you." "What's it all
about?" asked Loud. "Wait till we get there," answered Driscoll.[39]

When Driscoll arrived, he was accompanied by Elmer Bobst, a veteran
drug industry executive who had come out of retirement in 1945 to take
over the Warner Company chairmanship. Loud recalls,

They came in and their eyes were wild and their hair was on end. Ferd and I
sat down and said, "Now, what's the problem?" And they said, "A gentleman
[representing Revlon] came up to see us today and offered to buy the Pfeiffer
Foundation's stock in Warner-Hudnut."

Revlon was controlled by Charles Revson, the crude, tyrannical genius
whom Warner's management wanted to avoid if possible.[40]

Eberstadt told Bobst and Driscoll, "That's kind of a difficult spot.
You're trustees of the foundation. You must entertain the proposal."
Eberstadt added, "In the meantime, let us make a study of the business
and see what should be done. Maybe we can find someone else to buy
it." As soon as Bobst and Driscoll left, Eberstadt phoned André Meyer.[41]

Eberstadt and Meyer looked at the situation and decided to go ahead
and buy the stock—but not on their own. This time, in an effort to
spread the risk, they enlisted several other Wall Street firms, including
Ladenburg Thalmann, Lehman Brothers, Paine Webber, Wertheim, and
White Weld. Together they purchased the controlling block of 558,000
shares from the foundation for $11.2 million (of which $5.6 million was
financed by bank loans).[42]

The first order of business was to sell off the losing Hudnut division
and then embark upon a program of acquisitions and expansion to acquire companies heavily involved in ethical drugs with unique prescrip-
tion items as well as proprietary products that generated huge profit
margins. Eberstadt, as the investment banker for Pfizer, had seen how
that company had prospered with such items as Penicillin and Terra-
mycin.[43]

Eberstadt asked John Van Deventer, the Chemical Fund drug analyst,
to evaluate Bobst's plans for the company. When Van Deventer went
to see Elmer Bobst, he was not quite prepared for Bobst's unfortunate
lack of modesty. Bobst wanted to build another Hoffmann–La Roche,
the giant international drug company whose U.S. arm Bobst had headed
previously. Van Deventer recalled that when he got out his notes to ask

some questions, "Bobst sounded off for about two hours about himself and his accomplishments and what he planned to do for the company, but he didn't give me a single fact or figure."[44]

A former Eberstadt partner remarked, "Elmer Bobst had many good qualities, but humility was not one of them." Because of Bobst's many fine contributions to the humanities in later life, he was frequently feted at testimonial dinners in his honor, which Eberstadt felt obligated to attend. So frequent were these events that Eberstadt one day wearily remarked to an associate, "Last night I walked down memory lane once again with Elmer. I have walked down memory lane with Elmer so many times that I think the grass must be worn down by now."[45]

Although Bobst took credit for rebuilding Warner, the impetus came from Eberstadt and Lazard. Nelson Loud notes, "Eber and André came up with ideas; we figured out how to do the deals, negotiated them, made everybody happy, and did 'em." By October 1962, Warner-Lambert had blossomed into a company earning $200 million a year, and it had all been done by acquisitions. Says Loud, "We started with a company with two million three in earnings and ended up ultimately with a hundred times that."[46]

Eberstadt kept prodding the company into even bigger mergers including one with the mammoth Reynolds Tobacco Company, which was aborted over a dispute over who was to run the combined company. As Benenson related it,

Eber had the merger all worked out. It was a $750 million deal which would have been one of the biggest deals up to that time. The Reynolds guys came up in their huge airplane to fly everybody down to see the tobacco fields. Everyone got aboard and as the plane was taxiing out to the runway to take off Elmer Bobst got up and said, "I hope everyone understands that I am going to be chairman of the merged company." All the Southern colonels looked at each other and muttered something into the mike and the plane turned around and went back and they opened the doors and threw everybody out and closed the doors and flew away. That was the end of that. Eber wanted to kill Bobst [for blurting out that statement]. Nobody thought Bobst would have that much brass.[47]

Inevitably, Eberstadt's and Meyer's influence in the company began to weaken. "It was one of those evolutionary things," notes Frank Markoe, Jr., former chief financial officer of Warner-Lambert. "The company became more professionally managed, and when these things happen the role of an investment banker very often gets smaller." Warner-Lambert's new management was much less under the sway of Eberstadt than Bobst and Driscoll had been and was much less inclined to seek his advice.[48]

The final rupture came when the new Warner-Lambert president

Stuart Hemsley called Robert Zeller at Eberstadt to tell him that the company had decided to use Morgan Stanley as the lead manager of the next securities issue. Eberstadt could be comanager, Hemsley said, but Warner-Lambert was dropping Lazard. Zeller walked into Eberstadt's office to break the news. "No problem," Eberstadt shot back. "Call him back and tell him to forget it. We're partners with Meyer, and if he's not in it, we're not in it."[49]

The Warner-Lambert investment was even more rewarding than the Attapulgus–Minerals & Chemicals–Engelhard deal had been. After paying off bank loans, the Eberstadt-Lazard coventurers netted a $50 million profit—nearly ten times their original investment ten years earlier. Moreover, Eberstadt retained a large block of the stock, which he never sold and which continued to multiply in value.[50]

In another unusual deal, Eberstadt and Meyer owned briefly the entire northern coast of Haiti known as the Plantation Dauphin. What they owned, actually, was the world's largest sisal plantation, 35,000 acres, or 55 square miles, between the Santo Domingo border and Cap-Haitien. (Sisal is a fiber used to make rope, paperboard and kraftboard.) The plantation, the largest employer in Haiti, also owned securities in several U.S. and Japanese companies.[51]

Dauphin was owned principally by the André de Coppet estate. Modest interests were owned by a few former partners of de Coppet or trusts of their legatees. The trustees approached Nelson Loud about selling the property, and he obtained an option for Eberstadt at an initial price of $4 million subject to final appraisal.[52] First, however, the widow and the trustees of the estate asked Nelson Loud and Jarvis Slade, another Eberstadt partner, to come down and make an independent appraisal, as the U.S. Internal Revenue Service had challenged the earlier appraisals. They promptly flew down to Haiti to make their inspection. Loud recalls the incident:

It was the middle of August, hotter 'n' hell. But we found several intriguing things about the plantation: first, that it was a successful enterprise in itself; and second, that it owned several million dollars' worth of marketable Japanese and other foreign securities which were sitting in a custodian account in a vault in the Chemical Bank in New York.

The discovery led Loud to increase the original valuation from $4 million to $6.6 million. They returned to New York and reported to Eberstadt. "What are we going to do?" Loud asked Eberstadt. "Let's go see André," Eberstadt answered.[53]

Eberstadt and Meyer decided to bring in the English branch of Lazard Frères because they knew all about sisal in South Africa. (The London Lazards were cut in for a third of the pie since they did all of the technical work on the deal.) Over lunch at India House in downtown Manhattan, the sisal expert from Lazard's London branch made his report to Eberstadt and Loud. Eberstadt had no interest in a long, technical dissertation. "Is this thing any goddamn good?" he barked. The expert, who in earlier conversations with Lazard and Eberstadt people had praised the sisal operation, nervously replied, "It's too big, and it's going to be very hard to handle." Right after that meeting, Eberstadt phoned Meyer and reported the expert's findings. After a few minutes' conversation, they decided to call the whole thing off.[54]

Loud and Slade were flabbergasted. Here was an investment that, by their reckoning, was as close to riskless as they had ever seen. By liquidating the securities portfolio alone, they could have the plantation for nothing. Slade went to Loud and said, "Nelson, I think the firm should buy this even if Lazard doesn't want to go ahead." Loud said, "Really?" Slade said, "Yes, and if the firm doesn't want to buy it, I would like to have permission to buy it and pay the firm a modest fee."[55]

Loud looked at Slade and said, "Can you get the money?" Slade replied, "I have already got the money lined up." Loud said, "Well, I'd like to join you, Jarvis." Slade said, "Fine." Loud called Eberstadt and said, "Jarvis and I would like to come in to talk to you about Plantation Dauphin." They went to Eberstadt's office, and Loud said, "Jarvis and I would like to buy the plantation."[56]

Eberstadt was startled. "Nelson," he replied, "do you want to be an investment banker, or do you want to be in the sisal business?" But Loud wasn't going to be brushed off so easily.[57] He said, "Eber, let's have lunch and run through these numbers a little bit," which they did.

After lunch Eberstadt phoned Meyer and said "André, we are going ahead with this deal and you're still welcome to come in if you want; if not, that's fine." Meyer answered, "We're in."[58]

The investment fully lived up to Loud's and Slade's expectations: it was some of the easiest money Eberstadt and Meyer ever made. They bought the plantation in 1955 with $2 million of their own money (plus $4.6 million in bank loans) and within a few months turned around and resold it to the Haitian-American Sugar Company which, together with other asset sales (the securities portfolio), brought them $6 million, triple their original investment.[59]

In 1957, Eberstadt's old friend, Harry Hoyt, approached him with a block of stock owned by a group of Canadian stockholders of Carter Products, representing 20 percent of the company, who wished to sell at a price equivalent to $2.50 a share on the present stock. Eberstadt invited Lazard and some other investors to join him. The other investors included the securities firm of Reynolds & Co. and the Hoyt family which owned over 50 percent of Carter's stock through Bahdelan Corp., a family-owned investment company.[60]

Carter, a pharmaceutical specialty producer, had just developed Miltown, the first over-the-counter tranquillizer. Eberstadt perceived that this product had explosive growth potential. According to Van Deventer,

Carter's stock traded inactively over-the-counter at ridiculously low prices which made it difficult to value. Earnings from *Miltown* were increasing spectacularly. Finally, we bought some of it for *Chemical Fund*. The stock got up to 72 and I remember Eber coming into our noon meeting with "Well boys, things look good, why don't we add to this?"[61]

Porter recalled,

When Eber and André did the original Warner-Hudnut deal they cut Harry Hoyt in on the ground floor for a small piece . . . to open his eyes to what you could do with a controlling block of stock in an estate by creating a public company. Of course Hoyt made a pot full of money out of the Warner-Hudnut deal. . . . So when Hoyt saw this estate block in Carter come available he brought it to Eber to formulate a deal to do the same thing. So by casting bread on the water back in 1953, four years later it paid off in getting a similar opportunity with the Carter deal.[62]

But Hoyt had a penchant for maintaining over 50-percent control even when it violated the listing requirements of the Big Board. "The final blow to Eber," Porter recalled, "was when Harry tried to delist the company from the New York Stock Exchange."[63] To meet the Stock Exchange's listing requirements, Carter-Wallace would have to issue more stock to improve its market, but Hoyt did not want to dilute his interest below 51-percent control. He hit upon the idea of declaring a stock dividend in Class A nonvoting stock, but the Stock Exchange rules also forbid issuance of nonvoting stock.[64] Porter noted,

Hoyt did not want to comply with the Stock Exchange rules. Then some of the institutions who had bought the stock on the original offering came to Eber and said, "You know you represented this was going to be a listed security and we bought it on the strength of that assurance. . . . " Eber said, "Well I agree but I'm only a director, I can't control what Harry does."[65]

The institutions ultimately sued Carter to prevent delisting, and Eberstadt was forced off the board.

Despite these setbacks, Eberstadt and Meyer realized $40 million in profits on their Carter holdings—more than fifteen times their original investment, and Eberstadt continued to hold a large block thereafter.[66]

In early 1955, the management of Borax Consolidated, Ltd., enlisted the aid of Lazard Brothers in London in fending off an effort by a New York securities firm, Model, Roland & Stone, to gain control. As Loud described the deal, the London firm brought in Lazard of New York and Lazard of Paris to help. They in turn brought in Eberstadt to constitute a group to advise and assist Borax.[67]

In March, the Eberstadt-Lazard group purchased a substantial minority interest in Borax, which caused Model to cease its unwelcome activities. In June of the next year, the group formed Pacific Coast Borax Company to take over the business of Borax Consolidated's American division with additional debt financing of $18 million arranged privately by the group with several institutional lenders.[68]

"Eber and André felt that solid fuels were going to power space rockets and that a borax derivative, Boron, would be the primary vehicle," recalls Porter. But solid fuels did not turn out to be the technology used and Eberstadt and Meyer were forced to find new directions for their venture.[69]

By restructuring Borax Consolidated's American division into Pacific Coast Borax, the Eberstadt-Lazard group eliminated the double taxation caused by certain differences between U.S. and U.K. tax laws relating to the treatment of depletion.[70] They then, after providing substantial private financing for Pacific Coast Borax, merged it with U.S. Potash Company to form U.S. Borax and Chemical Company. Eberstadt and Lazard then purchased 200,000 shares for $2 million (plus $2 million in bank loans). Later they sold 150,000 shares of their holdings through First Boston Corporation and netted $5 million.[71]

Of course, other investment deals were made by Eberstadt and Lazard which were not as profitable as these transactions; some resulted in losses.[72] For example, the Eberstadt-Lazard team bought up Ziv Television and its library of hundreds of television shows that Fred Ziv, a pioneer independent television syndicator, had produced in the early years of television.[73]

Ziv seemed like a flourishing business, and when the founder, Fred Ziv, told Eberstadt he was interested in retiring, Eberstadt wasted no time making Ziv an offer. He and Meyer agreed to pay $14 million for the company, $12.5 million of which was financed by a loan from Chemical Bank.[74]

No sooner had the purchase been completed than Fred Ziv and his partner, John Sinn, approached Eberstadt and Meyer for more capital. The company, Ziv and Sinn explained, was in the middle of producing that season's series and needed an extra infusion of capital to complete the programs. "How much was needed?" Ziv and Sinn were asked. "Oh," they said, "about $6 or $7 million." "When we heard that," said Loud, "everyone turned pale."[75]

Having borrowed to the hilt to finance the acquisition, Eberstadt and Meyer were not about to go back to the banks for another $7 million. The television production business was changing, and the networks wanted to produce the shows themselves to lock in the huge flow of income from reruns that up to then accrued largely to the syndicators.[76]

Eberstadt and Meyer turned to their old friends, Benjamin and Krim at United Artists to find a solution. United Artists agreed to take over Ziv on terms that actually allowed Eberstadt and Meyer to make a modest profit. United Artists assumed responsibility for the $12.5 million bank loan and paid out another $4.75 million in notes and debentures. Over the next several years, United Artists lost heavily on Ziv, but the reruns of the old series eventually brought in enough income to offset most of these losses.[77]

By the early 1960s, however, Eberstadt and Meyer came to the realization that the market was beginning to change and that they could not initiate the type of deal that had been so successful in the previous decade. They could not compete with the rapidly expanding corporate conglomerates which, with the big bull market of the "go-go" 1960s, were able to use their overpriced stock to bid up everything in sight.[78]

The Eberstadt-Meyer relationship began to weaken as each of them turned his attention to his primary field. For Meyer, this was mergers; for Eberstadt, it was financing the little blue chips, especially those that were concentrated in the fields of expanding technology such as chemicals, drugs, electronics and medical diagnostics.

André Meyer was a more aggressive venture capital investor than Eberstadt. For example, when Lazard bought Avis, Eberstadt was offered his traditional interest but turned it down—he thought it was a little too risky for him. In his mind, it did not have what he always referred to as explosive growth—car rental was just not that exciting to him.[79]

Moreover, Lazard and Lehman were doing more deals in real estate— one of them that Eberstadt participated in near Dulles Airport was a difficult deal which took a considerable period of time to work out. Williams says that Lazard's "young turks"—Felix Rohaytin and others— kept bringing Eberstadt a lot of deals that in his mind were just too risky for him.[80]

Finally, some of Eberstadt's closest associates got the feeling on several occasions during meetings with Lazard that there was an element of distrust between the two men. The incident that may have accounted for the cooling of the Eberstadt-Meyer relationship involved a scandal that implicated Meyer with the convicted swindler, Edward Gilbert.[81]

Cary Reich describes Gilbert as a

gutsy stock market speculator who had come out of nowhere in the late 1950s to engineer the takeover of the country's leading manufacturer of hardwood flooring—E. L. Bruce and Company. Courted by the high and mighty of the financial world, he had slipped effortlessly into a "Gatsby-ish" life style with a ten-room Fifth Avenue apartment ... and an eleven-bedroom summer villa ... in the south of France.[82]

Gilbert was restless for another financial coup and had purchased 250,000 shares of Celotex, all on margin, with the intention of taking over the big building materials company. When the stock market collapsed in May and June of 1962, Gilbert embezzled funds from E. L. Bruce and Company to meet the margin calls of his brokers on the Celotex stock. The market drop was too great, however, and Gilbert escaped to Brazil before the fraud was discovered.[83]

Before this, Gilbert had been sought out by Meyer to determine how Lazard might help Gilbert take over Celotex by purchasing some of the Celotex stock that Gilbert needed to complete the takeover. When the stock market collapsed, Meyer abandoned Gilbert, and a month later Gilbert fled to Rio.[84]

According to Eberstadt's son Frederick, André Meyer repeatedly denied to Eberstadt any knowledge of Gilbert, claiming that Michel David-Weill, the principal family heir of the Lazard business, was involved with Gilbert, not he, Meyer. Frederick claims that his father never forgave Meyer for this lapse of integrity, and he became increasingly distrustful of Meyer thereafter. Frederick further recalled, "In the sixties there were conversations between my father and André about merging the two firms but that went nowhere ... probably because my father didn't trust Meyer."[85]

On top of this, after 1962 Eberstadt's firm was considerably changed from the firm that had initiated the fabulous deals in the 1950s—Nelson Loud and his highly skilled corporate finance partners departed to form New York Securities; Porter decided to leave and went to Shearson. Besides, Eberstadt's heirs apparent, his son-in-law and his nephew, wanted to shift the firm's emphasis to money management and away from investment banking. While the Eberstadt-Lazard relationship continued in the 1960s, especially on existing accounts such as Warner-Lambert and Engelhard Minerals & Chemicals, the opening of new coventures dropped off sharply.

Notes

1. Interview with James Benenson, former corporate finance associate of Eberstadt, April 9, 1984.

2. Interview with Nelson Loud, April 2, 1984.

3. Interview by Robert L. Newton with Robert C. Porter, January 1982, revised March 1984 (hereinafter referred to as the Newton-Porter interview).

4. Interview with James Benenson, April 9, 1984.

5. Preliminary prospectus, June 9, 1983, for NL Capital Associates, pp. 12–14.

6. Interview with Nelson Loud, April 2, 1984.

7. David E. Lilienthal, *The Journals of David E. Lilienthal* (New York, 1964–1981), vol. III, p. 591.

8. Lilienthal, *Journals*, p. 441.

9. Preliminary prospectus, NL Capital Associates, p. 12; also interview with Nelson Loud, April 2, 1984.

10. Letter to author from Robert C. Porter, September 28, 1987.

11. Cary Reich, *Financier: The Biography of André Meyer* (New York, 1983), p. 60.

12. Reich, *Financier*, pp. 33–34.

13. Newton-Porter interview.

14. Reich, *Financier*, p. 63.

15. Personal trust documents supplied to the author by several family members.

16. Reich, *Financier*, p. 63.

17. "Why Sell a Good Thing," *Forbes*, May 1, 1973, p. 54.

18. Statements to author by Eberstadt partners and associates.

19. Lilienthal, *Journals*, vol. III, p. 508.

20. Preliminary prospectus, NL Capital Associates, p. 20.

21. Interview with Nelson Loud, April 2, 1984; also internal Eberstadt background memorandum, April 13, 1972.

22. Ibid.

23. Reich, *Financier*, pp. 65–66.

24. Preliminary prospectus, NL Capital Associates, pp. 42–43.

25. Reich, *Financier*, pp. 66–67.

26. Interview with Francis S. Williams, May 8, 1984.

27. Ibid.

28. Reich, *Financier*, p. 67; also internal Eberstadt memorandum, April 13, 1972, and NL Capital Associates, p. 44.

29. Reich, *Financier*, pp. 67–68.

30. Ibid.

31. Interview with James Benenson, April 9, 1984.

32. Ibid.

33. Ibid.

34. Ibid.

35. Reich, *Financier*, p. 69.

36. Interview with James Benenson, April 9, 1984.

37. Preliminary prospectus, NL Capital Associates, p. 45.

38. Reich, *Financier*, p. 71; also internal Eberstadt memorandum, April 13, 1972.

39. Ibid.

40. Ibid.

41. Ibid.

42. Preliminary prospectus, NL Capital Associates, pp. 45–47.

43. Reich, *Financier*, pp. 72–73.

44. Interview by Robert L. Newton with John F. Van Deventer, January 19, 1982, revised in April 1984 (hereinafter referred to as the Newton–Van Deventer interview).

45. Reich, *Financier*, p. 73.

46. Reich, *Financier*, pp. 73–74.
47. Interview with James Benenson, April 9, 1984.
48. Reich, *Financier*, p. 74.
49. Reich, *Financier*, p. 75.
50. Preliminary prospectus, NL Capital Associates, p. 21.
51. Preliminary prospectus, NL Capital Associates, p. 47–48.
52. Ibid.
53. Reich, *Financier*, pp. 75–76.
54. Ibid.
55. Interview with Jarvis Slade, April 2, 1984.
56. Ibid.
57. Reich, *Financier*, pp. 76–77.
58. Ibid.
59. Preliminary prospectus, NL Capital Associates, p. 48.
60. Preliminary prospectus, NL Capital Associates, pp. 49–50; also internal Eberstadt memorandum, April 13, 1972.
61. Newton–Van Deventer interview.
62. Newton–Porter interview.
63. Ibid.
64. Interview with Peter Wastrom, October 29, 1985.
65. Newton–Porter interview, and interview with Wastrom, October 29, 1985.
66. Preliminary prospectus, NL Capital Associates, p. 50.
67. Ibid, pp. 50–51.
68. Internal Eberstadt memorandum, April 13, 1972.
69. Newton–Porter interview.
70. Interview with Nelson Loud, April 2, 1984.
71. Preliminary prospectus, NL Capital Associates, p. 51.
72. Preliminary prospectus, NL Capital Associates, p. 53.
73. Preliminary prospectus, NL Capital Associates, pp. 48–49.
74. Ibid.
75. Reich, *Financier*, p. 78.
76. Ibid.
77. Preliminary prospectus, NL Capital Associates, p. 49.
78. Reich, *Financier*, pp. 224–25.
79. Interview with John Payne, August 9, 1984.
80. Interview with Francis S. Williams, May 8, 1984.
81. Interview with Frederick Eberstadt, March 23, 1984.
82. Reich, *Financier*, p. 13.
83. Reich, *Financier*, p. 13–14.
84. Reich, *Financier*, p. 16.
85. Interview with Frederick Eberstadt, March 23, 1984.

8

Eberstadt's Private World

Away from the office, Eberstadt became a different person, maintaining his private world in absolute isolation from the world of business. Key to understanding this aspect of his life are Eberstadt's three greatest personal interests in life—his family, boating and fishing, and Target Rock. These intertwined interests formed a mosaic of his life away from Wall Street.

After their marriage in the early 1920s, the Eberstadts lived in apartments in New York City and spent their summers on Long Island. Eberstadt finally bought and developed into his estate a large tract of land jutting out into Long Island Sound which he named Target Rock after the huge, yellowish-brown boulder that lay just offshore. During the Revolutionary War the British fleet used the boulder as a target for gunnery practice, and it still bears shell marks from this activity.[1] The property was located in the heart of the millionaire's gold coast on the north shore of Long Island where the ultra-wealthy built enormous showplaces during the 1920s, financed out of the booming stock market.

After he had made his first millions at Dillon Read in the late 1920s, Eberstadt was anxious to rival his competitors by building a palatial mansion. Not born to riches, he needed to prove to the Wall Street community that he had arrived, and Target Rock was part of his answer to that need. Later in his social development, after he had arrived, he no longer wanted to associate with the leaders of that society. Target Rock then became his home and a retreat for his family. It was a sort of remote Wagnerian Valhalla sanctuary with all the mythical Teutonic connotations. His friends came out to admire it and to talk about Mary's plants; Eberstadt showed off his children and, eventually, his grandchildren; and he enjoyed the total environment of friends, family and admirers in a beautiful setting. Target Rock epitomized Eberstadt's lone wolf life-style.[2]

Before purchasing the main tract, Eberstadt had owned a narrow sliver of land on the far side of Lloyd Neck. Then former Ambassador James Gerard, who also owned property on Lloyd Neck near the Marshall Field estate, introduced him to a German named Rudolph E. F. Flinsch. Flinsch and his sister, Olga, agreed to sell Eberstadt a much larger piece of land. The transaction took place in Berlin in the fall of 1928; thus Eberstadt bought the land for Target Rock pretty much sight unseen, an error in judgment, which later caused quite a problem.[3]

After World War II, a real estate developer, Keith I. Hibner, bought the adjacent property, and Eberstadt found out to his dismay that Hibner's firm, Hawk Hill Development Company, was going to build on the ridge of its land homes that would threaten Eberstadt's privacy. Fortunately, Hibner was willing to sell to Eberstadt the portion of the land that included the ridge (about four acres) on the condition that Eberstadt pay him $24,000 and grant him a right of way to put in an access road to the beach. Eberstadt agreed to this proposal, and the crisis was solved to everyone's satisfaction. Eberstadt's son Frederick recalled ruefully, "God, it was hell to pay when my father found out that he had made a mistake."[4]

On the estate, Eberstadt built horse stables and tennis courts as well as the main house, which contained twenty-five rooms. To complement the main house, he built two guest cottages, Paddock and Pebble, opposite the orchard. With the gardens and the other facilities it probably cost him over $500,000 to develop the land and build the mansion. Eberstadt's nephew, Andrew, notes, however, that "it would probably cost $20 million today to buy and develop the estate on the scale that he did."[5] After World War II, he further enhanced his environment by commissioning the construction of several powerful yachts to cruise the waters off his estate and to use for deep-sea fishing in the Bahamas.

Eberstadt's boating interest began in the 1920s; he was a frequent participant in the small boat sailing competition off Huntington and Oyster Bay. He had a small Herreschoff-designed sailboat, named the "Tom Boy," which he sailed with his children on the Sound. Herreschoff had designed many of the America's Cup yachts. As the children grew up, they all sailed and crewed on this boat.[6]

Eberstadt's interest in power yachts and deep-sea fishing began after World War II. His son-in-law, Jack Payne, convinced him to become involved in power boating, and they soon became fast friends. His first venture in the power area was the *Mary Fran* (a name derived from the first names of his three daughters, *Mary*, *Frances* and *Ann*), a twenty-four-foot "Egg Harbor" class fishing boat which he purchased in 1952.[7]

In 1953 he bought a much larger power boat, the forty-one-foot sports cruiser, *Wild Goose*, which had two 160-horsepower Chrysler Royal engines, designed by Gear Handel and built by Malcolm Brewer in Camden, Maine. Eberstadt had come to Camden to look at another boat, but when he saw the *Wild Goose* he said, "Well, the boat I really want is that one over there." The person for whom it had been built had backed out at the last minute, and Eberstadt bought it. He kept the *Wild Goose* at Cat Cay in the Bahamas where he used it for sport fishing in the winter months.[8]

The first boat named *Target* was built by Huckins in Jacksonville, Florida, and came into service in April 1956. The *Target* measured fifty-three feet in length. Eberstadt's nephew, Andrew, recalled that

Huckins built PT boats in World War II and basically the *Target* was built on the same hull. It was a damn good boat for commuting and for fishing way out—the type of fishing he did up north where you want to get 15 or 20 miles off shore in a hurry—and this boat would get out there in a hurry. Today, I would assume a Huckins would go for half a million bucks. . . . My uncle kept it in German ship-shape condition; if the ash trays weren't clean, the captain would catch hell.[9]

After about five years, the first *Target* was donated to the Lerner Marine Institute on Bimini.[10] There was a big flap at the time as to whether the Internal Revenue Service would allow the donation as an eligible tax deduction. The second *Target*, even larger and more powerful, was also built by Huckins.[11]

Eberstadt's love of deep-sea fishing grew out of his intense competitiveness and his will to win. According to Robert Zeller, "Eber used to quote from Herbert Hoover's book about fishing to the effect that 'the gods give credit in a man's life for the years he spends fishing—those years don't really count in determining his mortality.' "[12] According to John J. McCloy, one of Roosevelt's top troubleshooters during World War II, Eberstadt's love of fishing grew out of his acquisitiveness. "He got great satisfaction from catching the biggest fish—it satisfied his ego."[13] William Cannell adds "grandfather enjoyed the hunt.' "[14]

After the mansion at Target Rock was completed, Eberstadt held frequent Sunday lunches there, primarily social meetings with many prominent guests present including former President Herbert Hoover, Mary Pickford, Gary Cooper and David Sarnoff, as well as the brothers Allen and John Foster Dulles and Franz Schneider, who lived close by.[15] Eberstadt's daughter, Mrs. Mary Harper, relates that her father insisted that each of his children attend Sunday lunch. Harper adds, "You could bring as many friends as you wanted to . . . but it was frowned on if I said I was going out on a Sunday at lunch time . . . that was a no-no."

Years later, when Mary Harper took her children to visit Lincoln Center for the Performing Arts in New York City, she was proud of the fact that half of the names on the list of major contributors to the center were names of persons she had met at Target Rock or at her father's New York City apartment in River House.[16]

For Eberstadt's grandchildren, the outside world did not exist. One grandson, William Cannell, remembers some summers when they never left Target Rock, "but for two or three times over the course of the entire summer." The idea was to be totally isolated and immersed in the flow of family life on the estate. Although friends would occasionally stop by in the evening, the family basically revolved around Target Rock.[17]

Some people claim that Target Rock was just a big act in Eberstadt's investment banking operation. Zeller, his closest partner in the last ten years of his life, doubts that, although he admitted,

Eberstadt, being an investment banker, used his connections with influential people in the business world and . . . Target Rock was in a sense a keystone of his ability to get things done. But I don't think Target Rock was any more a part of his business life than Cat Cay or Lyford Cay in the Bahamas.[18]

Mary Harper adds; "Target Rock was an extension of my father's energy. He clearly loved every square inch of it; for instance, he and mother got a stack of books this high to read up on [rose bushes] before they planted the rose garden."[19]

Once in the early 1960s, Eberstadt invited Howard Tierney, the head of Denver Chemical, and his wife Laura, along with Peter Wastrom, Eberstadt's partner who was working on a possible merger for Denver, to visit Target Rock for lunch one nice Sunday. Eberstadt sent his yacht over to the Stamford Yacht Club to pick them up, and they went across the Sound for lunch on the terrace with butler, cigars and all the fixings. When the Tierneys returned by boat after lunch and got off in Stamford, Laura Tierney turned to her husband and Wastrom and said, "Now I know how the Fresh Air Fund kids must feel when they have to go home to the city."[20]

Eberstadt's insistence on privacy when he spent time with his family at Target Rock was legendary. For example, one time William Sullivan, a long-time associate, was alone on the trading desk at the office on a Saturday morning. (Wall Street used to work a half day on Saturdays.) Another firm called and wanted to sell three thousand shares of Victor Chemical preferred stock, for which the firm was making a market, at $90 a share. Sullivan was still a junior in the department and buying that much stock would have exceeded his permitted position. Sullivan could not reach Maynard Simond, the managing partner at that time, or Eric Rodin, the head trader, so finally, reluctantly, he called Eberstadt at home. Furious, Eberstadt told Sullivan, "Don't you ever bother me again at home—you're there in charge—it's your decision." Sullivan thereupon took the block in and happily managed to sell it at a five-point profit on the following Monday.[21]

Eberstadt, the autocrat with his receding black hair and brown twinkling eyes, provided a study in contrast with the informality of his wife Mary. Mary loved Target Rock, but for different reasons. She had a major interest in gardening and her gardens contained among other attractions rhododendrons, gardenias, Korean box holly, clematis and ponds, with flagstone stepping-stones throughout.[22] Mary's gardening emphasized a much more informal pattern than the formal gardens of the French tradition; hers were more in keeping with English country gardens with paths cut through heavily bushed areas. The estate gardens, which comprised about ten acres, frequently received the first prize in the annual competitions of the Huntington Garden Association.[23]

One persistent conflict between Eberstadt and his wife concerned the density of the trees on the property. When the house was first built, Mary wanted more vistas so as to be able to see the Sound and Huntington Bay. To maintain his privacy, Eberstadt built the mansion close to the center of the property and away from the beach area. Thus it stood in a heavily wooded virgin wilderness, without any direct view to the water. The 1938 hurricane gave his wife part of her wish when it passed right over the center of the property and toppled many trees in its wake. Years later, Eberstadt consented to Mary's wish and agreed to selective cuttings to improve the sight lines.[24]

Eberstadt's routine at Target Rock emphasized his children and grandchildren. As many as ten of his eventual fourteen grandchildren spent their summers there. Typically, the grandchildren crowded into Eberstadt's bedroom upon rising to be with him and talk to him while he shaved; then he would have breakfast with them and walk down to the dock—sometimes they would have breakfast on the boat, especially if he was going to New York. Eberstadt, always the opportunist, would use the time going into the city to test the grandchildren's memory of the names of the buoys and lighthouses between Lloyd Neck and New York City.[25]

One long-lasting dispute with Long Island Lighting Company (LILCO) grew out of the company's proposal to condemn and acquire Eberstadt's land for a nuclear power plant. The battle, which began in 1945, continued for more than twenty years. When Eberstadt learned in early 1968 that he might lose his twenty-year battle with LILCO he went to Washington; shortly thereafter, Target Rock was given as a tax-deductible gift to the Department of the Interior as a wildlife refuge, safe forever from the encroachments of commerce, with the Eberstadts' retaining life tenancy. LILCO, rebuffed at Lloyd Neck by Eberstadt and other land-owners, then shifted its building plans to Shoreham where it continues to have problems with opposition to its nuclear power plant.[26]

Eberstadt had earlier considered giving the estate to his children, but his daughter, Ann Cannell, stressed, "None of the children was capable of taking care of it. . . . I think it is a shame that it didn't go to the New York Botanical Gardens . . . who, once they saw it, were very upset that they didn't get it."[27] Mary Harper relates,

We used to dream about . . . how he would divide it. . . . And [my father] sectioned it off into four pieces—Mary's Hill, Fred's Swamp or somebody's something or other. And really in a way I was kind of sorry when he came to all of us and he said "I know that if anything happens to Mother and me you can't handle this—you couldn't even handle the taxes, let alone the rest." So he came up with this idea [to give it to the Department of Interior] and he said "Do I have your permission?" And we all agreed, saying that we realized that it would be a lifetime job trying to keep up the place.[28]

In addition to Target Rock, Eberstadt maintained winter homes in several successive locations in the Bahamas. He had begun going to Nassau in the Bahamas in the 1920s. Frances Payne, the oldest child, recalls, "One winter we went to Nassau—Mom, Dad, sister Mary and myself. There was a yacht there with Mr. Cotton and some other people, possibly the Dulleses.[29]

After World War II, Eberstadt rented a house on Cat Cay in the Bahamas and then later he bought ten and a half acres and a house fronting on the ocean in Marchena Beach in the posh resort of Lyford Cay on New Providence Island in the Bahamas. Cat Cay and Lyford Cay were vastly different places, although both abounded in game and sport fishing. Cat Cay is a small island off Bimini owned by four families with beach houses approaching the size of Newport cottages. Lyford Cay was a much bigger, more developed place than Cat Cay.[30]

John Payne, Eberstadt's oldest grandson, recalled how impressed he was with the wealthy and prominent people that he had met at the Lyford Cay Club. Payne said to his grandfather, "Gee, the Fords [and other prominent members of the jet set] were there." Eberstadt however cautioned his grandson, "Now think about it, John. [The Fords] are only motor car manufacturers." He added, "For all their wealth, power and prestige, they are a cut below an investment banker who is a king maker in *all* fields of economic activity!"[31]

Eberstadt's concern for his family focused on his view of his role as the central galvanizing force shielding it from the outside world and revolving around Target Rock and his boating and fishing interests. He was far more successful in this with his grandchildren than with his own children. But he failed in his desire to unify his family into a dynasty. As John Payne, the oldest grandchild, put it,

Throughout all those years he pulled together the family at every opportunity and he made a great point that the family is a unified, loyal force, but as soon as he was dead, the family blew apart like a hand grenade. . . . there was a fundamental flaw in grandfather's theory that . . . you could make a unified whole—there wasn't any unifying force except for grandfather and the resources that grandfather had and the control and manipulation that he had over these people.[32]

Adds Eberstadt's oldest daughter, Frances Payne, "He never wanted us to be individuals—just puppets, his creations and his to dominate! None of his children has anything *at all* to do with any other really; we're all strangers; this was his legacy!"[33]

Isabel Nash, the daughter of poet Ogden Nash, who married Eberstadt's son Frederick, recollects her first visit to Target Rock, "a house where you couldn't count the number of rooms," and where Eberstadt could not resist ingeniously manipulating the members of the family against one another. She remembers particularly

a sort of game he'd play, when he'd invite me into a room where all the older women of the house were, and he'd ask me questions like, "How many miles of Metro are there under Paris?" Whatever I answered, he said it was perfect and would say to the others, "Look at this little girl, she's just a baby and she has the answers." Then he would go off to bed and leave me with these women positively hating me. It took me about four sessions to realize . . . he was mocking me, but I actually think . . . in our own way, we really loved one another.[34]

Although Eberstadt relished playing tricks on his family, he rarely enjoyed publicity about the exploits of his progeny. One close associate relates, "Eberstadt was in an absolute livid rage when Freddie's picture appeared with a bunch of chorus girls in the centerfold of *Look* magazine in the late 1940s."[35] Frederick also invited his father's displeasure when he was expelled from Princeton (like father, like son) for a prank that he and one of his college friends played during a recital given at one of Princeton's concert halls. He and his friend released a greased pig which, of course, caused a furor at staid old Princeton.[36] On the other hand, others believe that Eberstadt tolerated the jet-setters in his son's playboy life because Eberstadt got a vicarious thrill out of all the things he was doing—sort of a public recognition that Eberstadt had arrived.[37]

Eberstadt excelled in most outdoor sports, but he was a duffer in golf. He loved to deprecate his game with humorous golf anecdotes. In fact, Dean Mathey, his old Princeton friend and former Dillon Read partner, included one of Eberstadt's golf stories in his memoir "50 Years of Wall

Street." The setting was the Ausable Club in upstate New York where Mathey and Eberstadt frequently went to fish or play golf.

When the fishing isn't good, Eber, with an old set of clubs, would go golfing. On one occasion he was on very friendly terms with a caddy from a village a few miles further down the valley. On the very first hole, Eberstadt met with most of the disasters that face golfers—slices, hooks, bad lies, etc., so that when he holed out, he announced to his caddy, "That's 12 for me. You know, caddy," Eberstadt continued, "I believe that I am the worst player in this club." "Oh, no, you're not," said the caddy encouragingly, "there is another member who plays worse than you do."

"Is that so?" said Eber. "Who is he?"

The caddy replied, "It's a man named Eberstadt!"[38]

The best golfing story took place in the late 1930s during an all-day competition which involved tennis, golf and swimming—all of the sports between the two Eberstadt brothers, Rudy and Ferdinand. Eberstadt had told his and Rudy's children that he planned to play a practical joke on Rudy who was an excellent golfer. He had bribed the caddy to play all sorts of tricks on Rudy. For example, at one point, Rudy asked the caddy for a number seven iron, and the caddy gave him a number one driver wood with the statement that Rudy could not possibly make it with a number seven iron. Rudy took his advice and drove the ball way over the green as a result. Another time he put vaseline on the handle of the golf club Rudy asked for so that the club was slippery and Rudy was not able to control it properly. The caddy sneezed or coughed every time Rudy tried to putt or tee off, causing Rudy to duff his shot.[39]

Meanwhile both families—aware of what was happening—watched Rudy's predicaments gleefully from the sidelines as he systematically got himself in deep sand traps and water holes and what not. Ultimately Rudy, thoroughly defeated, came off the golf course. Ferdinand had beaten him. Ferdinand had his usual 150, but Rudy had wound up with a 199. At lunch afterward Ferdinand admitted to Rudy what kind of fun they had been having with him.[40]

These happy times only softened the Teutonic harshness that Eberstadt had inherited from his forefathers. He fitted the stereotype of the stern German father, who loves his family deeply but rules them with an iron hand. Despite his Prussian character, he adored his children and went to great lengths to be with them. For example, in June 1942 his daughter Mary graduated from the Garrison Forest School just outside of Baltimore. At that time, Eberstadt was working night and day in Washington to overcome the bottlenecks impeding vital war output, and it did not appear that he would be able to attend his daughter's graduation, much as he wanted to.[41]

Eberstadt, whose management techniques always emphasized the committee format, was proceeding with a crash program to solve war production problems, meeting continuously day in and day out with his staff of experts. In his post, he channeled the full force of his personality into this awesome task. He worked at a driving pace, arriving at the office at 8:00 A.M. or shortly thereafter and rarely leaving before 6:00 P.M. When he did leave, a briefcase of work for the evening usually went home with him. This represented his normal schedule for the entire week, including weekends.[42]

When the day for his daughter's graduation ceremony finally arrived, Eberstadt decisively solved his dilemma by taking the entire meeting with him; he simply packed everyone into a taxi so that they could continue their discussions en route to and from the ceremony. When they arrived, Eberstadt excused himself and the committee continued to work while he attended his daughter's graduation. After congratulating his daughter, he returned to the waiting taxi to return to the "war" back in Washington.[43]

Notes

1. Estelle Sammis, "A Natural Treasure for Long Island, Financier's Lands Now a Federal Preserve," *Long Island Press*, August 9, 1970, p. 21.

2. Interview with John Payne, August 9, 1984.

3. Interview with Frederick Eberstadt, March 23, 1984.

4. Ibid.

5. Interview with Andrew W. Eberstadt, April 11, 1984.

6. Interview with Franz Schneider, May 7, 1984.

7. Interview with Mrs. Mary Harper, April 11, 1985.

8. Interview with William Cannell, Eberstadt's grandson, June 15, 1984.

9. Interview with Andrew W. Eberstadt, Eberstadt's partner and nephew, April 11, 1984.

10. Interview with Mrs. Mary Harper, April 11, 1985.

11. Ibid.

12. Interview with Robert G. Zeller, May 1, 1984.

13. Interview with John J. McCloy, April 17, 1984.

14. Interview with William Cannell, June 15, 1984.

15. Interview with Mrs. Mary Harper, April 11, 1985.

16. Ibid.

17. Interview with William Cannell, June 15, 1984.

18. Interview with Robert G. Zeller, May 1, 1984.

19. Interview with Mrs. Mary Harper, April 11, 1985.

20. Interview with Peter L. Wastrom, March 29, 1984.

21. Telephone interview with William P. Sullivan, May 26, 1984.

22. Sammis, "A Natural Treasure for Long Island; Financier's Lands Now a Federal Preserve," *Long Island Press*, August 9, 1970, p. 21.

23. Interview with John Payne, August 9, 1984.

24. Interview with Mrs. Mary Harper, April 11, 1985; also "Wall Street Scene," *Wall Street Journal*, December 14, 1938, p. 6.

25. Interview with William Cannell, June 15, 1984.

26. Sammis, "A Natural Treasure for Long Island," *Long Island Press*, August 9, 1970, p. 21; also "LILCO Moves to Condemn L. I. Estate for Atomic Power Site," *Long Island Press*, February 12, 1968, p. 4.

27. Interview with Mrs. Ann Cannell, March 18, 1985.

28. Interview with Mrs. Mary Harper, April 11, 1985.

29. Letter to author from Mrs. Frances Payne, June 23, 1984.

30. Interview with Larry Harper, Eberstadt's grandson, September 11, 1984.

31. Interview with John Payne, August 9, 1984.

32. Ibid.

33. Letter to author from Mrs. Frances Payne, June 23, 1984.

34. "Isabel Eberstadt: An Original," *Women's Wear Daily*, May 6–13, 1983.

35. Telephone interview with William P. Sullivan, May 26, 1984.

36. Ibid.

37. Interview with Peter L. Wastrom, March 29, 1984.

38. Dean Mathey, *50 Years of Wall Street* (Princeton, N.J., 1966), pp. 50–51.

39. Interview with Mrs. Mary Harper, April 11, 1985.

40. Ibid.

41. "Eberstadt 'No' Man Ends Deadlock on War Materials," *Baltimore Evening Sun*, November 23, 1942, p. 15, and interview with Mrs. Mary Harper, April 11, 1985.

42. Ibid.

43. Ibid

9

The Collapse of the Dream of a Dynasty

If the decade of the 1950s was the flowering of the Eberstadt genius, then the decade of the 1960s was the withering away and deterioration of that genius. True, Eberstadt's total offerings reached a new record of nearly three-quarters of a billion dollars,[1] but new private capital deals fell off drastically due to the declining personal relationship between Eberstadt and Meyer and the split-up of the firm in 1962. However, additional profits from previous coventures with Lazard continued to enrich their coffers well into the 1960s.

Eberstadt, now over seventy years of age, increasingly sought to create a family dynasty in his business, but he was frustrated in this goal and he made grave errors in judgment in its pursuit. Finally, the trading and speculative environment was not favorable to a high-quality investment fund such as Chemical Fund. Although Chemical Fund regularly received above-average ratings for its performance in both rising and falling markets in *Forbes* annual mutual fund surveys,[2] it failed to keep pace with the spectacular performance of the increasingly popular high-risk speculative growth stock funds.

Although the decade of the 1960s in many respects mirrored that of the 1950s, with the growth of the economy and corporate profits unparalleled in the peacetime history of the nation, the soaring sixties started on a sour note for the Eberstadt firm. A new and aggressive group of lawyers, commonly referred to as "strike" lawyers, emerged and brought a number of derivative suits against mutual fund management companies. The suits sought to reduce the size of management fees which typically did not scale down to reflect the economies resulting from the increased size of assets under management. During the 1950s and the 1960s, many individual mutual funds reached and passed the billion-dollar mark.

In late 1959, one of the strike lawyers, Milton Paulson, brought a derivative suit against Eberstadt, claiming unreasonable compensation. The suit had no basis in fact for Eberstadt had years before voluntarily reduced his fees reflecting economies of size. In fact, Eberstadt had pioneered the idea of a tapered management fee much to the chagrin of his more greedy competitors and partners. After Paulson became aware of his oversight, he offered to settle the suit for payment of legal fees and expenses but Eberstadt, proud and incorruptible, refused. Although some of his partners thought that he should settle, Eberstadt doggedly stayed the course although it tied up his top talent for nine months and probably cost the firm as much as a million dollars in legal fees. Ultimately, Paulson's suit was dismissed by the Delaware Chancery Court as having no merit. [3]

The suit, however, had one important and lasting impact on the firm. It introduced Eberstadt to Robert G. Zeller, the trial lawyer at Cahill Gordon who coordinated Eberstadt's legal defense. Eberstadt liked Zeller's work on the preparation of the case so much that he later offered him a partnership in the firm shortly after the firm split in 1962. [4]

With the time-consuming and costly legal battle behind him, Eberstadt returned once again to his first love, investment banking. He had carefully honed the firm's investment banking partners who were the equal of any corporate finance group in Wall Street, each having been trained by the old maestro himself.

However, Peter Cannell, Eberstadt's son-in-law and partner, was aggressive and ambitious. He wanted to broaden the firm's presence in the rapidly expanding and profitable field of investment management. Eberstadt encouraged him, and he rapidly ascended the leadership ladder to take over the day-to-day administration of the investment management subsidiary in the early 1960s. In line with this, Eberstadt began to think in terms of transferring complete control of the parent firm from himself to Cannell and Andrew W. Eberstadt, his nephew.

What he had in mind was to create and perpetuate an Eberstadt dynasty. In order to achieve this, he felt that an investment banking firm's basic strength had to be family oriented. He was impressed with the longevity of such family-dominated European houses as the Rothschilds and the Warburgs and such American dynasties as the Lehmans and the Morgans, all of which were anchored in strong family ties. He was swayed by the successful merchant bankers in London and their traditions that were buttressed in family continuity. [5] Eberstadt's grandfather had played an indirect role in the formation of the prominent investment banking firm of Kuhn Loeb in the 1860s, and Eberstadt's first cousin, Otto Herman Kahn, had risen to the head of that family-dominated powerhouse.[6]

But that left the problem of what to do with his carefully trained investment banking partners, none of whom was a member of his family. These aggressive finance specialists were eager to do more deals and to gain a greater control of the business. Eberstadt was getting older, however, and he did not like many of the deals that his corporate finance partners were bringing to him. He became increasingly disenchanted with the quality of the investment banking deals generally in the Street as the "white hot" new issue market soared to a speculative peak in mid-1961. Eberstadt complained increasingly to his associates that "while I expect to look at 100 deals before I find one that I am willing to put my name on, now I have to look at 1,000 before finding a good one."[7] Reflecting his growing concerns, Eberstadt determined to curtail the investment banking business and concentrate on money management, in line with the wishes of his young heirs.[8]

In the early 1960s, Eberstadt suffered a series of nervous breakdowns probably brought on by the Paulson suit and the events leading to the subsequent split-up of his finely honed investment banking firm. Eberstadt's mental and physical condition was further weakened by a round-the-world tour he and his wife took in the fall of 1961.[9] The tour never got past India, where he was greatly depressed by the squalor and poverty he saw there. He lamented over the telephone to his secretary, Rita Higgins, "Humanity, humanity . . . people are lying dead in the streets. . . ."[10] Then, he caught a virus which forced him to end his tour abruptly in early December. Eberstadt was hospitalized three times in 1962 for mental breakdowns, and he received shock treatments at the Harkness Pavilion of Columbia Presbyterian Medical Center.[11]

His partners sensed that this was an opportunity for them to buy him out and put him out to pasture using him as a pinch hitter when needed but actually running the firm themselves. Looking back on those climactic days, Nelson Loud ruefully comments, "It was a classic misunderstanding. Ferd and I had prepared a program to perpetuate the firm but some of the partners were not too enthusiastic about it." [12] One of the departing partners, who requested anonymity, recalled,

What Eber had proposed was to reincorporate the business with Eberstadt receiving several million dollars for good will but retaining all . . . power . . . to fire anybody and take Chemical Fund back so that . . . the plan would not have accomplished anything for us.

Another former partner, Craig Severance, pointed out,

When we drew up an alternative plan to buy him out, which all the corporate finance partners initialled, Eberstadt took this as being tantamount to mutiny. He never wanted to give up control and after that he was determined to get rid of all of the partners who had wanted to buy him out.[13]

Loud acknowledges that Eberstadt never seriously considered giving up control, adding, "Ferd always told us it was his money . . . he was just letting us use it; any profits belonged to him."[14]

Before taking off on his round-the-world trip, Eberstadt directed Loud to develop another program to reconcile the various conflicting positions, but Loud's compromise program never reached Eberstadt who by then had taken sick in India and had left for home. When Eberstadt arrived back in New York, he was in a near rage as well as mentally depressed. He called Loud and read the riot act to him. Loud did not realize that he was talking about the previous plan of the partners and not about his alternative program. The next day, after Eberstadt had finally seen Loud's plan, he said, "This isn't so bad." But by then he had fired both Robert Porter and Jarvis Slade, two key corporate finance partners, although Eberstadt later relented and hired back both of these partners.[15]

About a week later, Eberstadt finally made up his mind. Eberstadt told his partners at their annual budget review meeting on December 18th:

It appears that I am standing in the way of some of my partners who want to do certain transactions which could be very rewarding to them . . . In order to allow them to fulfill their aspirations it is resolved that they go out and form a firm to consist of (and he listed the names of the eight partners who were to be separated).

When he had finished, Eberstadt asked, "Any questions?"[16]

There was silence—then a few halting questions—then pandemonium broke out. This was the first formal news that Eberstadt's corporate finance partners had received that they would have to leave the firm. Loud laments,

If Eber hadn't dug himself in so deep, it would never have happened. Hell, the whole thing was a tempest in a teapot; Eber was a tremendously stubborn and very proud man . . . when he got the bit in his teeth, he went all the way.[17]

When the firm split in early 1962, the agreement between the remaining Eberstadt partners and the departing partners, the so-called separation agreement, stipulated that Eberstadt would concentrate on money management and curtail the investment banking business. Eberstadt, however, retained certain investment banking accounts originated by him such as Becton-Dickinson, Warner-Lambert, Englehard Minerals

& Chemicals and Carter-Wallace; United Artists, Heller, Talcott, and numerous others were assigned to the new firm, named New York Securities, in return for an override to Eberstadt on any fees earned on these accounts for a period of time. But there was a provision in the agreement that permitted Eberstadt to recover any or all of these accounts if he did not like the way they were being handled or if any client preferred to return to Eberstadt.[18] For example, shortly after the split up, Krim and Benjamin asked to return and United Artists was transferred back to Eberstadt.

For the balance of the 1960s, New York Securities had 199 deals totalling $827 million, some $60 million greater than Eberstadt's total; only one-third of that volume came from transferred accounts.[19] After Nelson Loud left New York Securities in 1970, the remaining partners became involved in squabbling about partnership interests. Later, the firm became embroiled in lawsuits growing out of a massive fraud perpetrated by the management of one of its prime financing clients, Equity Funding Corporation.[20] Following this scandal, several of the corporate finance partners went over to Hallgarten, taking their capital with them, draining its resources.[21] After the severe stock market drop of 1973 and 1974, the remaining partners concluded that the days of the small boutique-type firm were numbered on Wall Street and that it was in their best interests to liquidate the company.[22]

Even before the split up of the Eberstadt firm, Cannell was working diligently to build up its investment management business. In the spring of 1961, he concluded that the firm needed a more aggressive fund to exploit the investment potential of science and technology. He proposed and began to shape a new fund to be offered by the firm to be known as Science Ventures, Inc. His merchandising skills, developed from his work with the advertising agency, Batten, Barton, Durston & Osborne, and the brokerage giant, Merrill Lynch, convinced him that it was better to bring out a family of funds with each fund positioned in an important niche in the market, an idea that took hold on a vast scale in the 1980s.

The firm's success in the chemical and related fields provided a springboard for the new fund to branch out into emerging science-based companies that would become the success stories of the future. Eberstadt was cautious, however, and he wanted to see the entire project fleshed out before he put his seal of approval on it.

Cannell organized a research team to work on the portfolio of the proposed fund which they managed and valued on a pro forma basis. By the end of the year, this paper portfolio had achieved a very impressive record; in the spring of 1962 the authorization was given to go ahead with the new fund project, and work began on the prospectus and a sales brochure.

But then in mid-1962 the market took a sharp drop, and Eberstadt pulled back from offering the new fund. Aggravating the situation was Eberstadt's mental condition. Moreover, he could never really tolerate initiatives that were not his own. Years later, Cannell recalled that sorry period: "I have never been so angry and disappointed in my life."[23] Despite several attempts to revive the fund, Science Ventures never got off the drawing board, and in the early 1970s the firm terminated the fund's registration and wrote off its development costs.

The firm finally did bring out a new fund, the Eberstadt Fund, in the late 1960s with a portfolio structured around the central value theories of Benjamin Graham. For portfolio manager, the firm hired Jeremy C. Jenks, a disciple of Graham who had perfected Graham's investment theories at Cyrus J. Lawrence & Sons into actual working formulas and had achieved considerable success.[24] The fund failed to achieve much sales success because the market in the late 1960s again became very speculative in contrast to the conservative investment approach of Graham.

Another decision in the early 1960s that Peter Cannell felt was critical to the future of the firm was to become a member of the New York Stock Exchange. Up to this time, Eberstadt had made its investment research available to institutional clients and in return received orders from these clients to purchase for their accounts new security offerings from underwriting syndicates thereby producing commission income for the firm. However, Cannell pointed out to Eberstadt that the firm was using a very inefficient means of being compensated for the value of its institutional research. Most institutions buy for their portfolios in the secondary markets rather than in the primary markets, except in the case of bonds. Since most of these stock transactions were on the Big Board, the firm had to become a member if it was to enlarge its institutional business base in the future.

Institutional investor trading activity was gaining on the Big Board, and it accounted in the early 1960s for more than 50 percent of the trading. Accordingly, the firm hired Pike Sullivan, a life-long friend of Cannell and a top institutional broker at White Weld, to head up its brokerage business and, on June 30, 1962, the firm became a member of the Exchange.[25]

Eberstadt put all of his prior business relationships to work to build up the firm's brokerage business including collecting on past favors or debts. One such "debtor" was George Champion, then head of the Chase Bank; the opportunity to collect presented itself over lunch one afternoon in Eberstadt's private dining room. Eberstadt began by reminiscing about Ivar Kreuger (the notorious Swedish Match King swindler of the 1920s) and how Eberstadt had gone over to Europe to represent the banks in their effort to recover on their loans to Kreuger. The banks offered Eberstadt either a percentage of the recovery or a straight fee for his efforts. Since Eberstadt recovered a great many millions of dollars for the banks, he would have made much more if he had taken the percentage, but he had, instead, opted for the flat fee.[26]

Champion recalled that he was always puzzled "why Eberstadt was so foolish as to take the fixed fee when he could have gotten much, much more if he had taken a percentage of the total recovery" and he asked, "Eber, why did you take the fee and not the percentage?"[27] Eberstadt came right back,

"Well, George, I thought about it way back then and I said to myself, one day, Eber, you're going to buy yourself a seat on the New York Stock Exchange and you're going to want the Chase Bank in your debt because they've got a lot of brokerage business to give out and if you just take this percentage and do them out of all that money, they're not going to feel kindly toward you when you buy that seat and you want that brokerage business."

Champion stared at the wall for a while and the lunch came to an end. That afternoon the firm received a massive amount of brokerage business directed to Eberstadt by Chase amounting to hundreds of thousands of shares. Eberstadt never lost an opportunity to exploit an opening if he had just a little edge.[28]

Eberstadt's earlier experience with the Otis failure, however, heavily influenced his thinking with respect to the brokerage business. He feared margin accounts and banned their use in the firm's brokerage business.[29] Another fear which troubled him was the growing back office problems suffered by several large retail brokers such as Goodbody and Bache. "Fails" to deliver securities on time became an increasing problem for the Street in the 1960s, and ultimately the Big Board had to arbitrarily close down on Wednesdays to permit member firms to clear up their backlogs. To protect his firm's capital, Eberstadt put a limit on the firm's daily brokerage volume so that it could not exceed 50,000 shares.[30]

What Eberstadt failed to recognize is that the problem of fails does not exist when you have a "cross" transaction, because with a cross the firm controlled both sides of the trade and no other broker was involved. Whenever the firm had a cross, Pike Sullivan could usually convince Eberstadt that there was no possibility of a fail. But late on one Friday in the summer of 1968, the firm had lined up a cross involving 65,000 shares of Pennzoil preferred at 125. The trade arose when Sullivan was en route to Lake Champlain in upstate New York for the weekend, and he could not clear the trade personally with Eberstadt. Eberstadt vetoed it, and the firm forfeited $82,000 in risk-free commissions on that one trade because of Eberstadt's fear of the brokerage business.[31]

While Eberstadt may have been over cautious in restricting his firm's total brokerage volume, he clearly was an early Cassandra of the monumental problems that swamped the securities business in the late 1960s. Wall Street's antiquated trading and clearing mechanism threatened to shut down the entire Wall Street community because of the interlocking nature of the securities business. Eberstadt was concerned that this might bring his own firm down if there was a widespread collapse.[32] Most of his gloomy fears ultimately came true, although after his death.[33] Goodbody, Wall Street's fifth-largest securities firm, overwhelmed by an avalanche of back office snarls and an accompanying sea of red ink, collapsed in the fall of 1970 and was ultimately taken over by Merrill Lynch.[34]

To deal with this escalating problem, Eberstadt became an early proponent of a joint effort by the securities business to protect against losses in the event of a failure of a Big Board member. As such, Eberstadt was a lonely voice in Wall Street at the time; most firms ignored the growing threat of a catastrophe. Thomas E. Dewey, the former governor of New York State and twice the Republican candidate for the presidency, who had become an adviser to Eberstadt on these problems, later wrote to an industry leader, "Ferdinand Eberstadt saved Wall Street by his courage and persistence in forcing Wall Street's highest echelons of authority to recognize and do something to solve this fatal flaw in the Street's clearing system."[35] Up to that point, the Street simply swept the problem under the rug.

Eberstadt also had other matters on his mind, one of them was a desire to reenter the investment banking business. Despite the statements to the contrary in the separation agreement, Eberstadt had never really given up his intention to develop investment banking deals. For example, immediately after the New York Securities spin off in the spring of 1962, Eberstadt syndicated the initial public offering of Becton-Dickinson common stock, consisting of 480,000 shares at $25 a share. Eberstadt had originated the Becton-Dickinson account in the late 1950s, initially raising $16 million for the company through several private placements with institutional investors.[36] The offering did very well despite the sharp fall in equity prices in May immediately after it took place, and the stock rose to a premium within a few weeks. Becton-Dickinson became Eberstadt's most prolific client, accounting for $195.5 million in financing in fifteen separate deals during the next decade.[37]

Other people were hired in addition to Zeller to flesh out the newly emerging investment banking operation. Peter Wastrom came over from Empire Trust Co., where he had worked with Dean Mathey, Eberstadt's old friend and business associate from Dillon Read. Edward B. (Ned) Conway also returned to the firm in the 1960s. Conway, a legal specialist, knew how to prepare and push a new securities registration through the Securities and Exchange Commission (SEC) quickly. He helped train Eberstadt's new investment banking team how to do a deal. Walter

Lubanko of Lehman and Douglas Brash of Paribas were also hired as corporate finance specialists.

In reconstituting his investment banking activities, Eberstadt decided to delegate more authority to his corporate finance staff and become less involved in the actual negotiation and implementation of the deals. Although Eberstadt remained firmly in control with complete power to veto any deal that he didn't like, he gave more freedom to his staff to fashion new deals with sometimes unfortunate results.[38]

One such financing that stumbled badly was United Foods. Lehman brought the deal to the attention of Walter Lubanko, who led for a time Eberstadt's newly emerging investment banking effort. Based on Lubanko's recommendation, Eberstadt arranged a private financing for United Foods consisting of $2.4 million in convertible subordinated notes placed with institutional clients to finance the construction of a new plant in Watsonville, California, and to repay some loans.[39]

Not long after the closing of that deal, Lubanko stepped into Wastrom's office and asked him if he would sit in when Irving Kaplin, the president and chief executive officer of United Foods, arrived for what Lubanko thought would be just a friendly get-together. Eberstadt was out of town and Wastrom and Lubanko met with Kaplin in the conference room. No sooner had they done with the pleasantries then Kaplin stated that all of the newly raised funds were gone and that he had "completely lost control of the company [with] financial records in disarray and the cost of the Watsonville plant escalating . . . far in excess of budget." United Foods was near bankruptcy. Thereafter, Eberstadt personally took over and reorganized the company, working out new schedules for the repayment of the debt issues. Ultimately, United Foods was merged with another food company but retained the United Foods name. It is now a stable but not spectacular company.[40]

Another deal that went bad was Elcor Chemical, an oil-field service company that had developed a new process for the recovery of sulphur from gypsum. For the process, Elcor had leased mineral rights on a vast acreage which had a high concentration of gypsum. Eberstadt underwrote a combination offering of bonds and stock raising about $40 million to finance the new process which proved to be a white elephant that drove the company to near bankruptcy. Fortunately, Elcor had a profitable engineering division that serviced oil-refining and chemical plants, but Eberstadt was forced to step in and reconstitute the debt by exchanging it for equity, reducing the company's debt service.[41]

The firm made a lot of money, however, on a number of other deals including Mitchell Energy and Tipperary Land both with Dean Mathey, another of Eberstadt's former partners from the Dillon Read era and a fellow Princetonian. Mathey had been involved in Dillon Read syndicate operations and had a great interest in energy companies; he had originated the legendary Louisiana Land and Exploration deal for Dillon Read in the late 1920s.

One of the most loyal Princeton graduates, Mathey helped finance Princeton's residential college system as well as other projects at Princeton from his prolific investment fund which featured Louisiana Land as its core holding.[42] Although he never matched Mathey's later-life largesse, Eberstadt over the years made regular annual contributions to numerous worthy organizations, including Princeton, through the Target Rock Foundation.[43]

Mathey left Dillon Read in the late 1930s and joined Empire Trust Company's investment banking unit[44] where he revived the close relationship that he had enjoyed with Eberstadt at Dillon Read and participated in a number of Eberstadt's energy ventures, many of which were quite profitable. According to Wastrom, Mathey respected Eberstadt's judgment but was wary in dealing with him. On Eberstadt deals, Mathey would tell Wastrom,

"Ok, Peter, I don't want to go through all the details with you. If it is good enough for Eber, it is good enough for me, but you must be sure that my position in this deal is exactly the same as Eberstadt's. I don't want to be in front of him; I don't want to be behind him; I want to be exactly on a par with him."[45]

In other words, if Eberstadt made a lot of money, Mathey would make a lot; if Mathey got hurt, so would Eberstadt. Both Mathey and Eberstadt dreamed of finding another Louisiana Land, and all their speculations contained some of the ingredients of that legendary deal.[46]

One of the most intriguing deals involving Mathey's participation was Tipperary Land Corp., a speculative Australian land development venture located south of Darwin in northern Australia. The vast land holding comprised 6,708 square miles—an area larger than the State of Connecticut. In March 1967 Eberstadt combined a $2.5 million private placement of senior notes and warrants with a $3.5 million unit offering to the public—each unit consisted of subordinated debentures and common stock—to raise $6 million of initial capital for the venture.[47] Long term, Tipperary hoped to become the breadbasket of Asia through farming methods that had never been tried on so vast a scale before.

The Tipperary operation contained some bizarre episodes. For example, among the many grandiose schemes of the company's founders was a plan to raise cattle. At about the time that they harvested their first crop of sorghum, Sir William A. Gunn, an Australian grazier and Tipperary's chief, hit upon the idea of feeding the sorghum to the cows, but since sorghum does not have any nutritional value for cattle, they all died.[48]

Another bizarre episode involved the shrimp venture. The Texans who controlled the company noticed massive pools of shrimp in the sea adjacent to their property in northern Australia, and they made a major investment in a fleet of shrimp boats to harvest the shrimp. By the time the boats were ready, however, the shrimp had all disappeared. The earlier appearance of the shrimp in the waters was an abnormality, and the shrimp venture was a total loss.[49]

In the speculative "go-go" market of the late 1960s, Tipperary initially soared to $42 a share from its original issue price of $1 a share. Then, adverse and abnormal weather conditions reduced the grain and sorghum harvest substantially below expectations, and the stock fell precipitously in the market. Tipperary was subsequently merged into another company allied to the group, but the Australian land venture has never been profitable. The dream of finding another Louisiana Land eluded Mathey and Eberstadt.[50]

The 1960s also included several outstanding financings such as North Central Airlines which involved the restructuring of a regional airline to eliminate the excessive debt incurred by the late founder, A. E. Mueller. Eberstadt's financial restructuring turned the carrier into a lean, aggressive competitor. As Porter put it, "To my mind, North Central was one of the most creative deals of Eber's later life."[51] Other noteworthy deals included a $30 million financing for Research Cottrell, an environmental control company brought to the firm by Francis Williams, and a series of financings for Denver Chemical, a specialty chemical firm, arranged by Wastrom which enabled Eberstadt and other conventurers to triple their money in about four years.[52]

Nor was Eberstadt inactive in mergers during this period—especially in McDonnell Aircraft's acquisition of Douglas Aircraft in 1967 and the acquisition of United Artists by Transamerica in 1968—both mega-sized deals at the time.

In the McDonnell-Douglas acquisition, Douglas had no more than six weeks left before the company would run out of money; in desperation, the company retained Lazard to solicit bids. Eberstadt was called at the last moment by his old friend, James McDonnell, to come out to help prepare McDonnell's bid for Douglas in competition with eight or ten other aircraft firms. Eberstadt counselled McDonnell to preserve the Douglas name by creating a new parent company, McDonnell-Douglas, to hold the shares of Douglas and McDonnell which would continue to operate as wholly owned but independent subsidiaries. This had a significant impact on the Douglas directors who had great pride in the achievements of the founder of the business who was still alive at that time. Zeller pointed out, "None of the other bidders had the vision that Eberstadt displayed in making that proposal."[53] As Eberstadt used to tell his partners, "Mergers are made in the heart not in the mind."[54]

In the case of United Artists (UA), Zeller called his old friend and

Stanford classmate, John Beckett, who headed Transamerica, and asked if they might be interested in acquiring UA. They definitely were, and after some hesitation Krim and Benjamin agreed. Previously, the UA management had wanted to sell the company to Consolidated Foods, but Eberstadt strongly opposed that course. With UA earnings down and with the need for additional funds to assure their future motion picture commitments, Eberstadt applied pressure on Krim and Benjamin to drop Consolidated Foods' proposal in favor of Transamerica. The $384 million deal went through; but Lazard performed a major share of the work of completing the transaction.[55]

Despite improved earnings and prospects, Eberstadt was encountering major personal problems in the late 1960s, problems that ultimately led to the failure of his dream to create a family dynasty. In the early 1950s, he had been disappointed in the lack of interest in the investment banking business shown by his son Frederick. His son had consented to try it out, but he lost interest and turned to commercial photography as a career.

However, Frederick Eberstadt's son Nicholas, who had a brilliant mind, seemed to be interested in the investment field. Frederick Eberstadt related a typical visit of his son Nicholas with his grandfather:

Grandfather and Nickie would go over the *Standard & Poor's* manual for fun. They would start at the beginning and go to the end and then start at the beginning again. When Nick was about ten or eleven years old, he would wait impatiently for dinner to be over and then he would go with grandfather to discuss what investments were good and what were bad; they would make up a portfolio into which they would invest theoretically either $10,000 or $100,000 and they would follow that for a year and see how they did. They did very well as a matter of fact.[56]

Nevertheless, Nicholas later lost interest in investments and became involved in social studies at Harvard's Center for Population Studies.

Eberstadt's nephew, Andrew W. Eberstadt, another hopeful to continue and foster the dynasty, had already achieved great success in developing dealer sales of Chemical Fund in the highly competitive New York market as a wholesale representative of the firm and had worked on syndicates as well. He became a partner of the firm in 1956, but he was not willing to assume the responsibility of running it. At this point, there was some indication that Andrew's older brother Rudy might also be interested in joining forces with his uncle in some way—perhaps as a deal maker, or a finder, or a venture capitalist. Rudy had shown his talent in putting together the highly successful Microdot through a series of mergers of small suppliers in the auto industry. Eberstadt's son-in-law, Peter B. Cannell, also rose rapidly in the ranks of the firm; he became a partner in 1956 and executive vice president of Chemical Fund in 1959. Since Andrew Eberstadt had no desire to lead the firm, Cannell seemed to be destined to inherit the mantle of leadership.

Zeller dismisses that idea, pointing out, "There is something about the father and son-in-law relationship, at least there was in that case." After Cannell became president of the fund in 1962, Eberstadt retained only a residual role as honorary chairman and a director.

But, when Eber became active again in the business, in the fall of 1962, he would attend the fund's portfolio meetings as a director and make recommendations. . . . At one point Cannell told Eberstadt that "he was not to have anything to do with the portfolio management except as a director and that he, Cannell, under the by-laws of the fund was its president and chief executive officer and would act as such!"[57]

Eberstadt controlled the parent firm that owned all of the stock of the Chemical Fund investment management subsidiary. Therefore Cannell was totally and completely powerless without the support of Eberstadt.[58] Once the feud between Eberstadt and his son-in-law got out of control, Eberstadt stripped Cannell of all of his authority, and the feud worsened. Not long thereafter Cannell withdrew as a partner in the firm, which infuriated Eberstadt; "The old man was mad as a hatter," Cannell later recalled.[59]

Zeller related that during this period Cannell occasionally had lunch with Eberstadt, generally with some outsider with whom Cannell had some business or personal relations. Eberstadt never missed the opportunity on these occasions to tell his Winston Churchill story. According to Zeller,

The story was that Churchill was being interviewed by a newspaper man towards the end of his career and one of the questions was, "Other than yourself, whom would you say was the greatest man of your age and generation?" And without the slightest hesitation, Churchill came back with, "Benito Mussolini." "Benito Mussolini? How on earth could you say that Benito Mussolini was the greatest man of your times?" "Very simple; he is the only man that I know of who had the sense and the guts to have his son-in-law shot."[60]

The blow-up between Cannell and Eberstadt had grave ramifications for the future of the firm. No one, of course, knows exactly how Eberstadt viewed the ultimate shape of the firm in its second generation but, according to Porter, "He had previously told his partners that the investment banking part of the firm would go to them and the money management part would go to his children."[61] At that point, he still clung to the dream of a family dynasty; but, as the feud with Cannell deepened, this dream receded and eluded Eberstadt's grasp.

Cannell's insurrection caused Zeller to become Eberstadt's closest partner and heir apparent. Others had ascended the ladder of authority at
breakneck speed in the past, only to trip up later and fall out of favor
with the old master. Zeller, however, had a strange hold over the "old
man."

Cannell and Eberstadt were both strong-willed individuals who could
brook no compromises. However, after Cannell resigned in 1964, Andrew Eberstadt and the partners and associates in the money management side of the business pleaded with Cannell to reconsider and to
return to the firm. Some of the older directors, lifelong friends of Eberstadt, also acted as peacemakers. As a result of their mediation, a rapprochement was worked out between Cannell and Eberstadt. Cannell
returned to the firm to head up the institutional research and brokerage
and investment advisory parts of the business, but he was to stay out
of the management of Chemical Fund.[62]

Shortly after this, Eberstadt approached his son Frederick in an attempt to persuade him to reenter the investment business. Frederick
consented with some reservations. Eberstadt told Frederick that he
would first have to go to school to get an education in finance. In the
summer of 1967, Frederick went to New York University graduate business school where he took several courses in finance.[63] When Frederick
returned to show his father his progress, Eberstadt seemed to waffle on
his prior commitment. The shock treatments he had taken earlier in the
decade for his mental condition may have affected his memory. Nelson
Loud noted that Eberstadt had had some difficulty with remembering
things during the late 1950s and thought he might have suffered a number of minor strokes that may have affected his memory at that time.[64]

Zeller questions whether Frederick could have been successful as an
investment banker based on what he had been told by others involved
with Frederick's earlier effort with the firm. Francis Williams, who
worked with Eberstadt's son in the early 1950s, had told Zeller, "Freddie
showed no interest in the business of any kind whatever."[65] Zeller con-
cedes that

if you hypothesize that [Freddie was making] a second try at it and that the
second try is successful . . . and he wants to keep it up, well, I don't have any
question but that Eber would have really welcomed that because he had a very
strong family feeling and he believed in the investment banking business as a
family business.[66]

Nelson Loud, who also was involved with Frederick's earlier training
program, differs with Williams and Zeller. Loud claims that

Freddie had the Eberstadt touch. Freddie worked on a couple of deals with me
and I told him he was good at it and I didn't understand why he didn't want

to pursue investment banking as a career. Ferd wanted Fred Eberstadt to be his heir and his continuance. He wanted to build a dynasty more than any one in the world.[67]

Peter Cannell and Andrew Eberstadt seemed to have little to lose by Freddie's entree into the firm as a link in the family dynasty. They recognized that Freddie would probably want to pursue investment banking deals rather than the money management field—their main interest. So the question remains why Eberstadt denied his son in the late 1960s. According to Frederick, "It was Zeller who scotched the idea."[68]

To fill the position vacated by Cannell, Eberstadt convinced Robert Porter to return to the firm in 1965 to become the president of Chemical Fund. Eberstadt assured Porter that while his primary responsibility would be to oversee the management of Chemical Fund, he could devote a major portion of his time to working on investment banking deals.[69] This was the way Eberstadt had run Chemical Fund in the past. But in the increasingly competitive money management world of the 1960s and the 1970s, Chemical Fund needed more than a part-time leader.

Eberstadt believed that Zeller could successfully lead the firm into its second generation and originate significant investment banking business. However, Zeller never developed any meaningful investment banking accounts for the firm. In a sense, Zeller made the perfect complement for Eberstadt in his later years. He never competed with the old man in his private preserve and therefore was never a threat to his primacy as the master investment banker. But Zeller lacked Eberstadt's ability to harmonize conflicting personalities to exploit a situation.

Eberstadt, now close to eighty years of age, became increasingly dependent on Zeller whom he considered his closest friend and confidant. For example, Eberstadt named Zeller an executor of his estate, the only partner of the firm so designated.[70] Zeller provided the kind of assurance and solace that the aging Eberstadt needed to assure himself that his family would be properly provided for and the firm would survive.

The feud with Cannell worsened. Ultimately Cannell withdrew from the firm for good, just two months before Eberstadt suffered his massive fatal heart attack. Even if Cannell had stayed on, it is doubtful that the end result would have been different; Zeller was Eberstadt's final choice to succeed him as head of the firm.

A longtime Eberstadt partner, who requested anonymity, stated that Cannell learned three things from his long, bitter relationship with Eberstadt. First, he made a mistake in thinking that he could work with

Eberstadt as a partner, given his own ambitions and Eberstadt's domineering character. Second, his dislike and distrust of Zeller contributed to his split with Eberstadt and his inability to work with him. Finally, Cannell felt that Eberstadt was the greatest manipulator of people that he had ever known—a Machiavellian type who set people against one another. It was this constant match playing, of course, that Eberstadt used to get the most out of people. In this, Eberstadt was no different from his old mentor, Clarence Dillon, who played personalities one against another to create healthy intramural rivalry. But Cannell intensely hated it.

The end came suddenly. On October 21, 1969, Eberstadt suffered a massive heart attack at National Airport in Washington, D.C., while he was en route to a meeting of the Blue Ribbon Defense Panel, a group appointed by President Richard Nixon to deal with national security. He thus literally gave his life for the country he had served so outstandingly throughout his career. Even as his life ebbed away at Walter Reed Hospital, Eberstadt ignored the inevitability of death and continued his vigorous pursuit of life. Ann Cannell, his daughter, noted, "He didn't act sick—flirting with nurses who were just crazy about him . . . there was something of the Spanish heritage in his look and in his attitude and . . . drive . . . he didn't waste much time."[71] Death came three weeks later on November 11. Eberstadt's body was cremated, and his ashes were strewn by his son over the grounds of his beloved Target Rock estate. At the funeral services held at St. John's Episcopal Church in nearby Cold Spring Harbor, members of his World War I unit, the 304th Field Artillery, stood as a color guard at each side of the altar.[72]

The incorporation of the firm had been accomplished at the last minute, after having been dragged out for more than a year, delayed by any number of matters including the last minute decision by Cannell in September 1969 to withdraw altogether from the firm. The incorporation of the firm was accomplished at the last-minute with the final papers signed by Eberstadt at Walter Reed Hospital just eleven days before his death. According to David Dievler, the firm's chief financial officer, if the firm had failed to incorporate before Eberstadt's death, it would in all likelihood have been dissolved because of the conflicting interests of the family trusts and the partners of the firm.[73]

In effect, the Eberstadt story was essentially a one-act play ending with the death of the founder. Like a character from a Greek tragedy, Eberstadt failed in his dream of creating a dynasty that could drive the firm forward in its second generation. Without his oversight and creativity, the firm's ability to originate innovative deals and manage the investment assets entrusted to it deteriorated badly; the guiding genius of Eberstadt was lost forever. Eberstadt's financial empire gradually disintegrated after his death.

Notes

1. Survey by author of Eberstadt underwritings as listed in the annual issues of the "Corporate Financing Directory" published by the *Investment Dealers' Digest* for the years covered.

2. *Forbes* Annual Mutual Fund Survey issues for the years 1960–1969.

3. Opinion of Chancellor Collins J. Seitz in Irwin Meiselman, Plaintiff, v. Ferdinand Eberstadt, et al., Court of Chancery of the State of Delaware, New Castle, May 4, 1961.

4. Interview with Robert G. Zeller, May 1, 1984.

5. Ibid.

6. Fritz Reuter, *Wormaisa 1000 Jahr Juden in Worms* (Worms, West Germany, 1984), p. 159.

7. Based on author's recollection.

8. Interview with Andrew W. Eberstadt, April 11, 1984.

9. Statements by various partners and family members.

10. Interview with Miss Rita Higgins, Eberstadt's private secretary, February 8, 1985.

11. Interview with Frederick Eberstadt, March 23, 1984 and Miss Higgins, February 8, 1985.

12. Interview with Nelson Loud, April 2, 1984.

13. Telephone interview with Craig Severance, May 26, 1984.

14. Interview with Nelson Loud, December 10, 1987.

15. Interview with Nelson Loud, April 2, 1984.

16. As related by a former Eberstadt partner who requested anonymity.

17. Interview with Nelson Loud, April 2, 1984.

18. Interview with Peter L. Wastrom, March 29, 1984.

19. "Cashing in on Specialization," *Business Week*, March 30, 1963, p. 90; also survey by author based on data in the annual issues of the "Corporate Financing Directory," published by the *Investment Dealers' Digest*.

20. Richard Baker, "Three Investment Underwriters Named in Equity Funding Suit," *New York Journal of Commerce*, November 7, 1974, p. 2.

21. Letter to author from F. Kenneth Melis, former Eberstadt partner and principal of New York Securities, June 15, 1985.

22. Telephone interview with Craig Severance, January 26, 1989.

23. Letter to author from Peter B. Cannell, May 20, 1985.

24. "The Money Men: The Disciple," *Forbes*, February 1, 1971, pp. 41–42.

25. "F. Eberstadt & Co. Becomes a NYSE Member," *New York Times*, July 31, 1962, p. 40.

26. Interview with James Benenson, April 9, 1984.

27. Ibid.

28. Ibid.

29. Interviews with Pike Sullivan, April 18, 1984, and Andrew W. Eberstadt, April 11, 1984.

30. Interviews with Pike Sullivan, April 18, 1984, and Walter Lubanko, a former Eberstadt partner, April 16, 1984.

31. Interview with Pike Sullivan, April 18, 1984.

32. Interview with Walter Lubanko, April 16, 1984.

33. Robert Metz, "Market Place: Potential Perils Found in 'Fails,' " *New York Times*, May 22, 1968, p. 62.

34. "Goodbody: The Great Rescue—Wall Street Prevails on Merrill Lynch," *New York Times*, November 1, 1970, III, p. 3.

35. Telephone interview with William P. Sullivan, May 26, 1984.

36. "1960–1969, A Decade of Corporate and International Finance," *Investment Dealers' Digest* and Investment Bankers Association, p. 76.

37. Author's survey of Eberstadt financings.

38. As related to the author by several Eberstadt partners and associates.

39. Letter to author from John M. Turner, a former corporate finance associate of Eberstadt, January 5, 1987.

40. Ibid.

41. Interview with N. J. Prestigiacomo, former Eberstadt partner, September 18, 1984.

42. "Princeton Creating Instant Traditions," *New York Times*, April 30, 1984, p. B2.

43. Interview with Miss Rita Higgins, Eberstadt's private secretary, February 8, 1985.

44. Empire Trust, a New York State chartered bank, was permitted under the 1933 Glass-Steagall Act to continue its prior activities as an investment bank.

45. Interview with Peter L. Wastrom, March 29, 1984.

46. Ibid.

47. Robert Metz, "Market Place: Sowing Cash Down Under," *New York Times*, September 13, 1967, p. 52.

48. Interview with Peter Wastrom, October 29, 1985, and telephone call, May 10, 1985.

49. Ibid.

50. Ibid.

51. Interview by Robert L. Newton with Robert C. Porter, January 1982, revised March 1984 (hereinafter referred to as the Newton-Porter interview).

52. Internal Eberstadt memorandum, April 13, 1972.

53. Interview with Robert G. Zeller, May 1, 1984.

54. Interview with Robert C. Porter, August 27, 1984.

55. Interview with Robert G. Zeller, May 1, 1984.

56. Interview with Frederick Eberstadt, March 23, 1984.

57. Interview with Robert G. Zeller, May 1, 1984.

58. Ibid.

59. Letter to author from Peter B. Cannell, May 20, 1985.

60. Interview with Robert G. Zeller, May 1, 1984.

61. Interview with Robert C. Porter, August 27, 1984.

62. Ibid.

63. Letter to author from Beth Rubin, director of records and registration,

New York University Graduate School of Business Administration, March 11, 1986.

64. Interview with Nelson Loud, April 2, 1984.

65. Interview with Francis S. Williams, May 8, 1984.

66. Interview with Robert G. Zeller, May 1, 1984.

67. Interview with Nelson Loud, April 2, 1984.

68. Interview with Frederick Eberstadt, March 23, 1984.

69. Interview with Robert C. Porter, August 27, 1984.

70. Codicil to Eberstadt's Will, December 19, 1967.

71. Interview with Mrs. Ann Cannell, March 18, 1985.

72. "The Pirate Piece," special holiday edition, 1969, *304th Field Artillery Association*.

73. Interview with David Dievler, former Eberstadt partner, April 10, 1984.

10

Aftermath

Most estimates of Eberstadt's final wealth put it at about $50 million (equivalent to several hundred million dollars if adjusted to the present value of the dollar). The taxable portion of his holdings—his taxable estate—came to $25 million according to the Suffolk County probate records.[1] Other estimates place the final value of his trusts, real estate in the Bahamas and the Target Rock estate on Long Island, together with his wife's and his own personal financial holdings, at $100 million or more.

If Eberstadt had kept until his death his original holdings of his most profitable investment banking deals, including Louisiana Land, Square D, Warner-Lambert, Carter-Wallace and Engelhard Minerals & Chemicals, the final value of his wealth could well have been considerably more than $100 million. But an examination of the Eberstadt probate records reveals that only small portions of these holdings were in his estate or in the many trust accounts he had created for the benefit of his children and grandchildren.[2]

After Eberstadt's death, the firm was run for a time by a triumvirate—Robert Zeller, the managing director, in charge of investment banking; Robert Porter, in charge of investment management; and Pike Sullivan, in charge of institutional research and brokerage. Triumvirates have never worked well from the time of the Caesars, and this was no exception.

The death of Eberstadt had a marked influence on the firm's relationships with its investment banking clients. Eberstadt's attitude had been: "If I have performed investment banking services for a firm, that business belongs to me and it should show me proper respect."[3] Whenever an Eberstadt partner wanted to approach a company with a financing idea, Eberstadt insisted that it first be cleared with the company's investment banker, including the split of the fee.

But the investment banking business had changed markedly from the days of Clarence Dillon when investment bankers respected the other fellow's "turf." Eberstadt had the personal charisma and ability to maintain these banking relations; the partners remaining after his death clearly did not. Even before Eberstadt's death Wall Street had entered a period of withering competition and past relationships were becoming increasingly vulnerable. As Ken Auletta states in his account of the fall of Lehman Brothers, "The psychology of Wall Street is becoming more speculative . . . The deal becomes all and the banker-client relationship is deteriorating."[4]

The second generation of investment banking partners hired by Eberstadt after the firm split in 1962 never really developed the close working harmony so necessary in a small, tightly knit organization. For example, the firm lost the Becton-Dickinson (B-D) business in 1975 when First Boston and Paine Webber comanaged a $53 million public offering of B-D common stock.[5] Eberstadt's partners had continued to maintain a close rapport with Fairleigh Dickinson, the son of the founder and the former chief executive officer, but after a younger, more aggressive management team came into control at B-D, they sought different financial advisers.

But all of the 1970s were not downhill for the firm and its partners. One investment banking deal, the Beker Industries financing, was a standout. Erol Beker, a native of Turkey, founded a fertilizer business in the United States which he sold to Hooker Chemical; Hooker then merged with Occidental Petroleum (Oxy). However, the Federal Trade Commission stipulated that Oxy had to sell off the fertilizer business before approving the merger.[6]

Beker, anxious to reenter the business, approached the Eberstadt partners to help negotiate a buyout of Hooker's fertilizer business which they achieved at bargain prices due to the depressed fertilizer business in the early 1970s. Beker's purchase was highly leveraged with debt—an early example of the leveraged buyout, a technique that Eberstadt and Meyer had pioneered twenty years earlier. The equity portion was supplied by Beker, the Eberstadt partners, and certain other investors.[7]

The fertilizer business then recovered and with expanded producing facilities, Beker's sales and earnings soared. Eberstadt brought Beker public in 1973 with an equity offering at $15 a share which valued the partners' investment at more than forty-five times their cost[8]—a level of profitability that even exceeded the profits from the legendary deals in the heyday of the Eberstadt-Meyer era. (The Eberstadt partners however, did not sell any of their shares in this offering.)

For a time, Beker was a stock market star soaring in 1975 to more than two times the original offering price. However, the fertilizer business continued to follow a roller-coaster path. Beker's highly leveraged operation caused earnings to fluctuate widely and in the 1985 fertilizer downturn, the company sustained $81.1 million in losses and Beker filed for reorganization under Chapter 11[9] with Erol Beker stepping down as chief executive officer.[10] Subsequently, the Bankruptcy trustee sold the business and it now operates under the name of Nu West Industries, Inc.[11]

Whether the Eberstadt partners were able to realize their profits before the collapse is not known, but the public investors who bought Beker on the original financing lost most of their investment as if they had continued to hold their shares.

In contrast to the dismal investment banking results, the firm's mutual fund management business thrived for a time after Eberstadt's death. In January 1973, Chemical Fund reached a billion dollars in assets for the first time, nearly double the level at the time of Eberstadt's death. With the favorable market of the early 1970s emphasizing the "nifty fifty" big blue chip growth stocks that dominated Chemical Fund's list of investments, new sales of Chemical Fund to the public reached over $200 million in 1972.[12] *Forbes'* 1973 mutual fund survey had ranked Chemical Fund's performance as "A" in both rising and falling markets and had included Chemical Fund on its Honor Roll of outstanding mutual funds.[13] However, these surveys were based on a cumulative performance over the previous decade when Eberstadt was alive and in charge. Thus, Chemical Fund's superlative ratings in the early 1970s were, in effect, a tribute to Eberstadt's stewardship during the last ten years of his life.

However, after the severe market drop in the mid-1970s, Chemical Fund's performance suffered badly and new sales dropped off sharply. The high-flying health care stocks which comprised over one-third of Chemical Fund's portfolio were particularly hard hit. Also, the price of petroleum, a key chemical raw material, soared as the Organization of Petroleum Exporting Countries (OPEC) cartel took charge of the world energy market. This had a devastating impact on the earnings and market value of many of the companies in Chemical Fund's investment portfolio.

The firm tried to exploit the favorable past performance of Chemical Fund by launching a number of new funds to create a "family of funds." In the mid-1970s, the firm acquired and merged the closed-end fund Surveyor Fund into the smaller Eberstadt Fund, with the surviving fund controlled by Eberstadt but taking the name Surveyor Fund. The merger added $100 million in assets to the firm's mutual fund assets and was an innovative "first" in the mutual fund industry. The firm then launched a bond and money market fund, but the magical touch of Eberstadt was missing in the new fund ventures and they failed to catch on with investors. After the deep bear markets of the mid-1970s, Chemical Fund's new sales slipped badly, and the fund fell into net redemptions, with total assets falling far below the record billion-dollar level reached two years earlier.

The sobering seventies were particularly harsh on the "buy/hold" growth stock philosophy of Chemical Fund and the firm's pension and other money management accounts. The fund's management stayed stubbornly with the big blue chips and paid dearly in performance. *Forbes* 1984 annual mutual fund survey rated Chemical Fund a dismal "D" in up markets and a grim "F" in down markets over the previous decade,[14] in sharp contrast to the "AA" ratings ten years before. Several major pension funds transferred their accounts from Eberstadt because of continued poor performance.[15]

After Eberstadt's death, the family interest in the business continued by virtue of its holdings of a special convertible preferred stock created as part of the incorporation of the firm just before Eberstadt's death in 1969. The Eberstadt children wanted to take an active interest in the business, but the existing partners would have no part of that and pushed instead to bring about the repurchase of this special preferred stock, resulting in tedious and at times acrimonious negotiations that took ten long years to complete. Porter points out, "Before he died, Eberstadt was telling us one thing and his children something else. The family thought their father had promised them the Chemical Fund management company and we thought that he had promised it to us." Porter added that, in a sense, "Eber . . . was a Jekyl and a Hyde [but] I guess any great person is that way."[16]

The special preferred stock gave Eberstadt the right to take back control of the firm. The family thought they had inherited that right,[17] but the papers incorporating the firm, which Eberstadt signed on his deathbed, contained a crucial inconsistency. At one point in the documents it stated that the owners of the new preferred stock (i.e., the Eberstadt family) had the right to convert that stock into voting stock that would give them control of the firm. Another clause, however, stated that if any provision in the documents had the effect of causing the firm to cease to be a member firm of the New York Stock Exchange, that provision would become null and void. Since the rules of the Stock Exchange provided that persons or groups not active in the securities business could not become members of the Exchange, that clause precluded the family from taking control of the firm.[18] One can only speculate about how this inconsistency in such a crucial document could have slipped by Eberstadt, a carefully trained lawyer, in all of the drafts that he reviewed over a period of two years prior to his death. The firm subsequently acquired in several stages the special preferred stock from the estate for various amounts totalling $3.5 million, and the Eberstadt family ceased to be a factor in its management.

Over the years, Eberstadt had developed extensive internal rules to deal with the inherent conflicts of interest growing out of the firm's overlapping activities in investment banking, money management and brokerage. After Eberstadt's death, these rules were codified into a written manual of conduct and distributed to all partners and employees.[19] Despite these efforts, the internal controls failed to prevent a fatal conflict of interest that emerged when the Sun Company attempted to take over Becton-Dickinson in 1978.

Fairleigh Dickinson, a major B-D stockholder, wanted to get rid of the Young Turks who had taken control of the company, and he found an ally in the Sun Company which wanted to diversify into new growth fields and reduce its dependence on the energy business.[20] Sun arranged with the Eberstadt firm and Salomon Brothers to bring about a whirlwind buyout whereby Sun privately bought up large blocks of B-D stock from several major institutional and other holders, including Eberstadt's Chemical Fund and Surveyor Fund, at about $45 a share, nearly double the market price of the stock in the open market. Using this technique, Sun quickly acquired 34 percent of the B-D stock, a commanding position for Sun's takeover attempt.[21]

Becton-Dickinson brought suit claiming that Sun violated various securities acts through an illegal tender offer. A number of other suits were brought in state and federal courts by various parties, including the Securities and Exchange Commission (SEC). The case came to trial in early 1979. After seven months of hearings, U.S. District Court Judge Robert L. Carter ruled that Sun's private purchase of B-D stock constituted a tender offer that violated the Williams Act and several other federal securities laws because there was no advance public disclosure.[22]

The adverse publicity following the damaging disclosures in the B-D suit caused the firm to recognize that it made more sense to break up the firm into separate and distinct segments. Porter wrote to the partners, "The [sale of the money management business] will eliminate . . . the potential conflicts between the investment banking and brokerage business on the one hand and the money management on the other."[23] The money management subsidiary was sold to Marsh & McLennan, and the investment banking and brokerage business continued as an independent securities firm assuming the name of the original firm, F. Eberstadt & Co., Inc.[24]

The investment banking–brokerage unit was very profitable in the early 1980s. The firm restructured Eberstadt's investment banking approach to fit into its institutional research expertise, which emphasized high-technology growth areas.[25] During the 1980s, new offerings soared to $850 million, more than three times the offerings made by the firm in the previous decade. However, after the high-technology stock boom peaked in 1983, several of the firm's major underwritings performed poorly in the air pockets that hit the smaller technology stocks.[26] One of the firm's financings that performed especially poorly was Diasonics, which damaged the firm's image and capital.[27] While the Dow-Jones stock average more than doubled between 1980 and 1989, an investor who bought shares in each of the firm's offerings during the decade of the 1980s would have lost over 25 percent of his capital.[28]

The firm encountered other problems shared by smaller securities firms in the increasingly competitive investment banking world of the 1980s. Much larger pools of capital were now needed to finance the mega-deals that transformed the business increasingly away from the traditional, safer syndicate format into more of a merchant banking business with accompanying larger capital requirements. Eberstadt's size precluded its ability to compete in this arena, and the business was sold in 1985 to Robert Fleming Holdings, Ltd., a prestigious, old-line British merchant banking firm that now operates under the name of Robert Fleming, Inc.[29]

The Eberstadt funds, under Marsh & McLennan, also fared poorly with redemptions sharply exceeding new sales. Chemical Fund's directors forced Marsh & McLennan to sell the management and distribution contracts for the two Eberstadt mutual funds to Alliance Capital, the investment management division of Donaldson, Lufkin & Jenrette (DLJ).[30] Chemical Fund continued to fare poorly under the new management, and massive redemptions in 1985 exceeded sales by over $300 million, reducing total assets to $710 million, well below the record of $1.1 billion in assets at the end of 1982. To help stem the tide, in 1987 Alliance Capital obtained stockholder approval to broaden the permissible scope of the fund's investments and to change the name to Alliance Fund.

In a career as far reaching and long lasting as Eberstadt's, any attempt to make a final evaluation of his life is difficult. Eberstadt played in the center of the power circles of government and finance for nearly fifty years, from 1919 to 1969. Only history can finally decide what lasting mark Eberstadt made on these worlds.

In sharp contrast to his brilliance as a negotiator, problem-solver and planner in both the private and public sectors, Eberstadt must be described as a failure in his relationships with people, whether his family, his partners and employees, or public figures (with a few notable exceptions such as Baruch and Forrestal).

Eberstadt loved to play the role of the lone wolf and, as such, he tended to run his business as a one-man show. That worked well as long as he was active but, after he was gone, his partners were unable to fill the void. Clearly, a number of unanswered questions remain about his life, his motives and the significance of his accomplishments.

Many believe that Eberstadt failed to achieve even greater prominence in life because he was a grasping opportunist and never kept to any predetermined mission other than wealth accumulation. Former Ambassador John J. McCloy, a Wall Street lawyer and one of Roosevelt's chief troubleshooters in World War II, recalled Eberstadt's feats while he was at Dillon Read but cautioned that Eberstadt's over-aggressiveness created distrust among his associates.

Eberstadt was a man to reckon with after the Chrysler-Dodge deal. . . . He was a legend then . . . on everybody's tongue . . . [but] I think . . . his ambitions were not tempered with enough wisdom and caution . . . his drive and pushiness and his inability to . . . suffer fools lightly [is] . . . where he fell short of reaching real heights. . . . [31]

However, for sheer brilliance, Eberstadt had few equals on Wall Street. In fact, Bernard Baruch told Pike Sullivan in the early 1960s, "Eberstadt was the most impressive and brightest guy I have run into in all my years in Wall Street."[32]

In his entire business career, Eberstadt never became really attached to anyone until he met Zeller. Prior to that, a long succession of associates served as his deputies only to be passed over, one for the next. Franz Schneider, Eberstadt's close personal friend and associate for over fifty years, notes "If Ferd had a weakness it was that he'd get over-enthusiastic about a fellow when he first met him. . . . When he found out the fellow wasn't as good as he originally thought, he'd have a reaction against him."[33] As Eberstadt's son Frederick aptly put it, "My father never left enough room on the bench for more than one to sit comfortably."[34]

Many of the post-Eberstadt problems of the firm relate to poor judgment by the managers Eberstadt finally chose to run the business after he was gone. For example, it is difficult to believe that Eberstadt would have gotten caught up in the Becton-Dickinson disaster. He would have manipulated the players tactfully as he had in tense situations in the past, and he would have avoided the conflict-of-interest situation that implicated the firm. One is reminded of Eberstadt's superb counselling to McDonnell, which helped assure the decision of Douglas Aircraft to merge with McDonnell instead of the other suitors.

The poor post-Eberstadt record contrasts sharply with the spectacular growth of Lazard after the death of its leader, André Meyer. Lazard's business has grown two or three times since Meyer's death in 1979 because the talent and leadership were in place to exploit the opportunities[35]—a sharp contrast to the record of the Eberstadt firm after his death.

As to lasting public service achievements, most observers believe that Eberstadt's masterpiece was his postwar work with James Forrestal in setting up a permanent national security apparatus to deal efficiently with international emergencies instead of the crash basis used in the first and second world wars. Out of that emerged the National Security Act with Eberstadt its prime architect. In 1948, Forrestal wrote to Eberstadt describing the new national security machinery as "the child of your brain."[36] Eberstadt himself believed, with others, that the national security organization and the Controlled Materials Plan of World War II were his major public service achievements.[37]

The key to Eberstadt's success in finance was his uncanny knack of recognizing long-term investment opportunities and then concentrating in that investment area to bring these opportunities to the public.

In the 1920s, that foresight was in financing German steel, coal and electrical businesses which were leading the industrial revival in Europe. In the 1930s, it was the "little blue chips"—the small, family-controlled temporarily depressed businesses that were poised to bounce back once the economy turned up. In the 1940s, it was the chemical companies that were developing new chemical processes and products to enhance living standards and boost the economy. In the 1950s, it was the drug companies with revolutionary new medicines to conquer major diseases. In the 1960s, it was the electronic revolution that helped American industry in its uphill battle to improve its productivity.

Eberstadt used to tell his aides,

Investment opportunity is somewhat similar to the bottle of milk delivered to your back door. If you get up early and get there first, you can skim off the three inches or so of cream at the top of the bottle; the lazy ones have to settle for plain milk, which is wholesome, but not as rich as cream.

Eberstadt skimmed the cream off the top of major investment values before the rest of Wall Street. In doing so, he enriched those who had confidence in his judgment.[38]

Perhaps Roger Murray, a long-time Chemical Fund director and professor emeritus of finance at Columbia University's Graduate School of Business and one of the foremost academic and professional investment experts in the field, said it best in this comment:

Eberstadt was [blessed with] a remarkable openness of mind to new developments and new technologies. [He had] great confidence in a proprietary interest as a motivating force . . . to build a business [and was] ready to back people who earned his confidence. . . . He was a strong-minded person with little patience for sloppy thinking.[39]

Ferdinand Eberstadt was not born to great wealth or influence. Like Clarence Dillon and André Meyer, he accumulated wealth and power by using his genius to develop important financial relationships with corporate and government titans. Today, the financial landscape is dominated by megafirms which compete with billions of dollars of capital in a twenty-four-hour global supermarket. Whether men cut from Eberstadt's mold will come to prominence in a financial world increasingly dominated by financial conglomerates is difficult to foresee. Eberstadt's achievements were spectacular in the relatively small-scale financial world of his time. One can only imagine with awe what an Eberstadt might achieve in today's financial superworld.

Notes

1. Estate of Ferdinand Eberstadt, file no. 1677 P1969, Surrogate's Court of Suffolk County, Riverhead, New York.

2. Ibid.

3. Interview with Peter Wastrom, March 29, 1984.

4. Ken Auletta, *Greed and Glory on Wall Street: The Fall of the House of Lehman* (New York, 1986); book review by Christopher Lehmann-Haupt, *New York Times*, January 6, 1986, III, 15:1.

5. "Corporate Financing Directory," 1970–1980, *Investment Dealer's Digest* (New York, 1982), p. 63.

6. Perez, *Inside Venture Capital*, pp. 81–82.

7. Ibid.

8. Beker Offering Prospectus, September 26, 1973, pp. 1, 29.

9. "Beker Industries and a U.S. Unit Filed for Reorganization under Chapter 11 of the Federal Bankruptcy Code," *Wall Street Journal*, October 22, 1985, p. 49, and "Beker Net Loss Dec. 31 year $81,064,000; Net Loss Dec. 31 quarter $29,279,000," *Wall Street Journal*, May 21, 1986, p. 40.

10. "The New York Stock Exchange Is Reviewing Beker Industries' Eligibility for Continued Listing Following Beker's Filing under Chapter 11 of the U.S. Bankruptcy Code; Separately, Erol Y. Beker, son of Erol Beker, Succeeds His Father as CEO," *Wall Street Journal*, October 23, 1985, p. 46.

11. "To Some, Beker Industries Bonds Are a Way to Profit from the '88 Drought," *Wall Street Journal*, August 23, 1988, p. 47.

12. The 1973 Annual Report to Eberstadt stockholders, section VI, p. 1.

13. *Forbes* Annual Mutual Fund Survey, August 15, 1973, p. 68.

14. *Forbes* Annual Mutual Fund Survey, August 27, 1984, p. 76.

15. Scott McMurrey, "Donaldson Lufkin Agrees to Acquire Marsh's Eberstadt," *Wall Street Journal*, October 29, 1984, p. 42.

16. Interview with Robert C. Porter, August 27, 1984.

17. Ibid.

18. Letter to author from Peter B. Cannell, May 20, 1985.

19. *Manual of Policies*, F. Eberstadt & Co., Inc., November 1, 1974.

20. Gail Bronson, "Row at the Top: A Bitter Battle Erupts at Becton Dickinson over Sale of 34% Stake," *Wall Street Journal*, February 1, 1978, pp. 1, 18, and

"Sun Co. Acquires 34% of Becton-Dickinson Shares," *Wall Street Journal*, January 20, 1978, p. 12.

21. Ibid.

22. "U.S. Judge Rules Sun Company Violated Securities Law," *Wall Street Journal*, July 10, 1979, p. 2.

23. Internal memorandum to Eberstadt partners from Robert C. Porter, January 19, 1979.

24. "Marsh & McLennan Completed Previously Announced Acquisition of F. Eberstadt & Co.'s Mutual Fund Management and Investment Advisory Services in Exchange for 142,858 Common Shares of Firm," *Wall Street Journal*, April 4, 1979, pp. 3, 4.

25. Interviews with Pike Sullivan, April 18, 1984, and Robert G. Zeller, May 1, 1984.

26. Lawrence J. Tell, "Bleeding Edge of Technology," *Barron's*, April 23, 1984, p. 20.

27. Norman Poser, "Diasonics' Disclosure Also Questioned," *Investment Dealers' Digest*, October 2, 1984, pp. 10, 37.

28. Based on a survey of Eberstadt offerings conducted by the author from data contained in the *Investment Dealers' Digest* Corporate Financing Directories.

29. "Robert Fleming Holdings, Ltd., Agreed to Acquire F. Eberstadt & Co., Inc. for at least $16.5 Million," *Wall Street Journal*, August 2, 1985, p. 16:2; also tombstone announcement advertisement of Robert Fleming Inc., *New York Times*, November 1, 1988, p. D18.

30. Robert McGough, "Cattle Auction," *Forbes*, December 3, 1984, pp. 276, 278.

31. Interview with John J. McCloy, April 17, 1984.

32. Interview with Pike Sullivan, April 18, 1984.

33. Interview with Franz Schneider, May 7, 1984.

34. Interview with Frederick Eberstadt, March 23, 1984.

35. Tim Metz and Gary Putka, "Wall Street Star: After Some Slow Years, Lazard Frères Regains Its Drive, Profitability," *Wall Street Journal*, September 6, 1984, p. 1.

36. Robert Cuff, "Ferdinand Eberstadt," *The Public Historian*, vol. 7, no. 4 (Fall 1985): p. 38.

37. Interview by Calvin Lee Christman with Ferdinand Eberstadt, July 17 and 18, 1969. July 17, 1969, side 2, pp. 3–4.

38. Telephone interview with William P. Sullivan, May 26, 1984.

39. Written to author from Roger L. Murray, received in May 1984.

APPENDIX

Underwriting Clients of F. Eberstadt & Co., Inc.

(year of initial public offering in parentheses)

Aeronca Aircraft (1944)

Aircraft Radio (1945)

Allen Industries (1936)

Allied Laboratories (1940)

American Barge Lines (1941)

American St. Gobain (1959)

Apex Electrical Manufacturing* (1936)

Armstrong Rubber (1945)

Baldwin Rubber* (1935)

Becton-Dickinson (1962)

Beech-Nut Packing (1947)

Bergen Drug (1963)

B. F. Avery & Sons (1937)

Braniff Airways (1941)

Caspers Tin Plate (1950)

Chamberlin Co. of America (1937)

Chock Full O'Nuts* (1958)

Clevite Corp. (1935)

Cliffs Corp.* (1935)

Cole Drug* (1966)

Denver Chemical* (1965)

Detroit Gasket & Manufacturing (1936)

*secondary offerings

Diversey (1950)

Elcor Chemical (1966)

Elliott Company (1943)

Emerson Radio (1943)

Emertron (1961)

First Realty Investment (1969)

Gleaner Harvester (1944)

Hastings Manufacturing (1950)

Walter E. Heller (1935)

Hewitt Robins (1937)

Hickok Oil* (1941)

Hydraulic Press Manufacturing (1939)

Ideal Cement* (1941)

International Resistance (1952)

International Salt* (1965)

Kalamazoo Stove & Furnace (1935)

King-Seeley (1945)

Kingsbury Breweries (1933)

McGraw-Hill Publishing (1936)

Mastic Asphalt (1940)

Maxson Food Systems (1946)

W. L. Maxson (1939)

Michigan Steel Tube Products (1936)

Mission Dry (1933)

Monarch Machine Tool (1937)

National Presto Industries (1968)

National Starch (1950)

New Park Mining (1947)

North Central Airlines* (1965)

N. Consolidated Airlines (1967)

Norwich Pharmacal* (1939)

Pennwalt* (1969)

Pfizer (1942)

Plymouth Rubber (1947)

Research Cottrell* (1967)

H. H. Robertson* (1938)

Rollins Broadcasting (1960)

Roosevelt Oil & Refining (1948)

Seeger Refrigerator (1945)

R. B. Semler (1944)

Sherwin-Williams* (1934)

Smith, Kline & French* (1951)

Smith-Douglass (1952)

Square D* (1934)

Standard Coil Products (1950)

Standard Products (1936)

James Talcott (1936)

Talon, Inc.* (1938)

Texas Gulf Sulphur* (1941)

Time, Inc.* (1951)

Tipperary Land (1967)

Union Carbide* (1941)

United Artists (1957)

Victor Chemical Works (1937)

Warner-Hudnut (1952)

Webster-Chicago (1950)

Wehr (1964)

Westvaco Chemical (1940)

Jack Winter* (1964)

Viviane Woodward* (1967)

Private Capital Deals

Carter-Wallace (1956)

Engelhard Minerals & Chemicals (1951)

Plantation Dauphin (1955)

U.S. Borax & Chemicals (1951)

Warner-Lambert (1952)

Ziv Television Programs, Inc. (1959)

Bibliography

Personal Interviews and Correspondence

Interviews and correspondence received by Calvin Lee Christman as part of his research for his dissertation, "Ferdinand Eberstadt and Economic Mobilization for War, 1941–1943," Ohio State University, 1971, for which he has granted the author permission to use in this biography:

Ernest C. Brelsford, letters, March 14, 1971 and April 18, 1971.

Eugene H. Catron, September 22, 1970.

Ferdinand Eberstadt, July 17 and 18, 1969.

E. Roland Harriman, letter, May 27, 1971.

John M. Turner, letter, October 30, 1970.

Interviews made available to the author by Robert L. Newton:

Robert C. Porter, January 1982, revised March 1984.

Franz Schneider, December 15, 1981, and February 10, 1982.

John F. Van Deventer, January 19, 1982, revised April 1984.

Francis S. Williams, November 18, 1981 (also an interview with Harry Ansbacher Long on June 15, 1978).

Interviews conducted by the author together with letters and telephone calls.

R. Palmer Baker, Jr., Lord, Day & Lord, letters, May 7, 1984, June 21, 1984, July 11, 1984, and January 15, 1985.

James Benenson, interview, April 9, 1984, and telephone call, July 30, 1985.

Edward J. Bermingham, Jr., letter, August 15, 1984.

Robert E. Blum, letter, May 7, 1984.

Nicholas F. Brady, Dillon, Read & Co., Inc., letter, May 30, 1984.

Hugh Bullock, interview, April 18, 1984.

Mrs. Ann Cannell, interview, March 18, 1985, and letter, July 13, 1984.

Peter B. Cannell, telephone, March 27, 1984, and letters, and May 20, 1985, and September 23, 1987.

William Cannell, interview, June 15, 1984.

Calvin Lee Christman, letters, April 9, 1984, June 11, 1984, July 1, 1984, July 13, 1984, December 3, 1984, February 25, 1985, June 3, 1985, February 8, 1987, August 9, 1987, August 28, 1987, and September 17, 1987.

John F. Connors, interview, April 10, 1984.

John Davenport, telephone interview, March 12, 1985.

Martin Davis, letter received in June 1984.

Fairleigh Dickinson, interview, September 19, 1984.

David Dievler, interview, April 10, 1984 and letter, June 12, 1984.

C. Douglas Dillon, interview, May 3, 1984.

Andrew W. Eberstadt, interview, April 11, 1984.

Frederick Eberstadt, interviews, March 23, 1984, and September 7, 1987, and telephone calls, March 1985, April 9, 1985, and December 5, 1988, and letters, July 16, 1984, April 5, 1985, April 25, 1985.

Rudolph Eberstadt, Jr., letters, April 6, 1984, and May 31, 1985.

Walter A. Eberstadt, letters, April 4, 1986, and June 2, 1986.

Bertrand Fox, undated letters received in April 1984 and September 1984.

George Franklin, Jr., interview, May 3, 1984.

Steven D. Fuller, interview, May 4, 1984.

David C. L. Gosling, letter, May 12, 1984.

Frank Greenwall, interview, National Starch, April 3, 1984 and letter, December 5, 1984.

Larry Harper, interview, September 11, 1984.

Lawrence K. Harper, Jr., interview, April 11, 1985, and letter, June 24, 1985.

Mrs. Mary Harper, interview, April 11, 1985, and letters, May 18, 1984 and February 22, 1986, as well as undated notes received from 1984 to 1989.

W. Averell Harriman, letters, March 26, 1984, April 9, 1984, and May 8, 1984.

Warren H. Henderson, letter, July 10, 1984.

Rita Higgins, interview, February 8, 1985, and various telephone calls.

Harry Hoyt, Sr., letters, April 16, 1984, and (to Robert C. Porter), November 19, 1984.

Eliot Janeway, interview, April 3, 1984.

Arthur Krim, United Artists, interview, April 12, 1984, and letter, February 7, 1986.

Marx Leva, letters to Robert C. Porter, October 15, 1984, November 28, 1984, February 12, 1985, and September 22, 1987. Written comment received in May 1984.

William H. Long, Doremus, interview, April 26, 1984.

Nelson Loud, interviews, April 2, 1984, and December 10, 1987, and telephone calls, July 8, 1985, February 28, 1986, December 15, 1986, and February 6, 1989.

Walter Lubanko, interview, April 16, 1984.

John J. McCloy, interview, April 17, 1984.

F. Kenneth Melis, letters, June 15, 1985, and March 3, 1986; also written comment received in June, 1984.

Daniel P. Moynihan, U.S. Senate, letter, February 23, 1988.

Charles J. V. Murphy, letters, (to Edward F. Willett), October 7, 1982, May 26, 1984, January 22, 1985, February 15, 1985, and March 3, 1985.

Roger L. Murray, written comment received in May 1984.

Robert L. Newton, interview, March 28, 1984.

Mrs. Frances Payne, letters, May 12, 1984, June 23, 1984, July 10, 1984, July 17, 1984, August 6, 1984, November 24, 1984, December 11, 1984, March 31, 1985, May 14, 1985, January 23, 1987, and December 26, 1988, and telephone call, November 26, 1984.

John Payne, interview, August 9, 1984, letters, April 20, 1984, April 26, 1985, May 20, 1986, June 4, 1986, and December 26, 1988, and telephone call, May 10, 1985.

Robert C. Porter, interview, August 27, 1984, and telephone calls, January 31, 1984, May 22, 1984, October 29, 1984, April 1985, and May 20, 1985, and letters, March 17, 1984, April 1, 1984, July 11, 1984, July 28, 1984, August 17, 1984, September 26, 1984, October 19, 1984, January 28, 1985, May 9, 1985, May 23, 1985, March 13, 1986, September 28, 1987, December 29, 1988 and January 23, 1989.

N. J. Prestigiacomo, interview, September 18, 1984.

Milton Rosenthal, Engelhard, Inc., interview, May 1, 1984.

Howard Rusk, M. D., interview, April 13, 1984.

Margaret Ryan, letter, May 13, 1986.

Franz Schneider, interview, May 7, 1984.

Alexander Schwartz, telephone call, May 1, 1984.

Craig Severance, telephone interview, May 26, 1984, and January 26, 1989, and letter, June 19, 1984.

Eliot Sharp, written comment received May 1984.

Jarvis Slade, interview, April 2, 1984.

Clifford N. Smith, letter, March 20, 1986.

Richard S. Storrs, letters, April 12, 1984 and May 31, 1984.

Pike H. Sullivan, interview, April 18, 1984, and letter, July 24, 1985.

William P. Sullivan, telephone interview, May 26, 1984.

Dudley B. Tenney, Cahill Gordon & Reindel, letter, March 22, 1985.

H. W. Tripp, letter and written comment, May 25, 1984.

John M. Turner, letters, July 5, 1984, August 1, 1984, August 9, 1984, February 14, 1986, and January 5, 1987.

Stansfield Turner, letters, September 8, 1987, and November 2, 1987.

Peter L. Wastrom, interviews, March 29, 1984, and October 29, 1985, letters, July 25, 1984, and March 4, 1986, and telephone call, May 10, 1985, October 8, 1985 and February 3, 1989.

Francis S. Williams, interviews, May 8, 1984, and October 1, 1985.

Donald A. Young, interview, April 5, 1984.

Robert G. Zeller, interview, May 1, 1984, and letter, December 2, 1985.

Books

Albion, Robert G., and Robert H. Connery. 1962. *Forrestal and the Navy*. New York: Columbia University Press.

Allen, Frederick Lewis. 1931. *Only Yesterday*. New York: Harper and Row.

Auletta, Ken. 1986. *Greed and Glory on Wall Street: The Fall of the House of Lehmann*. New York: Random House.

Baruch, Bernard M. 1960. *Baruch: The Public Years—My Own Story*. New York: Holt, Rinehart and Winston.

Birmingham, Stephen. 1967. *Our Crowd*. New York: Harper and Row.

Block, Maxine, ed. 1942. *Current Biography, 1942*. New York: H. W. Wilson Company.

Blum, Albert A. 1963. "Birth and Death of the M-Day Plan." In *American Civil-Military Decisions: A Book of Case Studies*, edited by Harold Stein. Twentieth Century Fund Study. Tuscaloosa: University of Alabama Press.

Brooks, John N. 1969. *Once in Golconda—A True Drama of Wall Street, 1920–1938*. New York: Harper & Row.

Carosso, Vincent. 1970. *Investment Banking in America*. Cambridge, Mass.: Harvard University Press.

Catton, Bruce. 1948. *The War Lords of Washington*. New York: Harcourt, Brace & Co., 1948.

Churchill, Allen. 1957. *The Incredible Ivar Kreuger*. New York: Holt Rinehart & Co.

Coit, Margaret L. 1957. *Mr. Baruch*. Boston, Mass.: Houghton Mifflin Co.

Connery, Robert H. 1951. *The Navy and the Industrial Mobilization in World War II*. Princeton, N.J.: Princeton University Press.

Dessauer, John H. 1971. *My Years with Xerox or the Billions Nobody Wanted*. Garden City, N. Y.: Doubleday.

Fennelly, John F. 1965. *Memoirs of a Bureaucrat: A Personal Story of the War Production Board*. Chicago: October House.

Galbraith, John Kenneth. 1955. *The Great Crash*. Boston, Mass.: Houghton Mifflin Co.

Gleisser, Marcus. 1965. *The World of Cyrus Eaton*. New York: A. S. Barnes & Company.

Grant, James. 1983. *Bernard M. Baruch, the Adventures of a Wall Street Legend*. New York: Simon and Schuster.

Hirsch, Felix. 1978. *Gustav Stresemann, 1878/1978*. Bonn, West Germany: Berlin Verlag in collaboration with Inter Nationes.

Howard, James M. 1920. *The Autobiography of a Regiment: A History of the 304th Field Artillery in the World War*. New York: n.p.

Isaacson, Walter, and Evan Thomas. 1986. *The Wise Men: Six Friends and the World They Made*. New York: Simon and Schuster.

Janeway, Eliot. 1968. *The Struggle for Survival*. 2d. ed. rev. New York: Weybright and Talley.

Jensen, Michael C. 1976. *The Financier*. New York: Weybright and Talley.

Lilienthal, David E. 1964–1981. *The Journals of David E. Lilienthal*. 7 vols. New York: Harper and Row.

Mathey, Dean. 1966. *50 Years of Wall Street*. Privately published in Princeton, N.J.

Matz, Mary Jane. 1963. *The Many Lives of Otto Kahn*. New York: Macmillan Co.

Millis, Walter, with collaboration of E. S. Duffield. 1951. *The Forrestal Diaries*. New York: The Viking Press.

The Nassau Herald of the Class of 1913. 1913. Princeton, N.J.: Princeton University Press.

Nelson, Donald. 1946. *Arsenal of Democracy: The Story of American War Production*. New York: Harcourt, Brace & Co.

Perez, Robert C. 1985. *Inside Investment Banking*. New York: Praeger.

―――. 1986. *Inside Venture Capital*. New York: Praeger.

Phalon, Richard. 1981. *The Takeover Barons of Wall Street*. New York: Putnam & Co.

Reich, Cary. 1983. *Financier: The Biography of André Meyer*. New York: William Morrow.

Reuter, Fritz. 1984. *Wormaisa 1000 Jahr Juden in Worms, Der Wormsgan*. Beiheft 29. Worms, West Germany: Verlag Stadtarchiv.

Robinson, Donald. 1952. *The 100 Most Important People in the World Today*. Boston, Mass.: Little, Brown & Co.

Rogow, Arnold A. 1963. *James Forrestal: A Study of Personality, Politics and Policy*. New York: Macmillan Co.

Rosenbloom, Morris V. 1953. *Peace through Strength: Bernard Baruch and a Blueprint for Security*. Washington, D.C.: American Surveys, in association with Farrar, Straus and Young, New York.

Schwarz, Jordan A. 1981. *The Speculator: Bernard M. Baruch in Washington. 1917–1965*. Chapel Hill, N. C.: University of North Carolina Press.

Shaplin, Robert. 1960. *Kreuger: Genius and Swindler*. New York: Knopf.

Sherwood, Robert E. 1950. *Roosevelt and Hopkins: An Intimate History*. New York: Grosset and Dunlap.

Smith, Clifford Neal, and Anna Piszczan-Czaja. 1976. *Jews in Southwestern Germany*. New York: R. R. Bowker Company.

Squadron A. Assn. 1951. *Squadron A: A History of the First 50 Years, 1889–1939*. Published privately by the ex-members of the Squadron A Assn. in New York City.

Sutton, Eric, ed. and trans. 1935–1940. *Gustav Stresemann, His Diaries, Letters and Papers*. Vols. 1–3. London: Macmillan & Co.

Twentieth Century Fund. 1980. *Abuse on Wall Street: Conflicts of Interest in the Securities Industry*. Westport, Conn: Greenwood Press.

Watzinges, Marc Otto. 1984. *History of the Jews in Mannheim [Germany], 1650–1945*. Mannheim, West Germany.

Wechsberg, Joseph. 1956. *The Merchant Bankers*. Boston: Little, Brown & Co.

White, William L. 1950. *Bernard Baruch: Portrait of a Citizen*. New York: Harcourt, Brace & Co.

Willett, Edward F. 1928. "Coal, Iron and Steel in Europe." Privately published by Dillon, Read & Co., by Papeterie de Publications La Finance, B. Garfunkel 4, Rue de la Bourse, Paris.

Business, Financial and Other Publications

1963. Cashing in on Specialization. *Business Week* (30 March): 90–92.

1935. Chrysler, *Fortune* (August): 31–35

1930. Clash of Steel. *Fortune* (June): 68–69.

Connelly, Julie. 1979. Dillon Read Refuses to Play the Game. *Institutional Investor* (January): 39–45.

Corporate Financing Directories. *Investment Dealers' Digest*, New York, annual issues, 1935–1986 (also ten-year summaries covering 1950–1960, 1960–1969, and 1970–1980).

1925. The Dodge Deal. *Literary Digest* 85 (25 April): 80–82.

1933. Empire Auction. *Fortune* (July): 4–6.

1942. Energetic Icicle. *Newsweek* (2 November): 42.

1939. Ferdinand Eberstadt. *Fortune* (April): 72–75.

1951. The $400 Million Colchem Question. *Fortune* (November): 76.

Greene, Richard. 1983. Why Underwriters Are Nervous. *Forbes* (12 September): 164.

Guzzardi, Walter, Jr. 1986. Life after Xerox. *Fortune* (6 January): 121–22.

Higgins, Carol. 1984. A Class Action Puts Three Underwriters in Jeopardy. *Investment Dealers' Digest* (18 September): 9, 10, 34.

1935. In the New Wall Street. *Fortune* (October): 78–93.

Janeway, Eliot. 1951. Mobilizing the Economy: Old Errors in a New Crisis. *The Yale Review* 40, no. 2 (Winter 1951, December 1950): 200–219.

———. 1943. Trials and Errors. *Fortune* (May): 64+.

Jansson, Solveig. 1979. How a "Midnight Raid" Turned into a Nightmare for Institutions. *Institutional Investor* (January): 157–161.

Jereski, Laura. 1987. Clarence Dillon: Using Other People's Money. *Forbes* (13 July): 270, 274.

1982. Liabilities of Underwriters: Implications of the Continental-Illinois Litigation. *Investment Dealers' Digest* (10 August): cover page, 62.

McGough, Robert. 1984. Cattle Auction. *Forbes* (3 December): 276, 278.

Merwin, John. J. P. Morgan: The Agglomerator. *Forbes* (13 July): 275, 278.

1971. The Money Men: The Disciple. *Forbes* (1 February): 41–42.

Mutual Fund Survey. *Forbes*, New York, annually, 1960–1988.

1973. Names & Faces: The Inside Story of Lazard Frères Merger and Acquisition Star, The Remarkable Felix F. Rohatyn. *Business Week* (10 March): 132–37.

1943. Nelson's Dismissal of Eberstadt Emphasizes Production Control. *Newsweek* (1 March): 54–56.

1942. New Order in WPB. *Business Week* (26 September): 14.

Newton, James Y. 1949. The Man behind the Big Brass. *American Magazine* (May): 30–31 + .

Noyes, P. H. 1933. The Last Days of Cyrus the Great. *The Nation* 136 (21 June): 701.

1942. Out of the Top Drawer. *Time* (28 September): 17–18.

1950. Policies & Principles: A Balance for Peace (based on excerpts of a speech by Ferdinand Eberstadt in Seattle, Washington). *Time* (30 October): 30.

Poser, Norman. 1984. Diasonics' Disclosure Also Questioned. *Investment Dealers' Digest* (2 October): 10, 37.

Robertson, Wyndham. 1973. Those Daring Young Con Men of Equity Funding. *Fortune* (August): 81–85 + .

Rohrer, Julie. 1985. The Reshaping of Alliance Capital. *Institutional Investor* (March): 85–88.

Stone, I. F. 1942. Brass-Hat Production. *The Nation* (5 December): 607–8.

———. 1943. The Charming Mr. Baruch. *The Nation* (27 February): 298–99.

———. 1942. The Return of Bernard Baruch. *The Nation* (17 October): 367.

1943. Struggle for Power. *Time* (15 February): 77.

Tell, Lawrence J. 1984. Bleeding Edge of Technology. *Barron's* (23 April): 20, 22, 24, 64, 65.

1928. A Third Motor Car Colossus, The Chrysler-Dodge Merger. *Literary Digest* 97 (16 June): 12.

1937. Wall Street Itself: A Simple Tour of the Canyon in 1937 Suggests That Economic Profundities Are Neither Welcome Nor Apropos. *Fortune* (June): 75.

1943. War Production Board: Is It? *Fortune* (March): 91–97.

1942. Washington Tip-Offs. *Time* (12 January): 62–65.

1973. Why Sell a Good Thing. *Forbes* (1 May): 54.

Williams, Frank J. 1926. A New Leader in Finance: Clarence Dillon. *American Review of Reviews* (February): 146–49.

Wise, T. A. 1967. How McDonnell Won Douglas. *Fortune* (March): 155–156.

Government Publications

The Commission on Organization of the Executive Branch of the Government. 1949. Task Force Report on National Security Organization (Appendix G), January.

Eberstadt, Ferdinand. 1941. *Report to Under Secretaries Patterson and Forrestal in Regard to the Army and Navy Munitions Board.* 26 November. Forrestal File, General Records of the Department of the Navy, National Archives.

U.S. Bureau of the Budget. 1946. *The United States at War: Development and Administration of the War Program by the Federal Government.* Washington, D.C.: U.S. Government Printing Office.

U.S. Civilian Production Administration. 1947. *Industrial Mobilization for War:*

History of the War Production Board and Predecessor Agencies, 1940–1945. Vol.
   I: *Program and Administration.* Washington, D.C.: U.S. Government Printing Office.

U.S. Congress. Senate. 1945. Committee on Naval Affairs. *Report to Hon. James
   Forrestal, Secretary of the Navy, on Unification of the War and Navy Departments
   and Post-war Organization for National Security* (Eberstadt Report). 79th
   Cong., 1st sess., 22 October.

————. 1947. *Hearings before Special Committee Investigating the National Defense
   Program.* 80th Cong., 1st sess.

————. *Industrial Mobilization Plan, Revision of 1939.* 76th Cong., 2d sess. S. Doc.
   134.

————. Senate. 1931. Subcommittee on Banking and Currency. Hearings Pursuant to Senate Resolution no. 71. 71st Cong., 3d sess., pt. 1.

Yoshpe, Harry B. 1965. Bernard Baruch: Civilian Godfather of the Military
   M-Day Plan. *Military Affairs* XXIX, no. 1 (Spring): 1–15.

Newspapers

1887. All about a Misfit. *New York Times,* 17 October, 2, col. 5.

1987. Arms in an Emergency. *New York Times,* 19 October, A20.

Baker, Richard, 1974. Three Investment Underwriters Named in Equity Funding
   Suit. *New York Journal of Commerce,* 7 November, 2.

Baldwin, Hanson W. 1947. New Defense Set-up Faces Obstacles. *New York Times*
   27 July, sec. 4, E5:3.

1985. Beker Industries and a U.S. Unit Filed for Reorganization under Chapter
   11 of the Federal Bankruptcy Code. *Wall Street Journal,* 22 October, 49.

1986. Beker Net Loss Dec. 31 Year $81,064,000; Net Loss Dec. 31 Quarter
   $29,279,000. *Wall Street Journal,* 21 May, 40.

1926. Big Steel Merger Formed in Germany. *New York Times,* 15 January, 1:5.

1947. Bill Creating National Military Establishment Signed; Secretary Forrestal
   Appointed Defense Secretary. *New York Times,* 27 July, 1:5.

Bronson, Gail. 1978. Row at the Top: A Bitter Battle Erupts at Becton Dickinson
   over Sale of 34% Stake. *Wall Street Journal,* 1 February, 1, 18.

1951. Business and Finance Leaders: Ferdinand Eberstadt. *New York Herald-
   Tribune,* 25 April, 30.

Cole, Robert J. 1980. SEC Drops Claim in Becton-Sun Case. *New York Times,* 15
   February, IV, 5:1.

————. 1979. Sun to Appeal on Becton; Opinions on Ruling Differ. *New York
   Times,* 11 July, IV, 20:5.

1972. Dean Mathey, 81, Banking Official. *New York Times,* 17 April, 36:3.

1983. Diasonics Debut on Wall Street Is Cheered by Investors; Medical-Gear
   Maker Raises $123 Million in Large Initial Public Offering of Shares at $22
   Each. *Wall Street Journal,* 24 February, 16: 2.

1925. Dillon Read Group Buys Dodge Motors for over $175,000,000. *New York
   Times,* 1 April, 1.

1928. Dillon Read Opens Paris Office. *New York Times,* 12 March, 35:1.

1928. Dodge Stock Buying Caps Chrysler Deal. *New York Times,* 31 July, 1.

1962. F. Eberstadt & Co. Becomes a NYSE Member. *New York Times*, 31 July, p. 40.

1942. Eberstadt Called Capital's Biggest "Yes and No" Man. *Washington Evening Star*, 20 December, A8.

1932. Eberstadt Hits Probe; Eaton Deals Bared. *New York Journal*, 17 June.

1926. Eberstadt in Dillon Read. *New York Times*, 5 February, 29:1.

1942. Eberstadt "No" Man Ends Deadlock on War Materials. *Baltimore Evening Sun*, 23 November, 15.

1932. F. Eberstadt & Co. Employees to Get Christmas Bonus. *New York Journal*, 14 December, 25.

1962. F. Eberstadt & Company Plans Split into Two Investment Companies. *New York Times*, 26 February, 38:2.

1969. Ferdinand Eberstadt, Investment Banker Active in Government Service, Dies. *New York Times*, 13 November, 43:2.

1951. Former Kahn Home to Be a Boys' School. *New York Times*, 21 August, 42:6.

1938. 4 Main Fields for Investment Finance Listed: Chemical, Oil, Airplane, Air-Conditioning Trades Are Cited by Eberstadt in Survey of Market. *New York Herald Tribune*, 27 March, 16.

1970. Goodbody: The Great Rescue—Wall Street Prevails on Merrill Lynch. *New York Times*, 1 November, III, 3:1

1927. Goodyear Fight Is Ended. *Akron Times-Press*, 12 May, 1.

1927. Goodyear Plaintiff Scores on Seiberling. *New York Times*, 9 February, 33:2.

1927. Goodyear Suit Ends outside of Court; Charges Dropped. Both Sides Agree to the Creation of Independent Board of Directors. End All Voting Trusts. Reorganization by Dillon, Read & Co. Is Recognized as Constructive; They Remain as Bankers. Compromise Agreement Is Result of Mediation Efforts of Owen. D. Young. *New York Times*, 16 May, 1:3.

1921. Goodyear Tire Plan Put into Operation; Bankers Announce Details by which a Readjustment Will Be Carried Out; Voting Trustees Selected; Disposition of Debt and Recapitalization Provided for in Plan of Committee. *New York Times*, 17 May, 25:2.

Gould, Leslie. 1930. Eaton, Eberstadt Score Again in Steel Victory. *New York Journal*, 23 December.

1932. Gray Reviews Fox Film; Ferdinand Eberstadt Testifies Regarding Continental Shares Inquiry. *Wall Street Journal*, 17 June.

1927. Has Faith in Germany; Representative of New York Banker Says Reich's Credit Is Strong Here. *New York Times*, 4 August, 32:4

1983. Isabel Eberstadt: An Original. *Women's Wear Daily*, 6–13 May.

1932. Ivar Kreuger a Suicide; His Stock Heavily Sold; Sweden to Protect Trust. *New York Times*, 13 March, 1.

1920. John Dodge Dead. *New York Times*, 15 January, 11:1.

Krock, Arthur. 1943. Tinder in WPB Set-up; Many Explosive Elements Remain to Threaten the War Program. *New York Times*, 17 February, 11:2.

Lawrence, W. H. 1943. Eberstadt Ousted; Wilson To Run WPB. *New York Times*, 17 February, 1:5.

Lehmann-Haupt, Christopher. 1986. Greed and Glory on Wall Street: The Fall of the House of Lehmann (review of book written by Ken Auletta). *New York Times*, 6 January, III, 15:1.

1968. Lilco Moves to Condemn L. I. Estate for Atomic Power Site. *Long Island Press*, 12 February, 4.

Lubasch, Arnold H. 1979. Judge Rules for Becton in Sun Case. *New York Times*, 10 July, D1, D4.

McMurrey, Scott. 1984. Donaldson Lufkin Agrees to Acquire Marsh's Eberstadt. *Wall Street Journal*, 29 October, 42.

1979. Marsh & McLennan Completed Previously Announced Acquisition of F. Eberstadt & Company's Mutual Fund Management and Investment Advisory Services in Exchange for 142,858 Common Shares of Firm. *Wall Street Journal*, 4 April, 3, 4.

Martyn, T. J. C. 1932. Kreuger's Juggling of Millions: An Amazing Story Now Unfolds. *New York Times*, 22 May, IX, 3:1.

Metz, Robert. 1968. Market Place: Chemical Fund 30 Years Later. *New York Times*, 9 August, 48:7.

———. 1968. Market Place: Potential Peril Found in "Fails." *New York Times*, 22 May, 62.

———. 1968. Market Place: SEC Moves on Paper Jam. *New York Times*, 25 May, 46.

———. 1967. Market Place: Sowing Cash Down Under. *New York Times*, 13 September, 52.

Metz, Tim, and Gary Putka. 1984. Wall Street Star: After Some Slow Years, Lazard Frères Regains Its Drive, Profitability. *Wall Street Journal*, 6 September, 1, 12.

1932. Moratorium Effective; Employees Prepare Statements for Government. *New York Times*, 14 March, 2:3.

1929. Morgan and Young Sail with Advisors. *New York Times*, 2 February, 1:4.

1883. Mr. Pondir's Assault Case. *New York Times*, 9 March, 8, col. 2.

1961. Mrs. Anne Douglass Dillon Dies. *New York Times*, 8 November, 35:5.

1942. Munitions Board, Obscure in Peace, Now a Key Agency. *Wall Street Journal*, 28 May, 1.

1985. The New York Stock Exchange Is Reviewing Beker Industries Eligibility for Continued Listing Following Beker's Filing Under Chapter 11 of the U.S. Bankruptcy Code; Separately, Erol Y. Beker, Son of Erol Beker, Succeeds His Father as CEO. *Wall Street Journal*, 23 October, 46.

1949. National Military Establishment Becomes Defense Department; Joint Staff Chiefs Chairman Created; Service Secretaries Subordinated to Give Defense Secretary More Power; Fiscal Methods Revised. *New York Times*, 11 August, 1.

1926. Offers $30,000,000 Reich Steel Bonds. *New York Times*, 26 June, 21:1.

1925. $146,000,000 Check Closes Dodge Deal. *New York Times*, 2 May, 1.

O'Neill, Thomas. 1942. Eberstadt, "No" Man, Ends Deadlock on War Materials. *Baltimore Evening Sun*, 23 November, 15.

1932. Pick Eberstadt to Aid Kreuger Salvagers. *New York Journal*, 15 August.

1984. Princeton Creating Instant Traditions. *New York Times*, 30 April B2.

1922. Private Financing to Europeans. *New York Times*, 18 July, 22:2.

1898. Produce Exchange Discipline. *New York Times*, 27 April, 12:6.

Reston, James. 1948. Wide Deficiencies; Eberstadt Group Alleges Security Plans Lag and Hits Joint Staff Chiefs. *New York Times*, 17 December, 1.

Sammis, Estelle. 1970. A Natural Treasure for Long Island; Financier's Lands Now a Federal Preserve. *Long Island Press*, 9 August, 21.

1985. Robert Fleming Holdings, Ltd., Agrees to Acquire F. Eberstadt & Co., Inc. for at Least $16.5 Million. *Wall Street Journal*, 2 August, 16:2.

1927. Sees Germany Advancing: Ferdinand Eberstadt Says 1927 Was Best Year under Dawes Plan. *New York Times*, 22 December, 34:3.

1979. Some Defendants in Sun Co.–Becton Case Vow an Appeal of Federal Court Decision. *Wall Street Journal*, 11 July, 16.

Steinberg, David. 1957. UA Plans First Public Offerings. *New York Herald-Tribune*, 20 March, sec. 2, p. 8.

Stone, I. F. 1942. The Nation: FDR Orders Ouster of Standard Oil Man. *PM*, 25 October, 9.

———. 1942. The Nation: N.J. Standard Oil Official Given Control of Exports. *PM*, 6 October, 1.

1926. Sues to Oust Board of Goodyear Tire: Prosecutor in Ohio Attacks Reorganization of Company in 1921 as Illegal: Raps "Management Stock": Action Begun to Take Control of Company "Away from Wall Street," Official Says. *New York Times*, 24 August, 26:4.

1978. Sun Co. Acquires 34% of Becton-Dickinson Shares. *Wall Street Journal*, 20 January, 12.

1978. Sun Company, Unit, Broker Firms, Others Sued by SEC on Sun Stake in Becton Dickinson. *Wall Street Journal*, 10 March, 24.

1928. $300,000,000 Bonds Return to Germany. Ferdinand Eberstadt Gives an Estimate on Dollar Issues Acquired Here. Exact Amount Unknown. Dillon, Read Partner Is Now in the Reich Negotiating Several Loans. *New York Times*, 19 February, II, 9:6.

1988. To Some, Beker Industries Bonds Are a Way to Profit from the '88 Drought. *Wall Street Journal*, 23 August, 47.

1957. United Artists to Make First Public Stock Offering of 350,000 Shares; $10 Million Convertible Debentures. *New York Times*, 20 March, 49:1.

1979. U.S. Judge Rules Sun Company Violated Securities Law. *Wall Street Journal*, 10 July, 2.

Waggoner, Walter H. 1948. Hoover Board Sees Waste in National Defense Set-up; Blow to Economy Feared. *New York Times*, 17 December, 1.

1925. Wall Street Keeps an Eye on Dillon. *New York Times*, 12 April, IX, 5:2.

1938. Wall Street Scene. *Wall Street Journal*, 14 December, 6.

1883. A Wall Street Sensation. *New York Times*, 3 March, 16, col. 1.

Williamson, Samuel T. 1957. The Mad Reign of the "Match King" (book review of "The Incredible Ivan Kreuger" by Allen Churchill). *New York Times*. 22 January, VIII, 6:3.

Young, James C. 1926. Clarence Dillon Became Banker through Chance. *New York Times*, January 10, VIII, 6:6.

Other Source Material

Address by Winston Churchill, Raido Broadcast, February 9, 1941.

Address by Ferdinand Eberstadt before the Rochester Security Analysts, Rochester, New York, June 12, 1962.

Address by Ferdinand Eberstadt, "Financing the Products of Research," before the Southern Research Institute. May 15, 1953.

Address by Ferdinand Eberstadt, "Trends in the Development of Our National Defense Organization," before the New York Chamber of Commerce, New York City, April 14, 1961.

Address by Robert C. Porter, "Importance of Financial Planning to a Growing Corporation," before the Pharmaceutical Advertising Club, New York City, May 9, 1957, reprinted in *Commercial and Financial Chronicle*, June 6, 1957.

Agreement of Settlement between F. Eberstadt & Co., Inc., the Executors of the Estate of Ferdinand Eberstadt, the Ferdinand Eberstadt Foundation, Inc., and certain others, Surrogate's Court of Suffolk County, New York, October 18, 1972.

American Underwriting Houses and their Issues, *National Statistical Service, Inc.* vol. I and II, 1925–1929.

Annual Reports to Stockholders of Chemical Fund, Inc., from 1938 to 1986 and its successor, Alliance Fund, thereafter.

Annual Reports to Stockholders of F. Eberstadt & Company, Inc., for the years 1972–1979.

Beker Offering Prospectus, September 26, 1973.

Broker-Dealer Financial Statements of F. Eberstadt & Co., Inc. and Eberstadt Fleming, Inc. filed with Securities and Exchange Commission.

Christman, Calvin Lee. 1971. Ferdinand Eberstadt and Economic Mobilization for War, 1941–1943, Ph.D. diss., Ohio State University.

Cuff, Robert. 1985. Ferdinand Eberstadt. *The Public Historian*. Regents of University of California, vol. 7, no. 14. Berkeley, Calif. (Fall): 37–52.

Eberstadt family personal trust documents supplied to author by various family members.

Encyclopedia Britannica, 1988 edition, Encyclopedia Britannica, Inc., Chicago, University of Chicago.

Estate of Ferdinand Eberstadt, file no. 1677 P1969, Surrogate's Court of Suffolk County, County Center, Riverhead, New York.

Estate of Mary V. T. Eberstadt, October 15, 1970, New York City Surrogate's Court.

"Financial Services to Industry and Investors," a brochure published privately by F. Eberstadt & Co., Inc., on the occasion of the firm's twentieth anniversary, 1953.

Financial Statements of F. Eberstadt & Company, Inc., and Eberstadt Fleming Inc., as filed with Securities and Exchange Commission.

First and Final Administration Account of Benjamin S. Tongue and Ferdinand Eberstadt, Executors of the Estate of Thomas T. Tongue, Deceased, in the Orphan's Court of Baltimore City, December 21, 1929.

Incorporation Papers of F. Eberstadt & Company, Inc., August 18, 1931, Division of Corporations, State of Delaware, Dover, Delaware.

Incorporation Papers of Science Ventures, Inc., December 12, 1961, State Department of Assessments and Taxation, Baltimore, Maryland.

Internal memorandum, F. Eberstadt & Co., Inc., regarding selected Eberstadt financings, April 13, 1972.

Internal memorandum from Robert C. Porter to partners of F. Eberstadt & Co., Inc., regarding the sale of the firm, January 19, 1979.

Jones, Drummond. "The Controlled Materials Plan of the War Production Board, November 1942 to November 1945." War Production Board Records, National Archives, June 1947. (Typescript draft)

Jones, Lewis Webster. 1929. The Young Plan Settlement. Foreign Policy Association. Vol. V, no. 12. New York City, 21 August.

Last Will and Testament of Ferdinand Eberstadt, June 27, 1967, together with codicils dated December 19, 1967, March, 15, 1968, and November 28, 1968, filed with Surrogate's Court, Suffolk County, New York.

Last Will and Testament of Mary V. T. Eberstadt, June 26, 1970, and filed with the Surrogate's Court of the City of New York.

Letter to author from Beth Rubin, director of records and registration, New York University Graduate School of Business Administration, March 11, 1986.

Letter with attachments from Das Staatsarchiv Sielemann, (Senat Der Freien un Hansestadt Hamburg, Staatsarchiv), March 17, 1987, relating to Lembcke and Rachal families and businesses.

Letter with attachments from Stadtarchivoberinspektor Berger, Archives of the City of Mannheim, West Germany, September 2, 1987.

Letter with attachments from Fritz Reuter, Archivdirecktor, Archives of the City of Worms, West Germany, March 11, 1986.

Letters to author from E. Leslie Byrnes, Jr., archivist of Newark Academy, October 15, 1984, October 24, 1984, and January 31, 1989.

Letters with attachments from Dr. W./Ha. Weisert, Universitatsarchivar, University of Heidelberg, Heidelberg, West Germany, March 10, 1986, and June 10, 1986.

Manual of Policies. F. Eberstadt & Co., Inc., November 1, 1974.

Letters from Andreas Pfeiffer, Consulate General of the Federal Republic of Germany, May 31, 1984, September 24, 1984, and November 23, 1984.

Memorandum of Law in Support of Motion to Compel Discovery in the matter of the Probate of the Last Will and Testament of Ferdinand Eberstadt, Deceased, Surrogate's Court, Suffolk County, State of New York, April 21, 1970, New York, Submitted by Frances Unnerstall, Objectant.

Moody's Industrial Manuals, various editions, 1930–1980.

New York City Department of Health, Record of Births.

Notice of Special Meeting and Proxy Statement for Proposed Merger of the Eberstadt Fund, Inc., with Surveyor Fund, Inc., July 20, 1973.

Offering Prospectuses of Various Eberstadt Financings, 1933–1969 (see appendix).

Opinion of Chancellor Collins J. Seitz in Irwin Meizelman, Plaintiff, v. Ferdinand Eberstadt, et al., Court of Chancellory of the State of Delaware, May 4, 1961.

Papers of Ferdinand Eberstadt, Seeley G. Mudd Manuscript Library, Princeton University, Princeton, New Jersey.

The Pirate Piece, special holiday edition. 1969. *304th Field Artillery Association*.

Poor's Industrials, various editions, 1920–1930.

Preliminary prospectus, NL Capital Associates, June 9, 1983.

Security Offerings by Dillon, Read & Co., 1921–1927, privately published, March 1, 1928.

Tombstone Announcement Advertisement, Robert Fleming Inc. *New York Times*, November 1, 1988, p. D18.

Wellman v. Dickinson. 1979. U.S. District Court, Second District of New York State. 475 F Supp 783.

Who's Who in America, *Marquis Who's Who, Inc.*, 40th edition.

Willett, Edward F. 1946. "Dialectical Materialism and Russian Objectives." Paper written at the request of James Forrestal, Secretary of the Navy. Not published, 14 January.

Zobel, Myron. Paper Parade: The Inside Story of the Controlled Materials Plan. Privately published in Washington, D.C., January 1944.

Index

About the Authors

ROBERT C. PEREZ, Ph.D., spent his entire business career with Ferdinand Eberstadt, beginning in 1950 as a marketing and public affairs specialist and later as a partner in the firm. A Yale graduate, Dr. Perez received his doctorate in finance from New York University Graduate School of Business Administration. His doctoral dissertation analyzed the mutual fund field and its distribution system; his research spurred a number of doctoral research efforts in the emerging field of marketing financial services. Dr. Perez has appeared as an expert witness at hearings before the Securities and Exchange Commission on mutual fund distribution, and he has conducted seminars here and abroad on marketing financial services. In the early 1980s, he left the firm to become a professor of finance, initially at Fordham and later at Iona College Hagan School of Business. Dr. Perez has authored a number of books and articles on financial subjects.

EDWARD F. WILLETT, Ph.D., co-author of the present biography, received his undergraduate and graduate degrees in economics from Princeton University. He first met Ferdinand Eberstadt at Dillon Read in 1924, and he had a close association with him that continued intermittently until 1956. Dr. Willett was one of the three founders of F. Eberstadt & Co. in 1931, and was an officer of that firm until he resigned in 1934 to embark on an academic career. After teaching initially at Princeton, he became a professor of economics at Smith College in 1938, where he taught until 1953 when he returned to Wall Street as an officer and economist at F. Eberstadt & Co., and later at Shields & Co., from which he retired in 1972. In 1945–1946, he spent his sabbatical year from Smith College as research assistant to Secretary of the Navy James V. Forrestal. Dr. Willett has authored a number of books, reports, and articles on economics and other subjects. He resides at 3030 Park Avenue in Bridgeport, Connecticut.